THE CHOIR

The Pacific Princess World Cruise Choir gathers on the grand staircase of the cruise ship once known as The Love Boat. This cluster of choir members brings to mind the famous Cerulean Neptune World Cruise Choir. Even their gifted choir director (the gentleman in black at the top of the stairs), bears a certain resemblance to the legendary Ted Rasmussen.

Sonia Harrison Jones

THE CHOIR

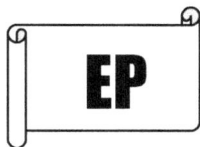

Erser & Pond

Published in Canada by Erser & Pond Publishers, Ltd.
1096 Queen St., Suite 225, Halifax, N.S., Canada B3H 2R9

Cover design by Benjamin Beaumont
Front cover photo of Sydney Opera House by Adele Marie Audet
Back cover photo of author by Terry J Alcorn

Library and Archives Canada Cataloguing in Publication

Jones, Sonia
    The choir / Sonia Harrison Jones.

ISBN 978-0-9865683-7-4

    I. Title.

PS8619.O54C46 2012   C813'.6   C2012-907912-X

This book is dedicated to
David Crathorne

God sent His singers unto earth
with songs of sadness and of mirth,
that they might touch the hearts of men
and bring them back to heav'n again.
— Henry Wadsworth Longfellow

MAIN CHARACTERS

Ted Rasmussen: piano player, singer and choir master on the Cerulean Neptune cruise ship

Dominique Perdue (the fake Maria Morgan), accidental stowaway on the Cerulean Neptune cruise ship

Selim, cabin attendant on Deck Six of the Cerulean Neptune

Ahmad (alias Angel), bartender in the Neptune Lounge

Carlos (Piglet) Casablanca, chef and owner of El Cerdito Bendito (The Blessed Piglet) in Algeciras

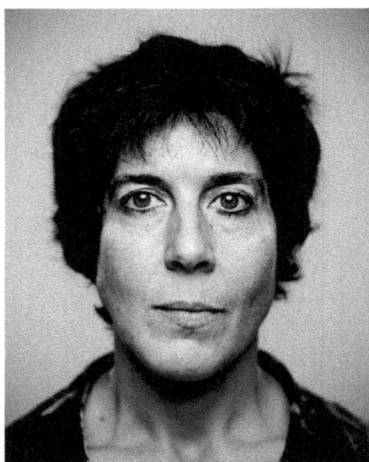

Paloma Casablanca, owner of Hotel de la Esquina (Hotel on the Corner) in Algeciras

Staff Captain Lars Jensen

Bella Boorsma, frequent cruiser and soprano in Ted's choir

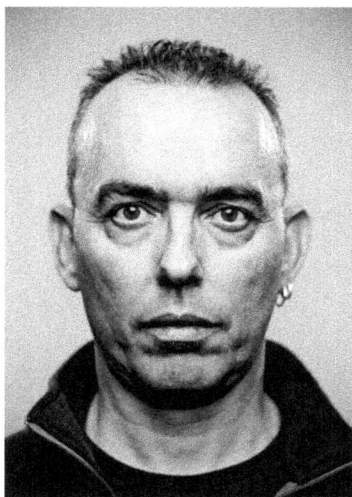

Federico Carpaggio, the Italian contact

Maria Morgan, undercover terrorist

CHAPTER ONE

Dominique Perdue didn't feel at all lost, even though her last name, meaning "lost" in French, suggested the contrary. This was made clear to her years before by her French teacher in the fifth form who, exasperated by her tendency to daydream, had scolded her for always being lost in thought instead of paying strict attention in class. The accusation had driven Dominique to the library to search for the derivation of her surname. It turned out it was originally "par Dieu," meaning "by God," and introduced to England in the wake of the Norman Conquest.

At first Dominique was glad to know that she had been sent into this world by God himself, but she was less pleased to learn that "par Dieu" was not only a common swear word but was also the usual message pinned onto the blankets of orphans and unwanted babies left on the steps of churches. So which was it to be? Was she an orphan or a child of God? The dichotomy of meanings left her feeling ambivalent.

She had lived in London all her life, and she felt content in her upscale West End neighborhood. Although she was what the French delicately refer to as "a woman of a certain age," she felt like an orphan since her father had abandoned her as an infant. Now her mother had passed away, leaving her a modest income and a townhouse in Mayfair. She had kept the apartment on the top floor for herself, and had added to her bottom line by renting the rest of the building to some tenants who were quiet, friendly, and paid their rent on time.

As for being a child of God, Dominique didn't consider herself to be very religious, although she did occasionally send some meandering thoughts Godward, thanking Him in a general sort of way for His blessings. But to whom, exactly, was she directing her gratitude? As far as the tenants were concerned, she congratulated herself for having chosen good people for the apartments downstairs. When it came to her robust health, she gave herself full credit for following a sensible diet and getting plenty of exercise. She was pleased with herself, too, for having reached her allotted time of three score years and ten, which happened to fall on the very day that she found the plastic card lying on the floor.

Dominique had no idea that this little piece of plastic was going to change her life. She knew that most of her days on earth were behind her, so she had accepted the fact that nothing of any particular consequence was likely to happen to her. But life is unpredictable, and sometimes we are thrust into the most peculiar situations when we least expect them.

It all began when she made a quick visit to the Mayfair Pharmacy. She was standing in the queue waiting to pay for her purchases and staring at the image of a woman in the line ahead of her, reflected in the mirror behind the counter. Was it just her imagination, or was this individual her look-alike? She was, in fact, almost a perfect carbon copy of herself. She had the same short gray hair, the same thin lips, the same long earlobes, and the same straight nose and tilted nostrils. She even looked about the same age, although Dominique believed that she herself was clearly the younger of the two.

"What an incredible coincidence!" she thought. "What in heaven's name can it mean?"

After living alone for many years, Dominique Perdue had acquired the habit of thinking out loud (but not loud enough for her to be overheard in the Mayfair Pharmacy), which helped her organize her thoughts and remember where her ideas were leading her. But it wasn't sufficient for her to have clearly-recalled, well-organized thoughts. What she really sought, insofar as possible, was the meaning of things, for why else would we be here on the planet Earth? Surely we must have some purpose, for if not, life would have long ago trapped us all in a quagmire of utter pointlessness.

Dominique reproached herself for attributing so much importance to the similarities she shared with the woman in the queue ahead of her. There was really nothing particularly remarkable about either one of them except for their rather old-fashioned wardrobes consisting of Cashmere twin sets and pleated skirts, so it was useless for her to be thinking about look-alikes or doubles or odd coincidences. If there was anything at all unusual about the two of them, it was that neither one had bothered to develop a unique persona. Most people liked to have a special look that made them stand out from the crowd, Dominique thought, but she had never taken the trouble to create a style of her own. She wore practically no make-up, and she wore no jewelry other than the pearls her mother had given her on her twenty-first birthday. Some people thought that Dominique's modest appearance had a somewhat arrogant side to it, as though she were thumbing her nose at the world, but her friends knew her well enough to understand that she was a quiet, introverted woman who preferred to stay in the background rather than push herself forward by means of fashion statements or brash behavior of any kind.

And then it happened. Dominique's doppelganger was rummaging in her handbag when suddenly one of the straps slipped from her grasp and the contents of the handbag fell to the ground. The woman gave a little cry of dismay and bent over to gather them up. Dominique did what she could to help, bending down and scooping up various items while at the same time feeling rather uncomfortable about touching the woman's personal belongings. The look-alike apparently shared her discomfort.

"Thank you, I can manage," she said with a tight smile, taking a comb and a mirror from Dominique and throwing them quickly into her handbag. "Thank you. I don't need any help. Thank you."

Dominique watched her as she nervously paid for her things and hurried out of the pharmacy.

Just then Dominique happened to notice the plastic card on the floor. She leaned over and picked it up, then ran to the door and looked outside to see if she could find the woman. She looked up and down the street in both directions, but the woman was nowhere to be seen. Dominique was left with the stranger's plastic card in her hand, wondering what to do. She went back to her old place in the line, still contemplating the card and thinking that she should give it to the cashier.

"Excuse me Madam," said the man behind her, tapping her on the shoulder. "I believe you belong at the end of the queue."

"But I was here before," Dominique replied.

"You lost your place, Madam. Please go to the back of the queue."

Dominique felt the blood rise to her face. What was this world coming to? She looked at the cashier to see if she would make a ruling, but she was busy packing a bag for the customer who had been directly in front of her.

"If you please, Madam," insisted the man behind her. "I have no time to waste."

Dominique didn't bother to protest. She had attempted to stand up for herself on other occasions, but had always found that getting into a quarrel was simply too upsetting to be worth the trouble, so without another word she reluctantly went to the end of the line, past all the other customers who looked off into the distance, pretending not to notice.

When she returned to her apartment she sat down at the kitchen table with a cup of green tea and two slightly stale biscotti. Then she put on her glasses and peered closely at the plastic card to see if it contained some information about the owner. As far as she knew it had no specific monetary value—it was just a laminex ID card issued by the Cerulean Neptune cruise ship. It was dated November 7th, that same day, and belonged to a passenger called Maria Morgan. She must have boarded the ship that morning, then disembarked to go up to London to do some last-minute shopping before the cruise ship got underway. By now, Dominique said to herself, the poor woman was probably searching frantically for her cruise card, as she would require it to board the ship again in Southampton.

Dominique regretted not leaving the cruise card with the cashier in case Maria Morgan went back to the pharmacy to see if anyone had turned it in, but she had felt so upset about the incident with the surly customer that it hadn't occurred to her to do so until she had arrived home. Now she would have to go all the way back to the pharmacy and ask the cashier if Miss Morgan had returned for her card. She finished her cup of green tea, then grabbed one of the biscotti and dashed out the door, swallowing the last bite as she walked briskly down the street.

"I was just wondering if anyone has reported a lost ID card," Dominique said to the cashier when she returned to the pharmacy. "It's a cruise card, actually" she explained. "She's a passenger on the Cerulean Neptune. She apparently got on board the ship this morning, but then she must have disembarked later and come to London to do some errands, and she dropped this on the floor when she was here."

"Nobody has reported anything," said the cashier.

"She's probably worried to death," Dominique replied.

"I imagine so, but there's not much I can do, is there?"

Dominique checked her watch. "I hope she doesn't miss her cruise," she declared, looking concerned. "Do you have her telephone number on file? Maybe I can ring her."

"What's her name?"

"Maria Morgan."

"Maria Morgan… that doesn't sound familiar. She isn't a regular customer here, so I'm afraid I can't help you."

"Well, do you want to keep the card so you can give it to her if she comes back?"

"I don't think that's a good idea. She may not know she dropped it here. She may never come back."

"So what do you recommend I do?"

"I expect there's nothing you really can do but go down to Southampton and give the card back to the authorities at the cruise terminal. They'll know what to do."

"That's rather a long way off," Dominique said, looking dismayed. "It takes an hour and a half by train, doesn't it?"

"I expect so," said the cashier. "Now I really must get on with it. I have customers."

It was almost four o'clock in the afternoon when Dominique finally arrived at the Mayflower Terminal in Southampton. There were large crowds of people milling about or standing in line waiting to be registered and admitted aboard. It was the last-minute crush, and all the passengers seemed nervous and cranky. The scene exemplified everything Dominique hated: crowds, pushiness, querulousness and general bedlam.

She looked about to see if she could spot Maria Morgan in the crowd, for if she were anywhere she would surely be here trying to explain to the authorities behind one of the counters that she had already been admitted aboard earlier in the day, but had misplaced her cruise card during her trip to London. But when she didn't see her anywhere, Dominique finally joined the shortest line she could find and waited to speak to someone behind the counter. Just as she was about to make it to the head of the line, she noticed a woman who looked just like Maria in the distance, talking to a Neptune representative who was patiently listening to her story.

"Maria!" Dominique called out as she drew close to the two of them. "Maria, I have your cruise card!"

As there was no response from either the woman or the Neptune rep, Dominique went and stood right next to them to get their attention. Then, much to her great dismay, she saw that the woman she thought was Maria was indeed not Maria at all—she was just another senior citizen with short gray hair and a conservative wardrobe. As she looked around the terminal, Dominique began to realize that these ladies of a certain age seemed to be sprinkled all over the place. Some were short and others were tall, some had gray hair and some had white, most were stout and a few were slim, and they out-numbered the men by a considerable margin. What was going on here? The crowd resembled the population of a senior citizens' retirement community.

"May I help you?" the Neptune rep said to Dominique, placing her hand reassuringly on the arm of the passenger with whom she had been conversing when Dominique had approached them. The rep must have seen the passenger's expression of anxiety and had been kind enough to divide her attention briefly without alienating the other woman.

"I'm so sorry," Dominique said. "I thought you were someone else."

"No problem," said the rep in a pleasant voice, turning to the other woman and continuing their conversation.

Dominique went back to her place in line by the counter, smiling at the woman who had been standing behind her.

"Hey! What do you think you're doing?"

"I was here before," Dominique said. "Remember?"

"Well, you lost your place," the woman said accusingly. "You can't cut in like that."

"But I just left for a minute. I went to speak to someone I knew. I wanted to catch her before she went away."

"I don't care what your excuse is. You can't cut in."

"I'm not cutting in. I was here before you were!"

"Go to the back of the line!" the other woman insisted, raising her voice.

"Just try to understand," Dominique said. "I've been in this queue for almost half an hour now. If I go to the end of the line I'll have to wait for another half hour. A passenger lost this cruise card, you see, and…"

"I told you," the other woman shouted, "get to the back of the line."

Dominique withdrew from the queue with her head held high, not wanting to spend another minute in the presence of such a bad-tempered character. What was the matter with people these days? Weren't they from the same generation? Hadn't they all lived through wars, lost husbands in combat, faced serious illness and other such hardships? Didn't any of them have any idea of what suffering was? Why would they want to perpetrate it rather than relieve it in some small way?

As she walked through the crowds she slowly began to realize that her anger was directed more at herself than at the hostile stranger. She was foolish to think that everyone was automatically going to be pleasant and helpful just because it was the right thing to do. She felt stupid to have expected too much. Worst of all, as she made her way obediently to the end of the line, she knew somehow that her face was flushed not so much with resentment as with shame for having let herself be pushed around so easily.

This time Dominique chose a different queue—one that was shorter than the first, and much closer to the wharf. As she stood there looking at the passengers going through the doorway to the wharf, she began to realize that they all had their cruise cards in their hands. They must have been told to have them ready for boarding now that they had completed the rest of their pre-boarding paperwork. It suddenly struck her that her look-alike, Maria Morgan, had obviously gone through the queues earlier that day and completed her pre-boarding paperwork too. Surely that must mean that she, Dominique Perdue, could go through that same doorway and up the gangplank and onto the cruise ship without having to wait in line to explain Maria's problem to someone at the counter in the terminal. She could then go to the purser's desk on the cruise ship and explain the situation and hand in Maria's cruise card so that they could return it to her if she managed to get in touch. Or better yet, they would probably know how to contact her themselves, since in all likelihood they had the information from her pre-boarding paperwork in the ship's computers by this time.

How do you solve a problem like Maria? Dominique decided to take the bull by the horns and just brazenly walk through the doorway with Maria's cruise card in her hand and see what happened. At best she would be able to solve Maria's problem at the purser's desk and then, perhaps, take a quick look around the ship before she got off again. At worst they might hand her over to the authorities for trying to gain illegal access to the vessel. At any rate, since Maria's cruise card had no photo on it, Dominique thought it unlikely that she would be apprehended before she could reach the purser's desk. With that happy thought in mind, she followed the crowd through the doorway and along the wharf until she arrived at the berth where the Cerulean Neptune was docked.

After navigating the widely-spaced metal bars on the gangplank—sometimes taking them just one at a time and sometimes two by two—Dominique found herself on one of the lower decks where the ship's security personnel asked her to insert her cruise card into a slot in a large box. *Beep* went the box, sounding a note that seemed like a D sharp to Dominique. She smiled to herself, fondly remembering her days in the church choir when she was a child. After putting her handbag through the X-ray machine and learning with relief that she didn't have to take off her shoes, she was told to move on through. What she didn't know was that as the D sharp beeps rang out, a security officer was scrutinizing the electronically-embedded snapshots in the cruise cards. After checking the invisible photo on the card that Dominique had inserted into the box, the officer was satisfied that she was indeed Maria Morgan.

"Welcome aboard, Mrs. Morgan," he said, returning the cruise card to Dominique, who thanked him and made her way to the stairwell. She wasn't about to join the crowd of people waiting for the elevator—she had been in enough crowds and line-ups for one day.

As the fake Mrs. Morgan emerged from the stairwell on Deck Four, she was greeted by the sight of yet another crowd of passengers standing around the purser's desk. Although the three attendees at the desk were handling their various problems with admirable speed and efficiency, Dominique Perdue was not then, and most likely never would be, in the mood to join the crowd. Instead, she thought it would be a good idea to look around the Cerulean Neptune to see if she could locate any other staff members who could help her.

The only trouble with that plan was that she would have to confess that she had boarded the cruise ship illegally with somebody else's card, and that made her feel more than a little anxious. It was probably just as well that the people at the purser's desk were too occupied to take care of her. She thought about leaving a note under the door of Maria's cabin, but she quickly discarded that notion when it occurred to her that Maria would not be able to get on board, let alone access her cabin, without her cruise card. Besides, after checking the card again she realized that even though the passenger's name was clearly printed on it, there was no cabin number. This made sense, for a lost cruise card with a name *and* a stateroom number could lead to obvious trouble. Dominique concluded that the best course of action was none at all, and with that in mind she decided to give herself a quick tour of the Cerulean Neptune before the ship set out to sea.

As Dominique was heading down one of the passenger hallways going from aft to fore, she was stopped by a cabin attendant.

"May I be of service, Madam?" he asked her.

"Well, as a matter of fact you can," Dominique replied. "I've forgotten the number of my stateroom, I fear."

"My name is Selim," he told her, with a little bow. "Let me have your cruise card for a moment. I can speedily find the number for you."

Dominique hesitated, then she thought how interesting it would be to see what a stateroom looked like.

"All right, then," she replied. "Here it is."

"I'll be back in less than a minute," Selim said, with a reassuring smile. "Stay where you are please, Madam."

Dominique watched with some trepidation as he made a right turn down another passageway. She wondered if she should follow him, but Selim was as good as his word.

"Good afternoon, Mrs. Morgan," he said, reappearing shortly afterward. "Let me show you to your cabin, number 6068. It's an easy number for you to remember."

He swiped the cruise card and opened the door for her.

"Your baggage will be coming soon," he told her. "I'll put it by your door and knock. If you are not here I'll put it inside your cabin. It's not good to leave it in the passageway. You never know who might be roaming about."

Dominique smiled at the irony of his remark. She was, after all, an illegal visitor herself. She could easily have been a pirate or a terrorist for all anyone knew.

"Thank you, Selim. I appreciate what you did."

Selim smiled and ran off to help someone else, while Dominique shut the cabin door behind her.

"What a beautiful stateroom," she thought, admiring the modern décor. There was a queen-sized bed, ample closet space, a narrow desk with two stacks of drawers, and a flat screen TV on the wall which could be viewed from either the bed or the couch. The bathroom was compact but functional, with shelves and a medicine chest and a spacious shower. Best of all, the cabin had a beautiful balcony with a white table and two matching chairs.

As Dominique opened the sliding doors to the balcony, she heard a scraping noise coming from outside. She went to the rail and looked down. There, about three decks below, she saw several crew members pulling up the gangplank.

What? Why hadn't they made an announcement? Or had she simply not been aware of it? Maybe passengers couldn't hear the announcements when their cabin doors were closed. At any rate, the cruise ship was about to get under way, and she was still on board! The rest of the passengers must have known somehow that the ship's departure was scheduled for exactly 5:00 PM.

Dominique Perdue's heart almost stopped beating when it dawned on her that she was now an accidental stowaway on the Cerulean Neptune, heading for parts unknown.

CHAPTER TWO

Ted Rasmussen was looking forward to resuming his job as an entertainer on the Cerulean Neptune. He felt rested and refreshed after spending three months at home in Bergen, Norway, and now he was eager to go back to work. He was an attractive, friendly man in his mid-fifties, and was very popular with everyone on board. He was a gifted pianist with a beautiful, resonant singing voice, so a solid group of regulars would go to the lounge every night to hear him perform. It was well known to the Neptune executives at the head office in Santa Marta, California, that he was a big draw for repeat customers.

Ted walked briskly through the passenger registration hall, wearing shorts and a T-shirt and carrying a knapsack on his back and a duffel bag in his right hand. As he headed for the doorway leading out onto the wharf, he was greeted by a number of passengers who knew him from previous cruises and whose facial expressions would change from reflections of tension and stress to ones of unqualified delight at seeing him in their midst once again.

"Ted! Over here!" they would cry.

"Hey!" Ted would call back. "Good to see you again!"

"How was Bergen?" another would ask.

"Fabulous. But I'm glad to be back here with you."

Another entertainer in Ted's position might have let his popularity go to his head, perhaps even squeezing the folks at the executive offices for some tangible compensation for going well beyond what was expected of him as far as public relations were concerned. But there was not even a hint of self-congratulation in Ted's heart, nor was there the slightest suggestion of insincerity about his love for the passengers. It was this very authenticity, this heartfelt genuineness of soul and spirit that attracted the passengers to him and made them feel at home with him from the first moment they met.

When Ted arrived at the ship's gangway he was greeted by the crew manager of the Cerulean Neptune and brought on board. Once he was on the ship, a security officer took his passport and put it in the crew office for safe keeping. Then another member of the security team took his photograph and issued him a laminex, which was his ID for getting on and off the ship for the rest of the world cruise. Once these formalities were completed, Ted hoisted his knapsack onto his back again and grabbed his duffel bag.

"See you guys later," he said over his shoulder as he made his way to the stairwell and headed for Deck Six. He was undaunted by the prospect of climbing three flights of stairs to his cabin, bearing his weighty knapsack and equally heavy duffel bag. He was a Norwegian, after all, and a real mountain goat when it came to climbing. A sculptor or a student of anatomy would have picked this up immediately by observing his legs—the calves, quadriceps, hamstrings and lateral compartments were all especially well developed.

"Hi, Paloma, good to see you again," Ted called out to a passenger whose looming figure almost blocked out the light in the hallway aft of his stateroom.

"*Hola*, Ted. Did you just get here?"

"About ten minutes ago."

"Well, it's good to see you on board again," she said, inserting her cruise card into the slot in her cabin door. "Are you playing in the Casino Lounge tonight?"

"As far as I know, but check your *Neptune News*."

"I'll do that," she replied, ducking her head as she let herself through the doorway to her stateroom.

Paloma was an exceptionally tall Spanish woman whose unusual height dated back to the genetic infusion of Dutch genes into the bloodlines of her Spanish ancestors during the conquest of the Low Countries in the sixteenth century. The genes responsible for her conspicuous height had apparently been successfully preserved by her family members through the ensuing centuries. She owned and operated a popular three-star hotel called *El Hotel de la Esquina* (the Hotel on the Corner) in Algeciras, which was frequented mainly by British tourists seeking a comfortable vacation on a modest budget in the warm climate of the south of Spain.

Paloma's husband, whose name was Carlos Casablanca, was a short, rotund, good-natured Andalusian who owned and operated the restaurant next door to her hotel, which he called *El Cerdo Asado* (The Roast Pig). Carlos had loved Paloma from the moment he first laid eyes on her, and he courted her with the same determination and intensity that had led his own forebears to succeed so admirably in their conquest of the Netherlands.

When Paloma finally consented to be his wife, Carlos was so ecstatically happy that he renamed his restaurant *El Cerdito Bendito* (the Blessed Piglet), and shortly afterward Paloma adopted *Piglet* as her pet name for him. Those who thought that he would be horrified by her choice were not the friends who knew him best. Piglet, in fact, was absolutely delighted with the nickname because it proved that they had come to know each other well enough to be comfortable with good-natured teasing and amicable humor.

After two decades of hard work and frugal living, Piglet and Paloma had succeeded so well with their enterprises that they were eventually able to leave them both in the hands of their most trustworthy and responsible employees every year while they enjoyed some well-earned rest and relaxation on the Neptune world cruises.

Even though Piglet and Paloma knew that some of their workers were occasionally skimming the profits and cooking the books, those particular employees were clever enough to leave sufficient funds in the coffers of the two enterprises to provide their employers with the profit necessary to have a comfortable life and to enjoy their cruises without losing too much in the process. Paloma and Piglet had agreed to turn a blind eye to their employees' shenanigans as long as they didn't get too greedy and kill the golden goose.

Just then Piglet appeared in the hallway where Ted was still standing. He was pulling two pieces of heavy luggage, with a carry-on under his right arm.

"Hello Ted," he said, pausing to greet his friend. "It is very chilly this English weather, is it not so?"

"Good to see you again, Piglet," Ted replied. "And yes, it's pretty cold, you're right about that."

"Did Paloma tell you the news?"

"No. What news?"

"I'm joining your choir."

"Really? That's great!" Ted exclaimed. "I never thought *that* would happen! What made you change your mind?"

"Well, I didn't have much choice, did I? Paloma joined you every sea day at noon for choir practice, so what was I supposed to do? I had to fight back."

"But you told me last year that you couldn't sing on key. Did Paloma give you lessons?"

"No, we quarrel too much when she tries to tell me what to do. She wears the trousers, you see, but she pretends she doesn't, for my sake. We Spaniards don't really like that sort of thing very much. We invented *macho*, you know. But mostly it's all just a pose," he admitted, with a wink.

"I know what you mean," Ted remarked, joining him in his good-natured laughter. "So what happened, then?"

"Well, Paloma doesn't know it, but when I went to the market to buy fresh fish and fruit and vegetables, I would go around the corner to take singing lessons with my friend who sings and plays the guitar. Paloma knew nothing about it. You must keep it a secret so she can show me her surprise."

"Don't worry. I'll keep your secret, Piglet."

"Thank you very much. And here is a surprise for you, too. What you see before you is a strong man, so you might therefore think that I have a deep, strong voice too, yes?"

"Well, I suppose…"

"But not so. Unhappily I'm not a deep bass, as I wished. I'm just a little tenor man. Not so much little, but short. Yes, that's the word. Short and round. Paloma, she explained me that there are too many estrogens in my fat. I told her I show her quickly how many androgens I have for her. We have a good time. Always a good time."

Suddenly Paloma opened her cabin door.

"*There* you are, Piglet!" she exclaimed. "Why are you standing around talking? I have waited all afternoon for you to arrive here. Come in right now!"

"The hen pecks but the rooster, he doesn't respond very quickly," Piglet smiled, as he strutted slowly down the hall.

"See you at choir practice!" Ted called after him.

Piglet waved at him without turning around.

After Ted finished unpacking his duffel bag, he flopped down on his sofa and swung his legs over the end, glad to be back in the familiar surroundings of the Cerulean Neptune, and eager to embark on this new voyage.

"I have salt water in my veins," he thought, "just like the rest of my Norwegian forebears."

It was a pity he couldn't see anything from his porthole, but the view was obstructed by a lifeboat. The unobstructed portholes were reserved for the paying passengers.

Did they see further and more clearly into the meaning of things, he wondered, with their unobstructed views? But if the panorama of the Cerulean Neptune meeting the distant horizon had to be blocked by something, it might as well be by one of the lifeboats.

"I could do with a lifeboat myself once in a while," Ted thought morosely, "for there are times when I feel very much at sea with nobody to talk to about the deeper things in life."

He quickly shook off these philosophical thoughts and got up from the sofa, giving himself a brief once-over in the mirror. It was time now to don a happy face and greet the passengers. His job was not only to entertain them with song and music, but he was also expected to do whatever he could to keep them relaxed and cheerful. This meant circulating among them and chatting about port lectures or travel plans or their families or the latest world news, or any other topic that happened to come up.

"Hi there, Ted!" cried a beautiful young woman as she caught sight of him opening the door to his stateroom.

"Hi Bella," he replied, his eyes lighting up at the sight of her. He was happy to see her back on board, for she was an even-tempered, tolerant woman who could be trusted to be discreet where matters of staff-passenger relationships were concerned.

The Neptune management, like that of most other cruise lines, had a strict policy forbidding any kind of fraternization between passengers and personnel that could be construed as overstepping the boundaries of social propriety. This was sometimes a rather thorny issue for the staff and crew who, after all, were sometimes at sea for weeks or even months at a time without access to spouses or partners. Management was aware of these hardships and did everything possible to facilitate visits from significant others, but there were always certain inevitable stretches of time when celibacy became an unwelcome reality. This made it necessary for management to mete out severe penalties to staff or crew members who flouted the anti-fraternization rules—those found guilty of doing so could be immediately dismissed. Lest the penalty seem inordinately severe, it should be kept in mind that the legal consequences for the cruise lines could be harsher still if sexual assault or other criminal activities were deemed to have taken place on board.

Bella felt sorry for the staff in this situation. Like it or not, they were forced to adopt a sort of parental stance where employees and passengers were concerned. It was the staff and crew, after all, whose jobs were at risk if the rules were flouted. In order to avoid all possible misunderstandings or temptations, the management of the cruise lines established a sort of "no fly zone" that governed certain areas of the ship. Passengers were strictly forbidden to visit the crew quarters or a staff member's stateroom, and likewise the staff was forbidden to set foot inside a passenger's stateroom unless his job required it; but if either one happened to be caught in the wrong location, it was curtains for the staff, and not for the passenger.

Bella knew it was mostly a question of the bottom line. Passengers were treated like spoiled children, coddled and catered to by hard-working personnel whose main purpose was to entice them to book a passage on future cruises. If a particular employee was seen to have failed to please the passengers or fulfill their requests, he or she would receive warnings or be given some explicit advice on how to handle the situation better in the future. If there were quarrels or disagreements between passengers and personnel, this could lead to dismissal or non-renewal of contract for the crew or staff member.

Bella realized, however, that management was aware that it was in everybody's best interest for matters to run as smoothly as possible on the ship. Like all good managers, the officers knew that the carrot works better than the stick, so every effort was made to inspire the staff and crew with rewards for excellent service. The passengers were also encouraged to vote for an employee of the month, and to put messages in the in-box at the purser's desk describing what they thought were truly outstanding qualities in those who served them.

During her first world cruise Bella did a sparkling write-up of Ted Rasmussen, presenting a detailed description of how, three years prior to the present world cruise, he had been invited to direct a small group of passengers who had started up a choir under the auspices of one of their fellow passengers. Ted's full-toned, resonant voice, musical talent, teaching savvy and personal charisma had attracted so many passengers to join the choir that it had grown to include three or four dozen members by the end of the next few cruises. By this time Ted and his choir had presented some extremely successful and much appreciated evening concerts.

Eventually Ted's noteworthy triumphs had come to the attention of various people in key positions at the head office of the Neptune Cruise Line in Santa Marta, California, who thought it would be excellent publicity for both the Neptune Cruise Line and the Sydney Opera if that highly-regarded company would invite the enthusiastic amateur singers and their inspired choir master to give an afternoon performance for the benefit of some favorite local causes. The number of cruise ships docking in Sydney's harbor had sky-rocketed in the last few years, so it would be an excellent opportunity for the Sydney Opera to thank the entire cruise industry for the huge increase in attendance.

But like many good ideas, it had fallen on ears that were not so much deaf as they were deadened by other issues and responsibilities that were taking priority over the Sydney Opera in the minds of the executive officers of the Neptune Cruise Line in California. Cruise vacations were growing in popularity and so, therefore, were the problems of safety, security, sanitation, environmental pollution and—since the sinking of the Costa Concordia—the issues of accountability, integrity, excellent training, and intelligent decision-making. These pressing concerns, therefore, left Ted Rasmussen and his ever-growing choir temporarily in limbo until a decision could be made about approaching the Sydney Opera.

It was already dark in the cabin when Dominique Perdue was suddenly awakened by a sharp rap on the door. At first she couldn't recall where she was, but then when it came back to her that she was a stowaway on the Cerulean Neptune cruise ship, she didn't know whether or not to open the door. What if they had come to arrest her? What if they held her in irons until they dumped her off in Le Havre on the other side of the English Channel? What on earth would she do then?

To her horror she saw the door open and a dark figure backed into her stateroom, dragging something heavy as he moved closer and closer to her bed. Suddenly the room was lit up with a blinding light, and she could do nothing but curl up and cover her face, hoping the figure wouldn't attack her and leave her for dead.

"Oh, I'm so sorry, Mrs. Morgan," came Selim's voice. "I didn't know you were here in your cabin. I knocked, you know. I knocked hard on the door, but you didn't answer."

"I was sleeping," Dominique mumbled. "I was taking a little nap."

"I'm very, very sorry, Mrs. Morgan."

"It's all right, Selim. You don't have to apologize."

"Thank you, Mrs. Morgan. I brought you your suitcase. I thought you would need it quickly. Shall I leave it for you here by the wardrobe?"

"Yes, certainly. That's fine."

"Your suitcase is very large, Mrs. Morgan. It is hard to move a suitcase that is so heavy, like this one. It will not fit easily in the closet."

"Thank you, Selim. Just put it over there. I'll take care of it later."

"I'm so sorry I disturbed you," he replied, taking a few steps towards the door. He hesitated a moment and looked at her closely, as though debating whether or not he should say something more. "You will be hearing from me very soon," he said finally, then he left her stateroom and closed the door behind him.

Dominique suddenly felt anxious. What did Selim mean by that last comment? Why would she be hearing from him very soon? Why should she hear from him at all? What was he planning to tell her, and on the subject of what? Did he suspect something? Did he find out about her? If so, how did he get the information? Was she about to be caught?

None of it made any sense to Dominique. Maria Morgan had already checked in and shown her passport and boarding information to the proper authorities in the cruise terminal that morning. The Neptune Cruise Line then issued Maria Morgan a laminex ID card which was now in Dominique's possession. It was therefore impossible for the authorities to question anything further about the transaction, for they had no information at all about Dominique herself, and therefore they could not possibly have compared Maria Morgan's ID against her own, for they knew nothing about her. In fact, they didn't know that she, Dominique Perdue, existed at all.

There had been only one moment of danger for her that afternoon, she mused, and that was when she had put her cruise card in the slot in the box after going up the gangway. If the security guard had questioned her likeness to the photo that was electronically embedded in the cruise card that she was using, he would have asked her for another picture ID for verification. But that didn't happen. Evidently she looked enough like Maria Morgan to pass muster, and she had been allowed to board the ship at the sound of the beep. She was relieved that they didn't have the equipment to check her fingerprints or her eyeballs, or she certainly would have been caught.

Dominique Perdue finally convinced herself that Selim's remark about hearing from him later was not a warning or a threat, but a perfectly harmless *goodbye, see you later* sort of comment. She decided to get up and take a shower, and let all her fears and worries go right down the drain.

It wasn't until the middle of her shower that it occurred to her that she had no clean clothes to change into. Why had she overlooked that detail? She must have been sleeping very deeply during her nap to have lost her concentration and her clarity of thought to that extent. There was nothing for it but to go through Maria's suitcase and find something to wear. After all, if everything went well she'd be cruising on the Cerulean Neptune for many more days to come.

To her great relief she discovered that the suitcase was brimming with clothes that were just her size. She felt it was best to put them all away in the drawers and closet so she could find whatever she was looking for when she needed it.

When she reached the bottom of the suitcase, she was surprised to discover about three dozen paperback copies of a little book called *Old Testament Alive!* What was *that* all about? The plot was thickening. Perhaps her doppelganger was a religious fanatic wanting to accost as many passengers as possible to try to convert them. She flipped through one of the copies and noticed that it was beautifully illustrated with color photos on just about every page. The characters had expressive faces, and the landscapes and cityscapes easily transported the reader straight back to the Holy Land itself. After reading through the first chapter of one of the copies, Dominique was surprised to discover it wasn't just a cheap religious tract. It was actually a very interesting, informative piece of literature, with a touch of humor here and there to make it more lively and enjoyable for the non-specialist. She looked forward to going through the whole book later during her spare time.

Then all at once something else occurred to her. What would happen if Maria Morgan reported her missing cruise card to the Neptune Cruise Line and asked to be allowed to board the ship at the next port of call? Dominique couldn't answer that question. She had no idea what the penalty was for being a stowaway. She would have to leave that difficult question up to her captors.

As Dominique put away the last of Maria's belongings, she saw an 8-ounce cylindrical polished cardboard container labeled *Natural Rock Salt.* Why on earth would she bring her own personal salt aboard? Did she intend to take it to the dining table? That would be pointless, Dominique thought, since there was bound to be plenty of salt available in the dining room. Did it have to be rock salt for some reason? Maybe this Maria Morgan was a particularly finicky eater. Dominique shrugged and stashed the salt on the top shelf of the closet, then promptly forgot about it.

All of a sudden she was startled by a knock on the door. It was Selim, bringing her *The Neptune News.* Maybe that's what he meant when he said she'd be hearing from him later. He was only telling her that he would be bringing her a copy of the ship's daily newsletter. How silly she was to worry so much about every little thing. She thanked him and sat down on the couch to read about the next day's activities.

Five minutes later the blood was rushing to her face again, for there, on page two of the *The Neptune News,* was a rather large announcement written in bold letters stating that she, Maria Morgan, would be leading a Bible study on the following Wednesday morning at eleven o'clock.

"Good Lord!" Dominique exclaimed out loud. "So that's what all those books are for! Now I'm going to have to give Maria Morgan's Bible study, and it's only three days from now. I hope I'll have enough time to prepare the class. I'll just have to wing it, I suppose, but at least I have a book to present to them. It's not a very scholarly book, though. Will the passengers like it even so? Maybe some of them will know a lot more than I do, and they may ask me some sticky questions. What will I do then? Will it become obvious that I'm an imposter?"

CHAPTER THREE

Dominique Perdue, trying to walk bravely under the shameful, burdensome weight of her false identity as Maria Morgan, was on her way to meet her fellow tablemates at the first seating in the Club Dining Room of the Cerulean Neptune, when suddenly she was stopped short by the most beautiful sound she had ever heard, coming from the lounge beside the casino. An impelling, expressive voice, filled with wonder, stunned veneration and inexpressible joy, was trying to tell a disinterested world that he had fallen in love with a girl named Maria.

> *Maria! I've just met a girl named Maria,*
> *and suddenly the name*
> *will never be the same to me.*
>
> *Maria! I've just kissed a girl named Maria,*
> *and suddenly I've found*
> *how wonderful a sound can be!*

As Dominique rounded the corner, the man playing the piano came into full view. He was looking toward the hall, singing his heartfelt song as he contemplated the passengers moving along in the direction of the dining room. Dominique stood there gazing at him with a sense of rapture, unable to make sense of the depth and strength of her emotions.

> *Maria! Say it loud and there's music playing,*
> *Say it soft and it's almost like praying.*
> *Maria... I'll never stop saying Maria!*

Dominique had the feeling that the world around her had disappeared, leaving her alone with this gifted musician who had given her permission to be herself, the woman she truly was, and whose name was Maria. From that moment on she would be Maria, not the real Maria Morgan whose identity she had assumed when she became an accidental stowaway on the Cerulean Neptune, but the glorious new Maria in the song from *West Side Story*, who was truer and more alive than her rather dull identity as Dominique Perdue. She gazed at the musician, enthralled by the metamorphosis that had been freely granted to her by a perfect stranger.

The piano player, whose name was Ted Rasmussen, was gazing at Dominique with much the same expression in his eyes. This woman, he said to himself, was known to him. He was sure that he had never seen her before, and yet somehow he knew that he had seen her always. It was as if he had been expecting her—as if, in fact, she had been sent.

Dominique was looking down at the floor, unable to stir, paralyzed with the acute shyness that overcomes us all when our feelings are new, sudden, and powerful beyond reason. For a "woman of a certain age," such a state is more than a little unsettling. For young people it is different. It is natural for them to be carried away on the wings of emotion, but their seniors are expected to be wise, unruffled examples of prudence, self-control, and rational behavior.

What, then, should she do about the present situation? She would do what older people are supposed to do in such circumstances. She would get a grip. She would get hold of herself. She would take herself in hand and lay aside all her notions of rebirth and transfiguration.

After reflecting on this powerful and totally unexpected occurrence, Dominique decided that she would not allow the moment to dwindle to nothing just for the sake of propriety. What had occurred that evening was inexplicable, but to Dominique it was something to be greatly treasured, for now she was no longer a furtive, frightened stowaway in a world of strangers. Her legal name was still Dominique Perdue, but her true name, the name she cherished above all others, had now become Maria Morgan, although if it had been up to her she would have preferred to be called Maria Trouvée—the Maria who was now found. She turned and smiled radiantly at the piano player as she continued down the hallway, and he smiled back.

When Dominique reached the dining room she was greeted by the maître d', who asked to see her cruise card.

"Maria Morgan?" he said, looking closely at her.

"Yes, that's me," she said brightly.

It astonished her to think that only five minutes earlier she would have been very nervous to answer that question, fearing that she would be caught in an egregious lie and dealt with accordingly. But now the name Maria had a magical quality that comforted her and gave her confidence.

"Welcome, Mrs. Morgan," he said, after handing the ID card back to her. He introduced her then to the head waiter, who showed her to a table close to the window where three other passengers sat chatting. The head waiter pulled out her chair and seated her with expertise, pushing the heavy piece of furniture close to the table just as she sat down.

"Your server will be here shortly to take your orders," he said, handing her a menu. "Enjoy your dinner," he added, heading back to the entrance of the dining room.

"Hi, I'm Bella," said the beautiful young blond woman sitting by the window. "Bella Boorsma. Welcome aboard."

"Thanks, Bella. I'm Maria Morgan. Glad to meet you," Dominique replied.

"And I'm Paloma Casablanca," said the slim, brunette, middle-aged woman sitting opposite Bella. "And this is my partner in crime, Carlos Casablanca."

Dominique decided that Paloma must be a particularly tall woman, for even though she was sitting down she was still about six inches taller than her husband.

"Happy to know you, Paloma and Carlos," Dominique declared, with a warm smile.

"Nobody ever calls me Carlos," he replied. "I'm known as Piglet, for obvious reasons," he laughed, leaning back in his chair. "The crime Paloma was talking about just now is that I'm only five feet tall and I like food too much," he said, fondly patting his protruding belly. "*Way* too much."

"Piglet is the head chef at the restaurant next door to my hotel in Algeciras, in the south of Spain," Paloma explained. "He is the best chef in the whole province of Andalusia, and don't let anyone tell you that it is not so."

"If I ever go to Andalusia, I'll be sure to stop by and try your creations," Dominique told him.

"The good kitchen is in the nostrils," Piglet explained. "I can even smell basil from across a crowded room. I can also smell a partridge in a pear tree before he is braised."

He turned to face the galley and sniffed the air. "I can tell you precisely what they are preparing for dinner tonight. That is because I have already checked the menu before you joined us, Maria," he admitted, with a sly wink. "I am going to order the *canard à l'orange*, which is my favorite dish. I will test it and then I will tell you what I think."

"And he will, too, you can be sure of that," Paloma said, giving him an affectionate nudge in the shoulder with her elbow. Dominique noticed that she didn't have to raise her elbow very high to hit the mark.

"So what do you do, Maria?" Bella asked her.

"Well, I used to be an English professor, but I'm retired now," she said. "What about you?"

"I'm in advertising, and I'm my own boss. I send myself all over the world doing projects for various corporations."

"Have you ever been on the Cerulean Neptune before?" Dominique asked her.

"Yes, three times. It's one of my favorite cruise ships. It has a real family atmosphere. People are mostly friendly and down-to-earth, although there are fights here and there, just as you'd expect to see in any family. You know, the usual thing… rivalries, jealousies, competitiveness, and all kinds of arguments about this and that, but it generally gets sorted out in the long run."

"So what are you working on now?" Dominique asked.

"Well, I'm taking a little break now. The only thing I care about at the moment is Ted Rasmussen's choir. He's fabulous. Everybody loves Ted. Do you like to sing?"

"I like to sing," Dominique said, "but I can't read music. I only sing along with the radio and that sort of thing."

"I like to do that too," Piglet chimed in. "I sing in the shower, just to drive Paloma crazy."

"You are never off key when Ted is playing the piano," Paloma remarked. "You have a beautiful soprano voice."

"Oh, shut up," Piglet said affectionately. "It's nothing compared to your lovely deep bass voice."

"I need a basso profundo since I wear the trousers in the family," Paloma said, elbowing Piglet's shoulder again.

"This choir director, Ted Rasmussen," Dominique said, "is he also the singer and the piano player in the lounge?"

"That's right," Bella replied. "He's the one."

Dominique was glad to find out the name of the singer who had affected her so deeply that evening. *Rasmussen* was a Norwegian name, she noticed. He did look Scandinavian, as a matter of fact. She couldn't quite picture him accurately in her imagination since she had only seen him once, but she remembered his closely-cropped gray hair and the lines on his cheeks and his intelligent blue eyes. But mostly it was his voice that echoed in her heart, singing "Maria, I'll never stop saying Maria!"

"You should really consider joining the choir, Maria," Bella said. "Seriously, you don't need to worry about not knowing how to read music. Believe me, there are plenty of people in the choir who can't read a note, but Ted repeats the lyrics and the melody often enough for us to get familiar with it, so eventually it all just falls into place."

"Bella's right, Maria," Paloma agreed. "You should join the choir. Just do it, and worry about it later. You won't be sorry. If you decide it's not for you, Ted will understand. He never forces anyone to do anything."

"Why would he?" Piglet piped up. "We're passengers, and he's staff. The staff is paid to keep us happy."

"It's a whole lot more than that," Bella frowned. "Ted is a hundred percent genuine, that's why everybody likes him and trusts him. And he likes us too, you can tell. That's why he's such a good teacher."

"It's you he likes most of all," Paloma said to Bella, in a teasing voice. "Everyone can see it."

Dominique felt that she was courting disaster by even considering joining the choir, if it meant she would make a complete fool of herself. She had never sung a note in her life except in Sunday school, and some Christmas carols on the streets of Mayfair when she was a child. She decided she would have to find a diplomatic way to turn down the choir invitation without seeming like an old bump on a log.

"I don't know if I'll have time for the choir," Dominique said finally. "I have to give a Bible study every morning at eleven o'clock, starting Wednesday, and I'll have to prepare for it every day. It'll take quite a bit of time."

"So *you're* the one who's giving the Bible study," said Bella. "I saw the announcement in the *The Neptune News* this morning. I guess I should have put two and two together, but your name wasn't familiar to me then, and I forgot it."

"Oh, don't let the Bible get in your way," Paloma said to Dominique. "You'll *love* the choir. Just wait and see."

"You must have known you were giving the Bible study before you came aboard," Bella said, looking bewildered. "Didn't you prepare it at home first, before you got here?"

Alarms went off in Dominique's head. If these people figured out that she didn't even know that she was expected to give a Bible study on the Cerulean Neptune, they might suspect that either she suffered from Alzheimer's disease, or she wasn't who she said she was. It was probably quite far-fetched for her to imagine that anybody would reach the conclusion that she had assumed a fake identity, but she had seen quite a few TV programs featuring guilty characters that tended to think their guilt was easily recognized by everyone around them.

"I did prepare some material," Dominique said vaguely, hoping to keep them off the scent. "But you know how it is. I'm retired now, and I haven't taught in quite a while. I know it sounds silly, but I'm going to have to devote a lot of time to this Bible study, so I won't be able to join the choir. I'm really sorry. I would have loved to, but I can't."

To Dominique's relief it turned out that Bella, Piglet, and Paloma felt guiltier about pushing her too hard to join the choir than she did herself about having to turn down their friendly invitation. It remained for her to figure out how to deal with all the rest of the guilt that she was feeling not only about assuming a false identity and being a stowaway on the Cerulean Neptune, but also because she was going to teach a Bible study without having enough time to prepare the topic.

"God has a very peculiar sense of humor," she thought ruefully. "First He gives me a full decade of post-retirement boredom, then He presents me with three new friends, an exciting Neptune voyage, and a strange attraction to a piano player I don't even know—all in one day."

"So, Maria, is this your first time on a world cruise?" Bella asked, thinking it best to lead the conversation away from the choir for the time being.

Dominique felt electrified by Bella's question. *What?* She was on a world cruise? *A world cruise?* How long would it take? Where would they go? Would she be getting on and off the ship? Had the real Maria paid in advance for the extras that were involved in a world cruise? Would she look like a complete idiot if she asked her new friends these basic questions? How was she to find out what she was expected to do? Maybe she could pretend she did have Alzheimer's after all. But it wouldn't work. No woman with Alzheimer's would be asked to teach a class on the Bible. She would do fine in the choir, but leading a Bible study? Not a good plan.

"Maria? Are you okay?" Bella inquired, looking at her with a concerned expression. Piglet and Paloma had both put down their knives and forks and were contemplating her with puzzled frowns.

"Sorry," Dominique said sheepishly. "I guess I was just having a senior moment. What did you ask me? What was the question again?"

"I was just wondering if you had ever been on a world cruise before, that's all."

"Oh, right... yes, of course. I mean no, actually. No, I haven't been on a world cruise before. I've never been on a world cruise in my life."

"Oh, what fun!" Paloma said, clasping her hands. "We'll have a marvelous time showing you what to do. We know all about what is world cruising. This is our third one, is that not so, Piglet?"

"I'm very fortunate to know some experienced guides like you," Dominique remarked, trying her best to speak with as much conviction as she could muster. "So tell me, are we going to visit any of your favorite places?"

"We're in my favorite place now," Piglet volunteered. "I love the Mediterranean. The countries have ancient cultures that date far back into the history. I wait with impatience to take the shore excursions about which they have spoken in the *Neptune News*. The guides, they have always interesting things to say about everything in the region here."

"Which is your favorite country in the Mediterranean, Maria?" Paloma wanted to know.

"Oh, it's a bit hard to say," Dominique replied. "Greece is hard to beat, but then so is Italy, and the Holy Land, and Egypt, and cities like Alexandria and Ephesus..."

"I'm sure that the people in your class will enjoy seeing those places after reading about them in the Bible," Bella declared. "After that we'll be cruising down the Red Sea and then eventually through the pirate-infested waters along the coast of Somalia."

"I've read about those pirates," Dominique remarked. "They must be desperate to help their people. They've had a drought for a long time now, and their government is in total disarray."

"You are right about that, Maria," Piglet agreed. "The people, they are starving. But you are mistaken about the intentions of the pirates, I think. They are not desperate to help their people. If it were thus, they would not interfere with aid workers who are trying to provide the Somalis with food, and water, and other good things like those."

"Why on earth would they try to stop the aid workers?" Dominique asked, astonished.

"The pirates are only interested in themselves, not their fellow citizens," Piglet explained. "So they keep their people subjected by preventing them from getting the food and the water. It does not serve their own interests to facilitate these supplies. Starving people do not have the strength to rebel."

"That's disgusting!" Dominique exclaimed. "That's the very essence of pure evil!"

"True enough," Bella agreed. "You can make that one of the themes of your Bible study."

"I do not wish to interrupt you," Paloma said, "but look around the room. Most of the people in the first seating have already gone to the floor show in the Cabaret Lounge, and the guests in the second seating are waiting for us to leave."

"Come on, let's go," said Bella. "Are you coming to the show tonight, Maria?"

"I have to prepare my Bible study," Dominique replied.

"Of course," Bella said, patting her on the shoulder. "See you tomorrow, then. I'll be attending your Bible study on Wednesday, too."

"Oh, good. Thanks, Bella. It'll be nice to see familiar faces on the first day of class."

As Dominique walked past the Casino Lounge on her way back to her cabin, she was disappointed to discover that Ted Rasmussen had gone away. The shiny black piano was no longer alive with the sound of music, and Dominique was left with a feeling of inexplicable sadness.

Down in the crew quarters Angel, one of the bartenders in the Neptune lounge, was taking his afternoon break. As he lay stretched out on the lower bunk, he stared resentfully at the two bunks across the narrow aisle. Why should the fat, useless passengers on the upper decks live in luxury, he said to himself, while he and all his other bunk mates had to stuff themselves into their cabins like so many olives in a jar? He was sick and tired of putting on a happy face and being nice to the passengers. Not a single one of those wretched infidels deserved to be pampered that way.

As far as Angel was concerned, it wouldn't go on that way much longer. He couldn't wait to see the passengers' faces when their comfortable little world came to a sudden and totally unexpected halt. And to think that he had come up with the scheme himself, and had put it all in place! His people would bow down to him and there would be dancing in the streets back home when it was all over.

Just then Selim arrived and squeezed himself into the bottom bunk across the aisle.

"You only have about five minutes before the second seating," Angel reminded him, "then you'll have to go up to Deck Six and start all over again. Don't forget to put the chocolates on the pillows."

"I know," Selim said. "You don't have to remind me."

"You better not talk to me that way, or I'll report you to the imam. I have rank over you in the mosque, you know."

"Sorry," Selim said apologetically. "I didn't mean any disrespect. I feel the way you do. I'm fed up with this job. I *hate* having to serve the rich passengers on the upper decks. They treat me like dirt. They look down on me."

"Who looks down on you?" Angel asked him. "Which ones, I mean? I'll make them pay."

"That tall woman who's married to a disgusting, fat little man she calls Piglet. *She* looks down on me."

"Piglet? Did you say *Piglet?*" said Angel, with a roar of laughter. "It's just like an infidel woman to marry herself with a pig! How does she treat him?"

"She has Piglet under her thumb."

"We'll put a stop to that. Our time is coming soon."

"Are you going to take the passengers hostage? Will you be holding them for ransom?"

"I'll tell you when the time comes. But right now it's on a need-to-know basis. I don't want to have to worry all the time about you shooting off your mouth."

"Who do you think I'm going to tell, anyway? I trust *you*. Why can't you trust *me,* too?"

"Because I know you, Selim. You can't keep your big mouth shut. If Security finds out that we're up to something, they'll be down our necks. We don't want that, now do we?"

"When have I ever ratted you out? Who am I going to tell, anyway? You think I'm stupid? I've seen it all. I know what kind of weapons the cruise ships are equipped to use against us, but none of them work."

"What do you mean, they don't work? What are you talking about?"

"They shoot us with high-pressure fire hoses, and we laugh in their faces. They deafen us with long-range acoustic devices, and we keep on coming. One time some passengers tried to repel us by throwing deck chairs down on our men when they were climbing aboard, but that didn't stop us. The problem with the infidels is that their superiors won't allow them to have firearms on board the ship. They're afraid we'll get their weapons away from them and shoot them with their own machine guns."

"Well, they're right," Angel said. "We're stronger and better trained than they are, and we're much smarter as well.

I've come up with an idea that they'll never figure out in a million years. They won't be ready for this one, Selim."

"Is it better than the Twin Towers?"

"The Twin Towers was the best one we've done so far, but this plan of mine will be just as good, if not better."

"We killed around 3,000 people that day in New York, you know."

"We won't get that many on this cruise ship," Angel said. "But it's not the number that counts. It's the way we do it that matters, and the great publicity we'll get afterwards. The Cerulean Neptune is a high-profile ship. It may not be the biggest one in the fleet, but it's the newest and the most modern one. The Neptune executives are very proud of it."

"So we're doing something new, something that's never been done before?"

"Yes, but that's all I'm going to tell you."

"No mother ship sending out little boats? No bombs? No explosions? No men coming aboard with grapple hooks?"

"Nothing like that."

"No rocket-propelled grenades?"

"No. We don't operate that way. That's what pirates do. They're the ones who use the RPGs. But we're not pirates, we're terrorists," Angel reminded him proudly. "That's what those cowardly infidels call us, anyway."

"Well, what's the difference?"

"Between an infidel and a terrorist?"

"No, between a *pirate* and a terrorist."

"Do I have to spell it out for you, Selim? Pirates want booty. Their mission is to get rich."

"What, by making the passengers pool their money?"

"They don't have cash on board. They charge everything on their credit cards, which are tied to their cruise cards."

"What about their jewelry? That's got to be worth a lot."

"It's just chump change compared to ransom money, and they get that by holding people hostage—officers, staff, crew, passengers—anyone they can get their hands on."

"Who pays the ransom?"

"Family, friends, the cruise lines, whoever is interested in the well-being of the passengers, or the well-being of their own treasuries, more like it. The cruise lines would rather pay ransom than get sued."

"I'd like to be a pirate," Selim said dreamily. "A pirate with a peg leg, and a patch over his eye, and a parrot on his shoulder, and a bandana covering his head. Someone just like Johnny Depp in *The Pirates of the Caribbean.*"

"Oh, grow up, Selim. Don't be such a crap head."

"Hey! You can't call me that. What's wrong with you? The imam says that using foul language is so bad even the angels can't tolerate it, and you call yourself Angel!"

"I've learned to use that kind of language so I can fit in. The infidels all say those sorts of words. They call it *cool.* So don't worry about it, Selim. I'll be forgiven because I'm on a jihad. I'm fighting for a just cause, and that's why you and I are different from the pirates."

"What do you mean?"

"When pirates attack a cruise ship, all they're thinking about is ransom money. They want to keep their captives alive so they can get paid. But we jihadists are fighting for Allah, bless his holy name, so we're helping him by sending the infidels to the gates of hell."

"Then tell me, Angel, do we have to commit suicide to do this holy deed?"

"I told you. You're on a need-to-know basis."

"Come on, Angel. I just want to know if I have to die. That's all I'm asking. I'm too young to die."

"What are you frightened of? Are you cowardly, like the infidels? Don't you want to go to heaven with the virgins? Your own personal virgins?"

"They'll only be virgins once, even in heaven."

"You don't know that. I'm sure Allah will heal them in the morning. Every morning."

"Allah be praised. But if I'm going to heaven anyway, why should I hurry to get there? I might as well get rid of as many infidels as I can while I'm still alive."

"I like your attitude, Selim. But you can stop worrying. You don't have to commit suicide. Now get your lazy butt off the bunk and get back to work."

"You're not my boss," said Selim, pushing himself out of the bottom bunk. "But can I ask you one more thing?"

"Go ahead."

"Why do you call yourself *Angel*?"

"Use your head, Selim. You know perfectly well that we're forbidden to touch alcohol. So how would it look if a passenger offered to buy me a drink and I refused?"

"The imam would pardon you if you drank alcohol for a holy cause," Selim remarked. "But you are virtuous, Angel. You found a better way when you decided to call yourself by a false name."

"So you like my idea, then, do you?"

"Absolutely. You decided to change your identity and become a man of Spanish heritage so that nobody will know that you serve Allah. Many Spanish men are called *Angel*. Some even call themselves *Jesus*. It is good for us to fool the infidels."

"You're right, Selim. That way I won't attract attention when I'm bartending. I can't allow anyone to prevent me from executing my plan."

"You have chosen well," Selim said. "Allah will help you and stand with you as you send the passengers to hell. You are truly the Angel of Death."

CHAPTER FOUR

Dominique intended to sit down right after breakfast and make an effort to prepare an introductory class for her Bible students who were scheduled to show up on the following Wednesday, but she became distracted by her curiosity about the meaning of all the names of the people she had encountered so far. She had been an English professor for most of her life, so words were for her what musical notes were for Ted Rasmussen. She had always had an interest in the meaning of surnames and given names, so she decided to make a list of the people she had encountered so far on the cruise, along with the meaning of their names. She went to the reference section of the surprisingly well-stocked library on Deck Nine and thumbed through a book of word origins. This is what she came up with:

TED, short for THEODORE: Gift of God, from Greek
    (theos) "god" and *(doron)* "gift"
RASMUSSEN, from Greek *(erasmios)*, "beloved"
DOMINIQUE, from French, "of the Lord"
MARIA, from Egyptian *mry,* "beloved"
MORGAN, from Welsh, "dweller on the sea"
SELIM, from Arabic *(Selima),* "to be safe"
CARLOS, from Germanic *(Karl),* "man"
PALOMA, from Latin, "dove"
CASABLANCA, from Italian and Spanish, "white house"
BELLA, from Italian, "beautiful"

Dominique contemplated the list for a while, thinking about the implications of the names. Ted had clearly drawn the best name of all: *beloved gift of God,* followed by that of her doppelganger Maria Morgan, whose name meant *beloved dweller on the sea.* She smiled when she realized that she had overlooked her own name, Dominique Perdue, meaning *lost child of the Lord,* from Latin *Domenici,* "of the Lord," and French *perdu,* "lost."

Dominique had indeed been feeling a bit lost ever since the real Maria had dropped her cruise card onto the floor of the pharmacy in Mayfair. From that moment forward she, the fake Maria, had felt as if she had been carried along on the waves of an unstoppable tsunami that had dumped her onto the decks of the Cerulean Neptune, where she had then fallen down Alice's rabbit hole into a wonderland of strange people and peculiar serendipities.

First there was the beautiful Bella, the young woman who had spoken to her so enthusiastically about the choir. Then there was the tall Paloma and her husband Piglet, the most oddly-matched couple that Maria had ever met. Finally there was Ted Rasmussen, who had left her feeling stunned not only by the quality of his voice and his depth of feeling, but by the extraordinary experience of having been greeted by her new name when she walked into the Casino Lounge, where he was singing *Maria* from *West Side Story.*

Dominique had been struck at that moment by a strange sense of destiny, awakened in her by the powerful effect of Ted's voice. She had no idea what that destiny would be or where it was leading her, but she had the impression that she was being called to follow the path wherever it went.

"*There* you are, Maria!" said a voice behind her chair in the library. "I've been looking all over for you!"

Dominique turned around and saw Bella standing there.

"Hi, Bella! What's up?"

"Have you forgotten? We have choir practice now."

"But I wasn't planning to join the choir, remember?"

"You don't have to join. Just sit in the back and listen."

"I have to prepare for the Bible class I'm giving. I don't have time to go to choir practice."

"But choir practice only takes an hour."

"What sorts of songs are you going to sing? Anything I know?" Dominique asked her.

"You're going to *love* the songs we're doing this year. Ted's taking us on a trip down Broadway. We're going to do songs from *West Side Story,* and *Les Misérables,* and *The Phantom of the Opera,* and oh yes, I almost forgot, some of the songs from *Man of La Mancha* as well."

"You're kidding!" Maria exclaimed. "Those songs are my absolute favorites! You're really going to sing all that?"

"You bet. We sure are! So are you coming?"

"Okay, then. Just let me put these books away first."

"You can leave them on the table if you like. Nobody will touch them. They'll still be here when you get back."

"The librarian won't mind?"

"There's no librarian on board. Everybody does their bit to keep the place neat and organized. But nobody will mind if you leave for just an hour or so. It'll be fine."

"So how many songs do you prepare for one concert?" Dominique asked, as the two women left the library.

"Oh, about a dozen or so," Bella said.

"So you'll sing three songs from each musical?"

"That's right," Bella replied, their voices fading as they made their way along the passageway and up the stairs to the Neptune Lounge, where Ted Rasmussen was just finishing the warm-up exercises. All the choir members had dragged their chairs onto the dance floor in four semi-circles around the stage, where Ted was now playing chords on the piano, followed by short finger exercises that the choir sang over and over, rising one note each time they sang the phrase.

I am a shining star, they sang.

I am a shining star, they sang, starting one note higher.

I am a shining star, one note higher again.

Paloma looked over at Bella and Dominique, and smiled at them from her place in the alto section.

When Ted was finally convinced that their throats and lungs were well warmed with these encouraging, reassuring sentences, he sat down on his piano bench and asked the choir members to pull out *Dulcinea* from the folders he had given them earlier, containing most of the songs that they would be rehearsing on sea days during the next segment of the cruise. He looked over his glasses at the members of the choir while they were rustling through their sheet music.

"I see we have a new member today," he observed. "Did you bring her, Bella?"

"Yes, she's our dinner companion at the first seating," Bella replied. "Her name is Maria."

"I'm glad to meet you, Maria," Ted said, with a warm smile. "Welcome to the choir. If you want to approach the piano, I can give you a folder with the scores for most of the songs we'll be singing on this segment of the cruise."

Dominique got up and went to the piano, where Ted was keeping the folders that he had prepared for any newcomers who might show up.

"Have you sung in a choir before?" he asked her.

"No, but I used to sing hymns in church. I can't exactly read music cold turkey, but I can follow it if you're playing the score on the piano."

"That'll do just fine," he said. "Are you familiar with Broadway musicals such as *Les Misérables* and *Man of la Mancha,* for example?"

"Yes, they're my all-time favorites!"

"Good, then. You'll find them all in your folder. Now, we'd better get started. We only have one hour to rehearse our songs."

Dominique went back to her place next to Bella in the soprano section. For the next hour she and the other choir members sang their hearts out, causing the Neptune Lounge to ring with the harmonies created by Ted himself during short pauses while he dictated the notes that he wanted each different section to sing. Once they learned their parts, Ted conducted them with great energy and growing fervor as the choir became more and more familiar with the music.

Ted's relentless, unflagging enthusiasm was contagious. He conducted them with inexhaustible energy, and the choir responded with notes and harmonies that Dominique would never have guessed possible coming from a mixed group of amateurs who gathered together every morning because they loved music and because they had come to love Ted as well.

"No wonder," Dominique thought. "*Amateur* means *one who loves* in French. We sing in the choir not for money but for the love of it."

Dominique was thrilled with the sounds of the song that they practiced that morning from *Man of la Mancha,* the musical with a book written by Dale Wasserman, lyrics by Joe Darion, and music by Mitch Leigh:

> *Dulcinea... Dulcinea...*
> *I see heaven when I see thee, Dulcinea,*
> *and thy name is like the prayer*
> *an angel whispers... Dulcinea... Dulcinea!*

As Dominique listened to the song it occurred to her that there were certain similarities between *Dulcinea* and *Maria.* In both scenarios the lover was deeply moved by the sound of the name of the woman he loved. How strange that she herself had just finished making up a list of the names of her new acquaintances on the cruise ship! Although she had lingered on the specific meanings of each of their names, she had now been exposed, through music, to the joy of hearing the *sound* of yet another set of names, which provided a sort of three-dimensional depth to the importance and splendor of merging language with music.

During a pause in the music, Dominique wondered for a moment if the beauty of the song would be enhanced for the members of the choir if they knew something about Don Quixote's life story. Why did he fall in love with Aldonza, a woman who was a lowly prostitute in the musical and a pig farmer's daughter in the original novel by Cervantes? In both cases she was rejected by Don Quixote's family, who found her objectionable on several different levels, and an obvious embarrassment to them all.

So was Don Quixote blind or insane to have loved her so much? His family thought he was probably both or maybe worse, but the truth was that Don Quixote loved Aldonza because he *saw* her for who she really was. His love allowed him to know her very heart and soul, and his tender insight, in turn, heightened his passion and deepened his love.

And then, Dominique thought, he decided to *change her name* to Dulcinea, which sounded more like that of a high-born lady of the Middle Ages and therefore suited her more perfectly. Dominique had also changed her name from *Lost child of the Lord* to *Beloved dweller on the sea,* and Ted had welcomed her twice while using her new name, the name provided by a stranger who herself was lost to Dominique when she simply disappeared without a trace in the streets of London.

"Love opens our eyes," Dominique said to herself, "and it helps us to know the loved one. A vicious circle, perhaps, but it's really love that causes love to deepen and grow. Love changes everything."

Dominique was reminded of the words from the musical *Aspects of Love,* with book and music by Andrew Lloyd Webber and lyrics by Don Black and Charles Hart:

> *Love, love changes everything,*
> *hands and faces, earth and sky.*
> *Love, love changes everything,*
> *How you live and how you die…*

Dulcinea's name was like the prayer an angel whispers, just as the meaning of Ted's name, *gift of God,* would slowly come to light and reveal to Dominique all its nuances during the course of the choir rehearsals. She looked over at Bella and smiled, glad that Bella had urged her so strongly to join the choir, and happy that Ted was their director. She couldn't wait to see how it would all develop. Dominique hoped, above all, that Ted would never stop saying *Maria*.

While Dominique, Bella, Paloma and the other members of the choir were singing songs from their favorite Broadway musicals, Piglet Casablanca was being given a private tour of the ship's galley as a professional courtesy. As a chef who had spent many years in a variety of kitchen settings, Piglet was able to appreciate the quality of the modern equipment that the Cerulean Neptune's chef, Giancarlo Giudicini, was proudly displaying.

The galley was a spectacle of gleaming stainless steel, arranged in an intelligent manner so as to accommodate the many requirements of planning, work flow, sanitation, and timing—all very carefully designed to produce the greatest number of dishes in the smallest space, in the shortest length of time, and with the fewest possible glitches. To top it all off, the end product had to achieve a clear level of excellence in order to avoid delays caused by food being sent back to the galley by dissatisfied passengers.

Scheduling was everything on a cruise ship the size of the Cerulean Neptune. None of the passengers visiting the galley that day could understand this better than Piglet who, in spite of all appearances, was an excellent conductor of culinary symphonies. When he worked in the kitchen of *El Cerdo Asado* in Algeciras, he grew in stature and bearing to such an extent that he seemed, in the eyes of his employees, to be every bit as tall as his wife, Paloma. This illusion of height, of course, was bolstered considerably by his white toque, or pleated chef's hat, which he always wore with great pride whenever he was "conducting" his kitchen staff in his restaurant in the south of Spain.

Piglet was delighted to be in the ship's galley that day, comparing notes with Chef Giancarlo Giudicini. The kitchen staff offered him dishes with small samples of the food items being prepared for the luncheon buffet, including skewered quail with tarragon pistachio pesto; peach, prosciutto and ricotta crostini; Moroccan spiced pasticcio with lamb and feta; Swiss chard lasagna with ricotta; and Piglet's favorite dessert—lavender sorbet—decorated that morning with mint sprigs and Queen Anne's Lace.

It seemed obvious to Piglet that the white flowers of the umbelliferous plant adorning the lavender sorbet were a poor choice of decoration for a food item destined for the dining room tables. Although he doubted that anyone would be tempted to take a small nibble of the Queen Anne's Lace, he nevertheless thought the staff was taking an unnecessary risk in presenting this particular type of plant to the passengers at meal time.

Suddenly Giancarlo Giudicini burst into life with a loud shout of angry indignation.

"Who put that Poison Hemlock on the sorbet dishes?" he thundered, his eyes bulging with outrage and disbelief.

The crew stared back at him, not knowing what to say.

"I asked you a question, and I'm waiting for an answer," he bellowed, staring daggers at the frightened galley crew assembled around the table. "Which one of you made this stupid decision?"

"P-P-Poison Hemlock, sir?" stammered one of them.

"You heard me. What's your name?"

"Selim, sir."

"Who the hell are you, and what are you doing here?"

"I'm a cabin attendant, sir. They asked me to help out for the special buffet luncheon. They're short-handed here in the galley, sir."

"Why did you put those flowers on the sorbet?"

"It looks like Queen Anne's Lace, sir."

"Only a fool would mistake it for Queen Anne's Lace!"

"Yes, sir," Selim said meekly. "But…"

"Want to know some other names for Poison Hemlock?"

"Yes, sir."

"How about Spotted Corobane, Musquash Root, Beaver Poison, Poison Parsley, or Spotted Hemlock? How's that for a start?"

"It's a good start, sir. A very good start."

"And would you also like to know what happens if you ingest Poison Hemlock?" Giudicini asked him pointedly.

"Yes, sir."

"You fall on the floor and become completely paralyzed. You can hear what people say, and you can understand what they're saying, but you can't speak and you can't move an inch. Eventually you die of asphyxia. Nice, isn't it Selim?"

"Well, I..."

"Of *course* it's not nice!" Giudicini yelled. "Stop trying to find a pleasing, acceptable answer. Now is not the time to be polite and subservient. Now is the time to find the right answer, and there is only one right answer, Selim! The right answer is that you are strictly forbidden to poison passengers on the Cerulean Neptune, do I make myself clear?"

"Yes, sir. Perfectly clear. But if some passengers *did* get hemlock poisoning, sir, what should we do?"

"Call the ship's doctor or the medical staff at once. They would provide antidotes such as stimulants and emetics and artificial respiration if necessary. But this is not the point, Selim!" he continued, still waving his arms in exasperation. "What I want to know is why you almost poisoned half the passengers on this ship with that Poison Hemlock of yours. Where did it come from, anyway?"

"Sir, the Poison Hemlock doesn't belong to me. I'm not in charge of stocking the galley, sir. I was just helping out today because I worked in the galley last year and I know something about food preparation."

Just then the swinging door opened, revealing the profile of Angel the bartender, who was listening in the hallway.

"What the hell are you doing skulking behind the door, Angel?" said Giudicini. "You have no business in the galley. What do you want?"

"I was looking for Selim, sir. I'm off duty now, and I was wondering if he'd finished his work."

"How did you know Selim was here? He's not normally part of the galley crew. Who sent him? Who is responsible?"

"He helps out sometimes for special occasions, sir. He has galley experience. He was supposed to be doing double duty today because of the special luncheon buffet."

Just then Piglet fell flat on the floor with a loud thump, inadvertently rescuing Angel from the need to give any more evasive explanations to the exasperated chef.

"For God's sake, what's happened to Mr. Casablanca?" cried Giudicini, leaning down to peer at him more closely. He suddenly noticed that Piglet was clutching a fork with a juicy piece of quail skewered on it. "Call the Medical Center at once," he shouted over his shoulder.

One of the crew grabbed the wall phone and dialed 911.

"Selim, get yourself over here!" Chef Giudicini yelled. "This man needs artificial respiration."

"Did he eat a flower, sir?" Angel asked nonchalantly, as he watched Selim give Piglet mouth-to-mouth resuscitation.

"No, he didn't eat a flower," Giudicini replied, irritated. "What do you know about these flowers, anyway?"

"You can see right away that they're Poison Hemlock," Angel said, in a bragging tone of voice. "I'm a bartender. I know all about herbs and flavorings. I also know that quails are immune to the poison of hemlock, but when they eat too much of it, their meat gets saturated with the poison so that they themselves become poisonous to other animals or to human beings. That's obviously what has happened to that man down there on the floor. There's a piece of quail on the fork in his hand, and another piece on the floor next to him."

Giancarlo Giudicini looked at Angel for a long moment.

"Report to my office and wait for me there," he said. "I want a little word with you."

The Cerulean Neptune medical team arrived just then and carried Piglet Casablanca away on a stretcher.

CHAPTER FIVE

Dominique Perdue, the accidental stowaway going by the name of Maria Morgan while she was on board the Cerulean Neptune, was sitting on the bed in her cabin with her Bible study notes spread out around her. After struggling for a good part of the evening to find a theme that would connect the pages of *Old Testament Alive!* with the songs they were singing in the choir, she had finally decided to talk about how love was brought to life and made more accessible to folks in today's world and in previous centuries too. Since she was more familiar with the musicals than with the Bible, she felt she would be on firmer ground if she took that approach.

During the previous choir practice, Ted had introduced a song from *Les Misérables* where Jean Valjean, the male lead, prays that the life of young Marius may be spared and that God might bring him safely back home. Ted had given Maria the shivers when he reached the high notes at the end:

> *God on high, hear my prayer,*
> *In my need you have always been there.*
> *He is young, he's afraid,*
> *Let him rest, heaven blessed.*
> *Bring him home, bring him home, bring him home!*
>
> *He's like the son I might have known*
> *if God had granted me a son.*
> *The summers die one by one,*
> *How soon they fly, on and on!*
> *And I am old, and will be gone.*
> *Bring him peace, bring him joy,*
> *He is young, he is only a boy.*

You can take, you can give,
Let him be, let him live.
If I die, let me die; let him live.
Bring him home, bring him home!

Dominique felt a catch in her throat when she thought about the child she might have known if God had granted her one. Even though she was childless, she knew in her gut that she would not have hesitated to die to save that child from harm or death. Greater love hath no man than this, that he should die for the sake of his friend—or child, or loved one.

But what about God? God was eternal, and couldn't die. Was His eternity like a ball and chain, then, preventing Him from making the ultimate sacrifice for His multitudes of beloved children? Dominique knew the answer. Most parents would willingly die for the sake of their children, but who among us would ask *our own child* to die for the sake of others? Surely there was no greater love than that, especially if the child in question was our only begotten son, and was totally good, innocent and sinless in every conceivable way.

It all boiled down to a basic truth, Dominique thought, as she looked at her notes. God is love. God is the essence of love, and that's why we can't live without Him. The very idea of a world without love is unthinkable. That being the case, the thought of a world without the presence of God is equally unthinkable. So when we nonchalantly deny that He exists, we ultimately condemn ourselves to the bleak reality of an orphanage where billions of little Olivers ask for more.

Who among us would willingly and knowingly choose to be an orphan? Dominique thought this might be a good opening question for the Bible study. Then all of a sudden she was struck by the unsettling thought that she herself was an orphan. Her mother and father were both gone and had no known relatives. She had always been very aware of this, but somehow she had not given much thought to the fact that the absence of her parents had made her officially an orphan.

"Orphan…" Dominique said to herself. "*Orphan* derives from a Latin word meaning *destitute,* which comes from the Greek word for *bereaved.*"

"God in His mercy protects us from feeling destitute every moment of every day," Dominique said to herself. "He bestows us with positive thoughts and feelings to help us get through life, but every once in a while He commits another act of mercy—He gives us a concomitantly negative wake-up call to remind us that we're all walking too close to a precipice that has no railing, and only He can save us from falling over the edge."

Dominique was not sure she liked being awakened to the harsh realities of life. In those moments when she noticed her solitude and the accompanying sense of desolation, her heart would yearn for a sponsor or an advocate to look out for her while she navigated the dark night of her soul.

As Dominique Perdue was awakening to these lugubrious but salubrious thoughts, Piglet was also awakening to find himself lying on a stretcher in the Cerulean Neptune Medical Center, attended by a nurse and the ship's doctor who was bending over him and massaging his heart.

"He seems to be coming to," Piglet heard the nurse say.

Her voice sounded dreamlike and far away, as if he were just recovering from anesthesia. His memory of the events leading up to his present situation was disturbingly shadowy.

"Where am I?" he asked, surprised by the pitiful little boy quality of his own voice.

"You're in the Medical Center," the nurse replied.

"What medical center? Where?" Piglet asked her.

"You're cruising on the Mediterranean Sea. Right now we're just off the coast of Spain."

"Spain?" he repeated. "What part of Spain?"

"Um, I think we're somewhere near Algeciras."

"Algeciras? This is where I get off! Let me out of here. I have to find Paloma! I need to find my wife!"

The nurse pressed a little harder on his chest to hold him in place.

"Mr. Casablanca, you mustn't struggle like that. Relax. You can't get off the ship. We're not stopping at Algeciras."

"What? Why not? How can you pass my home without stopping? That's where I live! I want to be with Paloma. Let me go home. Bring me home!"

"It's too soon for you to go home now, Mr. Casablanca. You have to finish the cruise first. You can't just jump ship."

"What am I doing on a cruise ship?"

"You're living your life. That's what we're all doing."

"I don't understand. Why can't I go home?"

"It's not time yet. We can't stop the ship. And besides, there's nobody here to bring you home right now, even if we *could* stop the ship."

"They could put me on a tender."

"Let me be perfectly blunt, Mr. Casablanca," the ship's doctor cut in. "Have you any idea how much it would cost to stop the ship and put you on a tender so you could go home? You can't do it on your own. It would cost a fortune."

"I have some savings."

"That wouldn't be enough, I'm afraid. You would need a millionaire to support you on your mission. Do you know someone who has that kind of money, someone who would be willing to spend it on you that way?"

"Yes, I know Paloma. My wife, Paloma. She would do that for me, but she doesn't have enough money. If I had the money I would use it to find a way to be with her, too."

"You shall soon be with her, Mr. Casablanca," the nurse assured him. "She's here on board the ship. She has already been contacted, and she's on her way right now. I'm sure she'll arrive very shortly."

By this time Piglet was wide awake and thinking a little more clearly, and the nurse was taking his vitals.

"His pulse is still a bit high, but his blood pressure is good," she said to the doctor.

"Excellent," he replied. "We'll let him rest a bit longer, and then we'll release him."

"Release me?" said Piglet, pushing himself up on his left elbow. "What do you mean? Release me where? How do you expect me to get home from here? Where is Paloma?"

"She's on her way, Mr. Casablanca," the nurse said.

"He's still out of it," the doctor remarked, removing his white coat. "Give him another ten or fifteen minutes or so, then check his vitals again. Get the paperwork ready for me to sign, would you? I'm going to grab something to eat."

Chef Giancarlo Giudicini was fit to be tied. He was pacing back and forth in his office, inveighing against the bartender, Angel, for skulking around outside the galley like a common criminal. What infuriated him most of all was Angel's facial expression, which flitted between disdainful and completely self-composed, with a touch of superiority that Giudicini found intolerable.

"How do you know so much about hemlock, anyway?" Chef Giudicini demanded.

"I'm a student of Socrates, sir," said Angel, with a smug expression. "As you undoubtedly know, there's a famous canvas by David depicting the death of Socrates..."

"Don't get smart with me, young man, if you want to keep your job."

"Do you want me to give you a different explanation then, sir, other than the real one?"

"I want to know why you're so interested in the subject of hemlock."

"As I said before, I'm a student of Socrates, sir, and of world literature too. *My heart aches, and a drowsy numbness pains my sense, as though of hemlock I had drunk.* I'm sure you must recognize those lines from *Ode to a Nightingale.*"

"Forget about Byron. Just answer my question, and stop beating around the bush."

"That's Keats, sir, not Byron," Angel said with a smirk.

"Never mind that," Giudicini shouted. "Get to the point, and stop all that ridiculous posturing. I'm not impressed."

"Surely you must have heard about the brilliant Bengali director Srijit Bannerjee, who directed the film known as the *Hemlock Society.* It's hard to be a cultured person these days without knowing something about hemlock, sir."

"I'm not going to stand here and play cat and mouse with you, Angel," said Giudicini, showing his lower teeth as he expressed his rage. "Get out of here. Just get out of here, and don't let me catch you anywhere *near* the galley again!"

"Yes, sir," said Angel, turning gracefully on his heel and heading for the door. "Please let me know if there's anything further I can do to help."

Chef Giudicini continued to pace the floor in his office, turning the whole situation over in his mind. There were two things that particularly bothered him: first of all, Angel knew too much about hemlock; and secondly, he was far too cocky and sure of himself not to have some sort of backup. He was up to no good, and not only that, he seemed to be part of a group or a plot of some sort. Chef Giancarlo Giudicini was determined to get to the bottom of it all.

Paloma Casablanca was deeply concerned when the nurse at the Medical Center called to inform her that her husband had collapsed during a cooking demonstration, but had recovered and was resting now.

"He must have had a heart attack, or maybe a stroke," she murmured as she hurried down the stairs to Deck Four. "Thank God I was in the stateroom when they called. What if he had died while I was in choir practice, singing away without a care in the world? Does anyone know I'm in the choir? Would they have found me somehow? What if he had died without me beside him, in the company of strangers?"

Paloma couldn't bear the thought of Piglet dying. In fact she wouldn't be able to live without him, and that was all there was to it. As simple as that. She couldn't even begin to imagine how widows and widowers got along without their other halves. How did they manage as just half a person? Yet couples did it all the time. It's rare for two people to die at exactly the same time, she said to herself, unless they are in an accident or some other sort of disaster of that nature.

Paloma took the stairs two at a time as she propelled herself on her long, thin legs toward the Cerulean Neptune Medical Center. She dearly wanted to wrap her arms around Piglet the way she had done seventeen years before, on the night when it had first dawned on her that she was in love with this unlikely little man who was a foot shorter than she was in stature but ten feet tall in terms of self-motivation and generosity of spirit.

Her life had been bathed in the sunlight of Andalusia ever since Piglet—her new neighbor whose real name was Carlos Casablanca—had opened the restaurant next door to her hotel. He had redesigned and reconstructed the building that had previously blocked out the warm light of day, and had planted, in the space between their two establishments, an exuberantly colorful garden of red geraniums, Spanish bluebells, pink Valencia roses, purple bougainvillea, yellow and lavender lantana, white lilies, red-striped gazania, and fragrant orange trees. The garden was dotted with chairs and tables strategically placed around a gazebo for guitarists and flamenco dancers.

Moments after the grand opening of *El Cerdo Asado,* the outside venue had come alive with strumming guitarists, stamping feet, clacking castanets and wailing voices singing of loves that had been lost long ago in the sands of the desert homes of Andalusia's ancient Moorish conquerors.

Paloma could not have known it at the time, but she, like the heroines of the mournful Andalusian songs, had already conquered Piglet's heart. As the weeks and months went by, he danced attendance on the dark, statuesque woman who owned and operated *El Hotel de la Esquina,* or the "Hotel on the Corner." She was not beautiful in the usual sense of the word, but her face shone with inner strength and intelligence, bespeaking a forceful yet kindly personality that reminded Piglet of the warm-hearted women in his own family.

Paloma, in turn, had been astonished to discover that she was slowly developing feelings for the thoughtful, energetic, creative chef and owner of the restaurant next door, the top of whose head, if he stood on his tiptoes, only just barely reached the level of her clavicle. But although Piglet saw the physical world from a relatively low perspective, he had an unusually broad overview of life itself, showing a depth of knowledge and understanding that never failed to impress Paloma when she turned to him for guidance.

His optimistic attitude eventually had a positive effect on her general approach to the problems that would normally come up during the course of an average business day at the Hotel on the Corner. Her friendship with Piglet had given her a sense of humor about the hotel's usual problems, and this decreased the overall tension of the daily activities. To her surprise the constant aggravations, when seen in this new light, seemed to melt away like butter in the hot Andalusian sun. Needless to say the guests themselves were beneficially affected by her more relaxed view of things, much to the delight of all concerned.

Nobody really understands the vast mysteries of love, no matter how much they may be studied, debated, or analyzed, and perhaps that's the way it should be. Suffice it to say that love eventually had its way with Piglet and Paloma, and they were married amid shouts of joy and endless toasts in the colorful, powerfully aromatic garden connecting Paloma's bustling hotel with Piglet's cozy restaurant.

Everybody loves a happy ending, so tourists and locals alike showed up frequently at the hotel, the restaurant, and the beautiful little garden to take pleasure in the exquisitely prepared meals and comfortable accommodations, both of which were enlivened by the most popular, talented, vibrant entertainers in the entire province of Andalusia.

"*There* you are Palomita, *mi vida*," Piglet cried when his wife appeared in the Medical Center. "I was just wondering where you were."

"Here I am, *amorcito,*" Paloma replied, with tears in her eyes. "I'm right here by your side."

Piglet tried to push himself up on his elbow, but he was strapped firmly onto the narrow stretcher.

"I seem to be tied down here… I'm not quite sure why."

"You've been ill, darling, but you're all right now. The nurse and the doctor have been taking good care of you."

"Well don't come too close then, Paloma. I don't want you to catch anything."

"You're not contagious, *mi amor.*"

"What's wrong with me, then?"

"You were poisoned, it seems."

"Poisoned?" Piglet exclaimed, looking alarmed. "Who poisoned me? And why would they want to do that?"

"Nobody poisoned you, my angel. It was an accident."

"Food poisoning? Was it food poisoning then?"

"I think so," Paloma said vaguely. "They didn't tell me the details when they called me in the stateroom. I hung up right away and came here as fast as I could."

"Well, was it staphylococcus, or E. coli, or what?"

Paloma glanced at the nurse with a questioning look.

"You'll have to ask the doctor to explain it to you," the nurse said. "He'll give you the diagnosis."

"Well, where is he, then?" Paloma asked.

"He just stepped out for a moment. He'll be right back."

"Could you at least untie my husband?" Paloma pleaded. "I'm right here beside him. I won't let him fall."

"I can't do that. We'll have to wait for the doctor."

"It's all right, *mi Palomita*," Piglet said, in his reassuring way. "You're here now, and we're together, so everything is going to be all right. Don't you worry about anything."

"You're always so cheerful and optimistic," said Paloma admiringly. "Even when you're in sick bay."

"That's because you're here beside me," he said, gazing at her tenderly.

Down in the crew quarters Selim and Angel were lying on their bunks discussing Piglet Casablanca's private tour of the ship's galley and the strange circumstances surrounding his sudden collapse.

"You were taking a huge risk by trying out that poison during the galley tour," Selim remarked.

"I had absolutely *nothing* to do with that!" Angel replied indignantly.

"Then how did the hemlock get on board?"

"How should I know? The seeds must have blown into the produce supplier's fields and sprouted there, and the stuff got gathered in with the vegetables. Hemlock grows wild in some parts of the English countryside, you know."

"Then why were you lurking near the door?"

"I was just casing the joint, as the Americans like to say. It's my job to know what's going on. I have to report back to the imam about everything I see."

"So you don't take credit for the poisoning, then?"

"Hell no!"

"You're a fool not to," Selim said. "The imam would be very proud of you."

"You've got a good point there."

"Hey, listen! If you don't want the credit, then give it to *me*," Selim said eagerly.

"Over my dead body," Angel said, giving him a whack on the head with his copy of *The Neptune News.*

CHAPTER SIX

Bella Boorsma was back in her stateroom again, after participating in a choir practice that was especially meaningful to her. Ted Rasmussen had introduced the fourth piece in the line-up, a familiar song that many of the choir members recalled from their school days long ago. Bella was quite a bit younger than most of the other people in the choir, but she was acquainted nevertheless with the familiar and well-loved words of "You'll Never Walk Alone" from Rodgers and Hammerstein's *Carousel:*

When you walk through a storm
hold your head up high,
and don't be afraid of the dark.
At the end of the storm
is a golden sky
and the sweet silver song of a lark.

Walk on through the wind,
walk on through the rain,
though your dreams be tossed and blown.
Walk on, walk on
with hope in your heart
and you'll never walk alone,
you'll never walk alone.

Bella had never wanted to be alone. Like most young women of her age, she had always taken it for granted that she would eventually meet the partner of her dreams and live happily ever after in an intimate, trusting relationship with someone who shared her desires and interests, and who would bravely go hand in hand with her through life to meet the various trials and adventures that lay in store for them. They would drink deeply together from the golden cup of their youth and then, when they were old and gray, they would sit on their rocking chairs and reminisce about the life they had made together, grateful for their blessings and rejoicing in their many opportunities to contribute to their family and to the world around them.

Bella had chosen the high road, however, avoiding deep relationships with others while she worked for her MBA at MIT Sloan School of Management in preparation for a career in marketing. She was fortunate to have been adopted by an intelligent mentor who was close to retirement age and who encouraged her to think for herself and to take the road less traveled. When she graduated she was offered a position in an advertising firm on Madison Avenue, where she greatly impressed the top executives with her stellar performance. At this point she felt she was ready to spread her wings and soar with the eagles, preferably in tandem with a soul mate with whom she could share her life at last.

The best laid plans, however, do not always materialize according to expectations. Bella, at the age of thirty-three, was diagnosed with UPSC, a rare and aggressive form of cancer that was known to metastasize quickly. After a major operation and the devastating news that she was already in stage four, she decided against chemo and radiation therapy, as these procedures were not thought to promise a cure in her case, and would only make her last months or years that much harder to bear. So Bella had walked through the storm with as much grace as possible, holding her head up high and enjoying whatever time she had left. She reluctantly resigned from her position in the New York City advertising and marketing firm, and dedicated herself to seeing the world in the time remaining to her. Of one thing she was utterly certain: she had greatly enjoyed being in Ted Rasmussen's choir on her two previous cruises, so she had signed up for the present tour knowing without the slightest doubt that at the end of the storm she would see a golden sky and hear the sweet silver song of a lark. What else she would see or hear was by no means clear to her.

There was one other inducement, however, that drew Bella Boorsma back to the Cerulean Neptune, and that was the fact that she had fallen in love with Lars Jensen, the staff captain. It had all begun rather suddenly the previous year when a heated argument broke out among some passengers who had boarded a bus to take a shore excursion, and Staff Captain Jensen had been called in to settle the problem.

Lars Jensen had already completed a good number of tasks earlier that morning, starting out with a meeting on the bridge with the captain before the ship arrived in Marseilles. They discussed the day's agenda as they waited for the local pilot, then the captain instructed Jensen to bring the ship into the pier. After completing the task, he had joined the captain for breakfast and then he had returned to his office to read the communications from other Neptune ships and from the head office in California. He also had made several calls to various authorities on the dock, as it was his responsibility to handle security matters as well as vendor relations. He had spent two hours overseeing the off-loading of waste material and the on-loading of supplies, including fresh fruit and vegetables in large wooden crates that had recently arrived in port from the outlying farms of Provence.

Just as Lars Jensen was contemplating the possibility of taking time out for a fresh cup of hot coffee, he was alerted to the problem of a disruption among the guests on the bus that was waiting to take a group of passengers on a wine-tasting tour. The guide had put her personal belongings on the two seats at the front of the bus, indicating that the guests were not to sit there.

After the bus was fully loaded, two passengers hesitated for a moment in the front by the driver, looking down the aisle to see where they could find a place to sit. Seeing no empty seats, they turned to the guide and asked her what they should do. She told them to wait while she consulted her passenger list, and was surprised to see that she actually had two extra passengers that day. She conferred with the ship's shore excursion organizer, and it was finally decided that a miscount had somehow taken place.

"No problem," the guide said to the two passengers who were waiting to be seated. "You can sit here in the front, and I'll take the folding seat just below you by the door."

"No way! That's not fair!" protested the man across the aisle from the seats that the guide had originally reserved for herself. "My wife and I were here first! We could have had your seats with the unobstructed view if you hadn't put your things there and made us sit behind the driver's booth where we can't see through the front window."

"I'm sorry, sir, but there's not very much I can do about that," said the guide politely. "These people are seated now, and I can't ask them to move," she explained.

"Yes you can," the man argued. "We were the first to get into the bus, and they were the *last* ones in. They have no right to sit in the best seat."

If the people who had taken the guide's former seat had been willing to change places with the protesters across the aisle, or if they had simply kept their mouths shut and let the guide remain in control of the situation, they would have saved everyone a lot of time. Instead, they chose to engage in a shouting match with the protesters, who then rose to their feet so that they could yell back at their challengers. Push inevitably came to shove, while the guide tried in vain to separate the warring parties. The bus driver jumped up and joined the fray, while two other passengers did their best to keep the infuriated guests from injuring one another.

It was at that moment that Staff Captain Jensen received a call from an agitated tourist guide telling him about the fight that had erupted on the bus that was about to depart on a tour of the wineries of Provence.

"I'm sorry, sir," she said as she finished her story. "I did my best, but I just couldn't get them to listen."

"Hold tight," said Jensen calmly. "I'm on the way."

Two or three minutes later the staff captain had stepped into the bus and politely invited the four antagonists to exit the vehicle with him for a moment so he could have a private word with them.

Bella's eyes, and those of the passengers in the window seats along the right side of the bus, were glued to the little group of five standing outside on the dock. At first there was a lot of arm waving going on, but within a minute or two Jensen had come up with a solution that appeared to satisfy everyone. The angry faces morphed into gratified smiles, and soon the group was laughing heartily at something the staff captain was telling them. With his arms around the shoulders of the couple who had been the first to board, he guided them back to the open door of the bus and watched while they settled into the seats with the unobstructed view. The couple who had been the last to board the bus remained on the dock, waving to their friends as Lars Jensen joined them in saying goodbye to the passengers on the departing bus.

"What the hell was *that* all about?" said the man in the aisle across from the couple who had now won the seats with the unobstructed view.

"Ah, it was just a little misunderstanding," said the other man. "That couple was supposed to go on the wineries tour that leaves this afternoon. They misread their ticket, is all."

"Well, you'd think the tour guide could have checked their tickets before all this happened," said the man's wife, in a loud voice. "The Neptune administration should train these people better."

"They don't work for Neptune," said her husband. "It's a private local company. The tour guide got rattled, I guess."

"Well, Neptune should find another company, then," the woman said huffily. "This was nothing but a big waste of time for everyone. What's *wrong* with people these days?"

"Human error, my pet," her husband said. "You need to make room for human error."

"Look who's talking. Since when have you ever made room for *my* errors?"

"You don't make errors, my dear," he replied, patting her gingerly on the knee. "Maybe a few miscalculations or misunderstandings, but never any errors."

As the bus pulled away from the dock, Bella Boorsma looked out her window at Staff Captain Lars Jensen standing there, looking proud and handsome in his white uniform. He was second in command to the captain, and was sufficiently trained in seamanship to be able to take over for the captain if he became ill or incapacitated. He also acted as the ship's chief of police, religious and psychological counselor, and the judge of all matters pertaining to conflict between either crew or passengers, or both at the same time. It was a rare person, Bella thought, who had the intelligence, diplomatic skills, technical proficiency and wisdom to succeed in these disparate areas of responsibility. She looked admiringly at him as the bus moved on, and it seemed to her that he was smiling back at her as they drove away.

Bella found herself thinking about Lars Jensen far more than she would have expected to think about a man she had never even spoken to before. She tried to imagine what it might be like to share the day with him, looking over the rolling vineyards of the south of France and enjoying the wine-tasting along with some delicious canapés. They would give each other little nibbles of their favorite tidbits, and they would drink from each other's glasses as they savored the vintages. The sun would shine down on them as they strolled along together, hand in hand, feeling blessed by the warmth of their new love.

Meanwhile Lars Jensen was back in his office again, sipping the coffee that had eluded him all morning and thinking of the lovely young woman who had been sitting at the window and smiling at him as the bus pulled away from the wharf. What was it about her that he found so unusually attractive? She had gentle eyes—that was it. He liked women with soft expressions and kind eyes. He detested confrontations with bossy, brassy, abrasive, strident women. They were all so verbal that he had learned long ago to let them talk themselves out at the beginning of the argument, leaving him with the opportunity to come up with something soothing to say to cool them off and calm them down. He usually succeeded, but at great cost to his nervous system. He was always ready for a stiff drink after one of those unpleasant showdowns, and he wasn't even a drinker. He would have practiced the avoidance technique in the case of those overbearing women and their male counterparts if it weren't for the part of his job description that required him to be the soother-in-chief of the guests of the Cerulean Neptune where controversies and angry disputes were concerned.

When it came to the beautiful young woman in the bus window, however, avoidance didn't come into the picture at all. He would have to make some discreet inquiries here and there to see if he could find out more about her. He shook his head and almost laughed out loud at the very thought of a "discreet" inquiry. It was a contradiction in terms, for the minute a man made inquiries about a particular woman, the rumor mill would immediately start grinding away, followed by gossip that would turn into a series of guessing games that kept everybody happy and occupied for weeks at a time.

Most of the guys he knew would be all over him to find out if he had "scored," and if not, why not? They would line up for the privilege of teasing him and giving him invaluable advice on how to achieve the highest possible score in the shortest available time, and he would be expected to put up with them in a good-natured way, pretending that all the banter and nudges were the greatest fun he had experienced in years. At least if he didn't score they would let him off the hook by blaming the woman for being a prude or a tease.

No, he thought, he would keep this one all to himself. He didn't want to risk having the gossip or the rumors get back to her in a form that would turn her off before he even had a chance to talk to her himself. He would have to move as slowly and carefully as possible. The only problem with the slow and careful approach, however, was that a cruise, any cruise, has an expiration date that creates a sense of urgency—one has to move forward with a certain amount of alacrity or the cruise ends before the romance begins.

As he sat at his desk musing about the woman at the bus window, it occurred to him that he had seen her somewhere before. But where? Was it around the ship in the lounge or in the passageways or the casino or in one of the restaurants? Then he suddenly remembered that he had seen her at an evening choir performance the year before. *That's* why she looked so familiar. She was in the choir. That meant she was in choir practice with Ted Rasmussen at noon every sea day. Could Ted be trusted with a discreet inquiry? Ted was quite a bit older than he was himself, and probably a good deal more mature than the guys in his orbit who would no doubt enjoy the opportunity of teasing him, which might even end up destroying his chances with the woman at the window.

But wait! Maybe Ted was interested in her himself. How could he not be? His only hope, Lars thought, was that Ted was already involved with somebody else. No, it was better not to say anything to anyone at all. There was no real need to make discreet inquiries, for there was always the risk that an inquiry could arouse the interest of the one to whom it was made, and that could mean that Lars would be shooting himself in the foot. The only thing for him to do was to find out where she liked to go and what she liked to do, and then make sure to be there, preferably ahead of time, before she showed up. Bumping into her here and there would give him the chance to talk to her without appearing to be stalking her, and best of all nobody would know how he felt about this woman. He wanted her all to himself—no games, no gossip, no inquiries. He wiped his forehead with his hand, surprised to find that he had broken out in a cold sweat. This had never happened to him before. Why was he nervous? He was not a teenager, after all. He was a well-trained, competent man, and had spent years studying every aspect of managing a ship and the people on it, yet here he was, wondering how to approach a woman he barely knew and with whom he had never even spoken, as if his very life depended on his being successful in developing a relationship with her. Now he was fearful of being seen as a stalker or a seducer, worried that Ted Rasmussen might already have her in his sights, and shy about approaching her in a straightforward way. There was too much to lose if he made a blunder, and too much at risk if he made a misstep.

"God help me," Lars thought as he drained the last drop of coffee from his cup. "I don't recognize myself anymore."

He glanced at his watch and realized that it was already noon. The people in the choir had probably already finished pulling their chairs into rows on the dance floor in front of the piano in the Neptune Lounge. He had hoped to be able to slip unnoticed into the room while they were busy with this task, but now they would be warming up and getting ready to sing, so he would attract their attention if he simply appeared and took a seat nearby, like an audience of one. He hoped there would be somebody else in the lounge who was busy doing something, so that he could approach him as though he had official business to discuss.

As luck would have it, Angel was behind the bar at the back of the lounge, setting up glasses for an upcoming event. The Francophone Club had arranged a welcome party so that all the French speakers on board could become acquainted. Most of them were from Quebec, and they welcomed the opportunity to speak with their fellow Canadians in their native language.

Lars went over to the bar and struck up a conversation with Angel, asking him if he had everything he needed for the Francophones, and if there was anything he could do to be of service.

"No, not really," Angel replied, shooting him a puzzled look. "I have everything I need. It's all under control."

"Good. Carry on then," Lars said, turning to go. "By the way," he continued, changing his mind and facing Angel again. "What are they planning for hors d'oeuvres?"

"They've ordered some sandwiches on French bread... jambon de Paris with Gruyère and cornichons, followed by assorted petits fours."

"Excellent. I might stop by myself for a few minutes. It sounds like something I wouldn't want to miss."

Just then Ted Rasmussen played a chord on the piano, and the choir began singing *You Raise me Up.*

Lars Jensen smiled to himself as he turned to go. As far as he was concerned there was only one person who raised him up and that was the woman who had smiled at him from her window as the local bus and its passengers set off early that morning for a tour of the wineries of Provence. He saw her profile now in the front row of the choir. He watched her, enraptured, as she sang with great feeling about being raised up to stand on mountains.

Angel watched the staff captain with great interest as he walked reluctantly in the direction of the starboard doorway of the Neptune Lounge. He took particular notice of the fact that Jensen hesitated by the door and turned around to take one last look at the soprano section of the choir.

"Perfect," Angel said under his breath. "Now all I have to do is find out which one he's got the hots for, and I'll have him right where I want him."

CHAPTER SEVEN

Dominique Perdue, the fake Maria Morgan, returned to her stateroom right after choir practice, too timid to hang around Ted Rasmussen along with the other choir members who were vying with one another to get him to sit at their table at the luncheon buffet. Ted watched her as she left the Neptune Lounge, wishing they could sit down for lunch alone together so he could get to know her. He had noticed her looking at him as he was singing and playing the piano in the Casino Lounge on the first night of the cruise, and somehow he knew that he wanted to see her again and again. He had been surprised by his reaction to this woman, for he was not unused to having passengers linger near the piano, listening spellbound to his songs. But this time it was different. He had felt attracted to her in a way that was not easy for him to understand. All he knew was that when he looked at her he felt as though he could find happiness by her side, the kind of quiet happiness that comes from being known and appreciated on the deepest levels.

The warning bells sounded, of course, for he knew very well that ship board romances between staff and guests could lead to the dismissal of the staff member if they got out of hand, or even if they were seen to be indiscreet in any way. This was fine by Ted, who was not the kind of person who sought superficial, short-lived relationships that were carried out publicly for all to see. He felt that he was fortunate to have enjoyed some highly successful bonds with significant others in his life. He had also experienced some inevitable failures, due in great measure to the fact that his contracts on world cruises were only three months long. The separations would become either incredibly frustrating to his partners, or the two would grow apart to such an extent that the original form of the relationship would be hard to maintain. Yet the fabric of his friendships almost always withstood the test of time, and he enjoyed keeping in contact with passengers with whom an initial attraction had eventually developed into an enduring and mutually satisfying friendship.

"How on earth does he do it?" these friends would say to one another when they happened to meet.

"Ted Rasmussen is a good man, and we can all see it," some would reply, not knowing how else to explain it.

"He can't sing without feeling," others would say, "so he touches our hearts and makes our spirits soar."

"That's true. And how often do you get a chance to feel that way? It usually takes a whole night on Broadway to get me to achieve lift-off like that."

"I've heard him go through an entire Broadway musical from beginning to end all by himself in one evening, singing every one of the parts."

"Me too. That's what I'm saying."

"He's a very talented performer. We're fortunate to have him on board, you know."

"I've heard there are passengers who book cruises over and over again, just to hear Ted Rasmussen sing and play the piano."

"Lucky for the Neptune Cruise Line."

"Lucky for us, too!"

"I wonder how many people realize that."

"We appreciate him because we know him and we've seen him perform, but it's too bad he doesn't have a larger audience. He could be famous!"

Bella Boorsma was one of the passengers on the Cerulean Neptune who held Ted in particularly high esteem. She had known him for three years now, and had long been troubled by the fact that he was essentially being underutilized. He had talent and charisma that went far beyond what one could normally expect from the average singer and piano player on a cruise ship, she thought, yet she didn't see any clear-cut signs of advancement on the horizon for him. In some ways she almost hoped that he wouldn't be tempted to accept any other offers, because she looked forward to seeing him on her yearly world cruise, and she hated the thought of not being able to sing in his choir if he were to leave the Neptune Cruise Line to pursue other options. But she always felt mortified by her selfish thoughts, and she would promise herself to find an opportunity for Ted that would keep him with the cruise line and at the same time provide him with the advancement he so clearly deserved. It occurred to her that Staff Captain Lars Jensen would be just the right person to consult.

"You've brought up a very interesting question," said Lars, delighted that Bella had thought to seek his advice on the matter. For the last few days he had been casting around in his mind for an excuse to get together with her, and here she was, sitting in the Casino Lounge with him, chatting over coffee and pastries. "Ted Rasmussen is a great asset to the Neptune Cruise Line, though," Lars continued. "I'd hate to see him leave us and move on."

"I feel exactly the same way," Bella agreed. "That's why I wanted to bounce this idea off you. I think I might have a plan that could be viable, but I wanted to see what you thought about it before I went any further down that road."

"Yes, tell me about it," Lars said, leaning a bit closer.

"Well, here's what I was thinking. First and foremost, we want to keep Ted with the Neptune Cruise Line. If that's what Ted wants too, of course."

"Of course," Lars nodded.

"And secondly, we want to attract more passengers to the Cruise Line so that both parties can benefit."

"Absolutely."

"So I was thinking that if Ted and the choir got off the ship once in a while and sang in outside venues, it would be exciting for the passengers, while at the same time it would give Ted a bit more exposure. If it worked out well, it would give the Neptune Cruise Line some good publicity too, and it would be a win/win for everybody."

"That sounds very interesting," Lars said. "But it could be costly. Have you given any thought to that?"

"Not yet. I wanted to run it by you first."

"Well, I like your idea in theory. I like it very much. But there are a number of things to work out first, before it would be ready to present to head office. Do you know anyone who could write up a professional proposal?"

"I could," Bella suggested.

"*You* could?" Lars exclaimed, immediately regretting having sounded so surprised. The last thing he wanted was for Bella to think he underestimated her abilities.

"I have an MBA from MIT's Sloane School of Business, so I'm well trained in that area."

"You're a Sloanie? I had no idea!"

"Well, of course not. How could you have known?"

Bella and Lars spent the better part of an hour discussing the project and talking about the best way to present it to the Neptune headquarters in Santa Marta. By the end of the hour each one knew quite a bit more about the other as far as their business knowledge was concerned, and they were beginning to form some opinions about their basic attitude toward life in general.

Both of them liked what they had heard.

Dominique Perdue, the accidental stowaway who had Maria Morgan's ID but who saw herself as Maria Trouvée, was probably the one passenger on the Cerulean Neptune who appreciated Ted the most. Not only did she feel inspired by his interpretation and performance of her favorite songs in the Casino Lounge and during choir practice, but she had gained some useful insights into the connections between the Broadway musicals and the Bible. She would never have the time to read all the Scriptures before giving her first Bible class, but perhaps she could add something to *Old Testament Alive!* to make her presentation more understandable if she combined Broadway with the stories from the Bible.

Les Misérables, for example, was a case in point. Jean Valjean was sick, starving and destitute because he had been in prison for stealing a loaf of bread and now, as a released convict, he was unable to earn a living. The Bishop of Digne invited him home for dinner and a warm place to sleep, but Jean Valjean, knowing that his prison record would forever prevent him from finding work, could not resist stealing the bishop's silverware. Inspector Javert catches him and drags him back to the bishop's house to get a statement from him so that he can throw Valjean into jail again. But the bishop claims that he gave him the silver as a gift, and besides, he points out, Valjean neglected to take the candelabra with him when he left. Valjean is so touched by the bishop's kindness and so grateful for his having saved him from Javert's clutches that he decides to dedicate his life to God.

Dominique knew enough about history to be familiar with the conflict between Catholics and Protestants at the time of the Reformation. The former believed in salvation through obedience to God's law (works/Javert), whereas the latter maintained that we have *all* sinned and fall short of God's standards, yet we are saved by the mercy God shows to those who love Him and trust Him (faith/Valjean). Once one understands that Jean Valjean knows that his true home is with God, then it is easier to see the dual meaning of his prayer when he asks God to bring Marius home.

Dominique also knew history well enough to understand what the Spanish Inquisition was all about. The inquisitors thought that if one could get rid of all the so-called heretics and Protestant sympathizers by means of a cruel and ruthless inquiry into their beliefs and behavior, one could thereby protect Church and nation. But Miguel de Cervantes (the author of *Don Quixote de la Mancha*, Spain's greatest literary masterpiece) was secretly in agreement with Erasmus of Rotterdam, the tolerant humanist who wanted to reform the Church from within by demonstrating the reality and the universality of God's love for *all* His children. So Cervantes created a humorous, apparently crazy knight who went about righting wrongs and rescuing maidens in distress. To do this he had to gaze into their very souls, recognizing that Aldonza the Prostitute, for example, was really Dulcinea the Princess. He saw her for who she really was, and he was therefore able to touch her heart and soul, and inspire her to change her life by following him on his great quest, just as Jean Valjean was inspired by the kind mercy of the Bishop of Digne to change his life by dedicating himself fully to God.

Dominique was starting to see connections everywhere. Jean Valjean and Don Quixote had much in common in spite of the fact that the former was a competent entrepreneur and the latter was a dreamer and a hopelessly impractical knight covered in armor cobbled together from pieces of old tin he had collected from a garbage dump. But they both shared the same quest to make this a better world by bringing God into the picture, God as He really is—the God who loves us just as we are, but too much to leave us that way, as theologian Dietrich Bonhoeffer once put it. God yearns to raise us up so we can stand on mountains and be the best that we can be.

Dominique was reminded of a song that Ted had taught the choir the previous day—a song made popular by singer Josh Groban, composed by Secret Garden's Rolf Løvland, and with lyrics by Brendan Graham:

When I am down and, oh my soul, so weary,
when troubles come and my heart burdened be,
then I am still and wait here in the silence,
until you come and sit a while with me.

You raise me up, so I can stand on mountains,
you raise me up, to walk on stormy sea,

I am strong, when I am on your shoulders,
you raise me up to more than I can be.

There is no life, no life without its hunger,
each restless heart beats so imperfectly,
but when you come and I am filled with wonder,
sometimes I think I glimpse eternity.

Like Moses, whom God raised up to stand on Mount Sinai where he was given the Ten Commandments, and like Peter, who walked on the stormy Sea of Galilee, Jesus raises us up onto His shoulders so we too can stand on mountains and become more than we can be by our own puny efforts.

Dominique was surprised by how clearly her Sunday School classes were coming back to her. Just about every song in the choir had its roots somewhere in the Bible, but she had long ago turned her back on what she considered to be the themes espoused by uptight conservatives with middle class morals. She recalled how much she had enjoyed the satirical parody of the American lifestyle epitomized by the Simpsons, and how she had laughed at the priceless spoofs created by *The Committee,* a talented improvisation group from San Francisco whose performances she had attended at a dinner theater in London when they were on tour there.

She felt ashamed now of her disdainful laughter and by the way she had looked down on the conservative men in uninspiring suits who were being mocked by *The Committee.* Scornful laughter had been her natural weapon of choice too, when it came to debating the socio-political problems of the day, for her opinions were based almost exclusively on the information she had harvested on a regular basis from *I.F. Stone's Weekly*, a highly-regarded and widely-read left-wing newsletter written and published by a humorous, iconoclastic American journalist.

But Dominique's scoffing laughter had now disappeared along with the self-confident opinions she had held in her youth. She came to appreciate the famous comment made by Winston Churchill, who remarked that if you're not a liberal when you're young, you have no heart; but if you're not a conservative when you're old, you have no brain. Now that she had acquired a certain measure of insight in her mature years, Dominique was not at all certain that she had a brain, but she did suspect that she had a heart. She was also quite certain that Ted Rasmussen had a particularly tender heart, judging from the songs he had chosen for the choir and the sincere feeling with which he sang them in the lounge. Some might say he selected those specific songs only to please his audience, a group consisting primarily of retired older folks who had the means and the leisure time to enjoy a world cruise. This might well have been the case, since most of the passengers would have come of age at some point during the fifties or sixties, but Maria could see that Ted, who seemed to be from a somewhat younger generation, was nevertheless genuinely moved by all the songs that she loved too, and which he sang with a depth of feeling that touched her heart.

As she sat in her stateroom trying to find an inspiring way to present her Bible study, Dominique looked for ways to merge the themes from Ted's chosen songs with similar themes from the Bible. She shared with Ted an enthusiasm for three Broadway musicals: *The Phantom of the Opera, Les Misérables,* and *Man of la Mancha.* What did these musicals have in common with one another, and what did they have in common with the Bible? There was one theme that bound them all together, and that was the topic of love— a topic that fundamentally connects the entire human race. What, then, were the types of love described in these three different musicals?

After spending most of the afternoon thinking carefully about each musical in turn, Dominique finally came up with a sort of synthesis that focused her thinking while she re-examined the musicals in greater depth. As far as she could tell, *The Phantom of the Opera* could perhaps be subtitled

"Love as Seduction," in that the Phantom's main purpose in taking on the role of Christine's mentor was to bind her to himself by making her his personal *chef d'œuvre,* just as Pygmalion created Galatea in his own image. If Maria was correct about the Phantom's intentions, his love for Christine could be interpreted as fundamentally self-serving, which is the key purpose of a seduction. *To seduce,* Dominique knew, means *to lead away,* that is, to lead the loved-one away from everything she believes and from everyone she loves, so that she is essentially bound, body and soul, to the lover himself, with nowhere else to turn.

But why would any woman willingly submit to such a claustrophobic life? The theme brings to mind the celebrated Stockholm syndrome, or capture-bonding—a psychological phenomenon in which hostages basically fall in love with their captors, who tend to grow more and more abusive as time goes by. The Phantom, however, becomes the exception to the rule, for in the long run he proves his sincere love for Christine by granting her the freedom to be with the suitor whom she herself truly loves.

"This is a great musical," Dominique said to herself. "The Phantom has passion, subtlety, and a wicked temper, but he redeems himself in the end by his magnanimity. What started out as a selfish desire proves to be true love when he sacrifices that desire for the sake of Christine's happiness."

What fascinated Dominique most about this musical was the symbolism of the chandelier that was being auctioned off in the opening scene, tagged as Lot 666. In Revelation, the last book of the Bible, the number 666 represents the number of Satan, who has been banished forever to hell, the realm of eternal darkness. Dominique liked the contrast between this darkness and the light of the chandelier, for the symbolism of dark and light, after all, represents the conflict between good and evil that plays out in every human soul. *Lucifer* in Latin means *Bearer of Light,* the name originally given by God to His leading angel. But when God expelled him and his vast minions from heaven because of their rebellion against Him, He changed Lucifer's name to Satan, which means *Opposer* in Hebrew, because he seizes every opportunity to challenge God's will and humankind's nascent faith.

"What a fantastic introduction to the book of Genesis, which explores the battle between good and evil," thought Dominique. "They both exist in all our hearts, just as they both exist in the chandelier, which was originally made for the purpose of providing light. But it ends up crashing down on the audience, causing darkness, death and destruction, just like the mayhem brought about by the fallen angel whose number is 666."

Dominique was pleased to have come up with the idea of including her three favorite Broadway musicals with the material introduced in *Old Testament Alive!*.

"There's no end of things to talk about when it comes to *The Phantom of the Opera*," she thought. "I'm not so sure I should subtitle it *Love as Seduction*, though. Maybe I could call it something like *The Phantom of Darkness and Light*, or maybe *The Chiaroscuro of the Human Heart*. Yes, perhaps that's it. I'll have to give that some more thought."

Just then there came a loud knock on her cabin door, bringing her back to reality with an unpleasant start.

"Why do the cabin attendants always have to bang so hard on the door?" she wondered. "We're not deaf."

"Come in," she shouted.

"The passengers always yell at us to come in when we knock," Angel thought. "They must think we're deaf."

He opened the door and smiled pleasantly at Dominique, who was sitting on the bed surrounded with books from the ship's library and notes she had made on pieces of paper.

"Good morning, Maria," he said amiably.

"Good morning," Dominique replied, wondering why he was calling her by her first name. "Are you quite sure you've come to the right stateroom?" she continued, noticing that he was carrying a tray of cans and bottles. "I don't remember ordering anything to drink."

"Don't play dumb with me, Maria. I went to a lot of trouble to get permission to take inventory on Deck Six so I could come to your cabin with a bottle of the special wine."

"That's what I mean. I haven't taken anything from the fridge, so you can save yourself the trouble."

Dominique got up from the bed and approached him, noticing that his name tag read "Angel".

"I just got through telling you, I have to fill out this inventory sheet," Angel said, opening the door of the fridge and peering inside.

Dominique stared at him, wondering what kind of non-work he could possibly find in a fridge whose contents she had not touched or even glanced at since the day she'd made the astonishing discovery that she was a stowaway on the Cerulean Neptune. She of all people! She'd always been more or less timid, retiring, and bookish—perfectly content to go unnoticed and to remain generally out of sight. She was the ideal candidate for stowaway status, in other words.

Angel took a pen from his shirt pocket and started to make check marks on a printed list.

"Do you have to go to all the trouble of taking inventory even though I haven't touched anything?" Dominique asked.

"I have to hand in this inventory sheet later to prove I've done my job. I wouldn't be allowed into your stateroom if I didn't have a specific job to do. You know that."

"Well, it seems like such a waste of time, that's all."

Angel gave her a sort of puzzled smile.

"You don't have to pretend with me, Maria. You can let your guard down. Nobody can hear us while we're in here with the door closed."

"What do you mean?" Dominique asked him nervously. "What are you talking about?"

"I'm here with the back-up," he said, looking irritated. "You know the boss's policy. We're supposed to have back-up every step of the way, to make sure it all goes smoothly. So I'm leaving it in your cabin just in case we need it."

Dominique looked at him closely. What boss was he talking about? Did he think that his boss was her boss too? And what back-up was he referring to? She would have to be very careful with her responses in case he began to suspect that she wasn't who he thought she was.

"We're lucky," he said, with the suggestion of a sneer. "They gave me a case of *1971 Château Apollyon Belial Grand Cru Classe Pauillac Bordeaux,* with new labels. It's a nice deep red, the color of blood," he said, smacking his lips. "Anyway, remember it's the *1971 Château Apollyon Belial Bordeaux*, got that? And keep your hands off it. Do *not* put it in the refrigerator, either."

With that bit of advice Angel turned and left the cabin, winking at her as he shut the door.

"What was *that* all about?" Dominique asked herself. "First he checks my fridge when he doesn't have to. Then he puts a bottle of wine next to the fridge that I didn't ask for. So why did he put it in my room if he doesn't want me to touch it? And what was that wink all about?"

Dominique picked up the bottle of *Château Apollyon Belial Grand Cru Classe Pauillac Bordeaux*. It was full right up to the top, but the bottle had been opened, for the seal was gone and the cork was showing about half in inch above the rim. She put the bottle back and sat down on her bed again to review *Man of la Mancha* to see what connections she could make with *The Phantom of the Opera,* but she kept thinking about the strange visit from the man called Angel.

"What did he mean when he said the bottle of *Château Apollyon Belial* was back-up?" she asked herself. "Who *was* that crew member, anyway? I didn't like his cheeky attitude, and the way he told me not to play dumb with him. That look-alike of mine has some very unpleasant friends."

CHAPTER EIGHT

T ed Rasmussen was sitting in his stateroom, wondering
whether or not to tell the members of the choir that he
had been given some exciting news from the Neptune
Cruise Line's executive offices in Santa Marta, California.
Apparently a certain Marty Goldbloom, the creative director
of the Neptune Cruise Line, had been sent an interesting
proposal from Staff Captain Lars Jensen and elite passenger
Bella Boorsma, outlining some ideas that would provide Ted
and his choir with more exposure by having them perform in
ports around the world. This happened to square up nicely
with the long-standing idea of successfully promoting the
Cerulean Neptune choir to the Sydney Opera, so Marty had
formed a team of experienced researchers, a talented copy
writer and a skillful in-house art director. They had all put
their heads together to discuss the intriguing presentation
that Bella Boorsma had put together for the Sydney Opera.
Now all that was needed before making the presentation to
the executives at the Sydney Opera was the go-ahead from
Neptune's board of directors.

The success of the Neptune presentation to the Sydney
Opera would be more certain if Ted Rasmussen's choir were
to perform at various venues around the globe. Although
many choirs of all types and sizes were already traveling to
countries on every continent, the choirs could not function
without the services of professional tour companies that were
experienced in accommodating the choirs and musicians by
organizing transportation and itineraries as well as making
reservations at numerous hotels, restaurants, and appropriate
venues for the concerts.

A great deal of planning was required to shepherd choir members in countries that were foreign to them, however, for there were many possible traps and loopholes that could only be avoided by exercising the knowledge and foresight that comes with experience. But this specialized knowledge has a price. The typical traveling choir had to spend a considerable amount of time raising the funds to pay for their world tours, or they had to pay a professional fund raiser to do the job for them. Either way, the project was always expensive, time-consuming and discouraging to all concerned when the choir failed to meet their financial goals.

But what if the choir members already enjoyed excellent accommodations, restaurant services, and tour facilities on a cruise ship that was taking them on a trip around the world? The fact that the Cerulean Neptune choir members had paid up front for their travel expenses seemed to be the solution to the financial exigencies.

Thanks to the Cerulean Neptune's highly professional presentation by elite passenger Bella Boorsma, the Neptune Cruise Line's creative team was finally ready to present the new concept of the choir's program to their executive board, emphasizing the suitability of starting with one major venue and progressing from there to smaller ones that had less experience managing traveling choirs. Marty Goldbloom, the creative director for the Neptune Cruise Lines, was the first to speak to the executives sitting around the boardroom table that day to hear what he had to say about getting permission for Ted Rasmussen and his choir to perform at the famous Sydney Opera House.

"It's all in the way you present yourself," Marty began. "If the presentation shows Ted's choir as a group that can give a polished performance, you've already cleared the first hurdle. Our art director will take care of the glossies and the CDs and the promotional material, so we have no problem there. Then the tour director on the Cerulean Neptune will handle the transportation and logistics of getting the choir from A to B in the various ports of call, so the extra expenses in that area will be minimal too, and the choir runs less risk of getting lost or being late."

Marty paused for a few moments to give his audience an opportunity to absorb the fact that his ambitious hopes and plans for the Cerulean Neptune choir did not involve a plea for funding. *Show me the money* was the principal hurdle for any new project that went before the board, but this time the executives of the Neptune Cruise Line had not yet raised any objections to the arrangements that Marty Goldbloom had presented to them so far.

"The next step," Marty went on, smiling at the interested faces of the Neptune executives sitting at the boardroom table, "the next step is to appeal to the self-interest of all the parties involved in this project. So what have we got so far? We've got a great choir with a fantastic choir director who chooses inspirational, well-loved songs that the choir sings with genuine feeling. We have no problem understanding what's in it for Rasmussen—if we succeed in getting him some extra exposure and a couple of new paragraphs on his CV, he'll be happy. The same goes for the choir members, who'll be able to boast to their friends that they sang at the Sydney Opera House."

Marty paused for effect before continuing. "And what's in it for *us*?" he said, looking at the expectant faces around the boardroom table. "We'll get far more passengers signing up for our world cruises if they can do something special or unusual, and I hardly need to point out that being part of a touring choir is pretty hard to beat, especially if the price tag can be swallowed without too much choking. So therefore it's a win/win situation, no matter which way you look at it. And last but not least, we'll also get a lot of publicity. Check out the banner that my creative team has designed. Geoffrey, would you and your graphic art team please show the board what I'm talking about?"

"With pleasure," Geoffrey said.

Several men and women got up, stood in line, and rolled out a fifteen-foot, blue-and-white oil-cloth banner displaying the Neptune logo followed by the words "THE NEPTUNE CRUISE LINE'S WORLD CHOIR".

"The banner will be pinned up on the wall behind the choir," Marty explained. "If there's no wall, then the choir members in the front row will hold it up if they have no sheet music, and if they do have sheet music they'll fasten it to their waists with a hook-and-eye system that we'll provide."

The creative director paused for a moment while Geoff and his team of graphic artists took their seats again.

"But the big question is," Marty continued after the team had settled down, "the really major question here is what's in it for the Sydney Opera House. Well, the way I see it is that instead of starting off small, playing to minor, penny ante little venues, we should start off big, and make the Sydney Opera house our sponsor. So my team designed another oil-cloth banner for the purpose, which they'll show you now.

The creative director's team arose and held up a longer banner which read, "THE SYDNEY OPERA PRESENTS THE NEPTUNE CRUISE LINE'S WORLD CHOIR."

"We've pretty much got all the bases covered," Marty said proudly. "If the Sydney Opera wants to sponsor us, they get the banner with their name on it. If they decide not to have anything to do with us, then the front row of the choir won't have to be weighed down so much with the extra length of oil cloth. But if they do decide to sponsor us we'll put THE SYDNEY OPERA PRESENTS on the top, and THE NEPTUNE CRUISE LINE'S WORLD CHOIR on the bottom. Either way, if the front line of the choir holds the banner, it'll stretch from the first sopranos right over to the end of the altos. The effect will be *amazing*. So to sum it up, we start from the top and work our way down to the minor leagues. I know it sounds crazy because it's counterintuitive, but that's what creativity is all about. Expect the unexpected. I rest my case."

The Neptune Cruise Line's creative director sat down while the rest of the executives conferred among themselves. After a while the Chief Executive Officer of the Neptune Cruise Line stood up and addressed the board.

"My friends," she began, "I've lived too long to be taken in by the mistaken assumption that *different* is automatically *better*. I see no reason why we should start at the top and work our way down to the smaller venues. The whole idea is topsy-turvy. What's more, I can see no reason to believe that we can convince the executives of the Sydney Opera that they should take a chance on a choir that has no proven track record yet. Sure, the choir is good. It could be excellent, for all I know. It might even be the best choir in the world, but I have no way of determining that. I've heard a lot of fabulous things about Ted Rasmussen, but he may not be the only remarkable choir director in the whole world. We here at the Neptune Cruise Line have a sterling reputation, but we have been in business for a long time, and we got our reputation the hard way—we earned it. We weren't given any free lunches or honorary kudos, which is what you seem to be asking for, Marty," she said, turning to face the creative director.

"I didn't mean it that way," Marty stammered. "I was just trying to say that…"

"You've done a good job with your presentation, don't get me wrong," the CEO continued. "But you should stick to what you do best, rather than getting involved with executive decisions. I appreciate your enthusiasm and the trouble you took to work out what you thought would be a successful way to land an important client, but let's put first things first, shall we? I love what you said about combining our Cerulean Neptune world tour with the chance to have Ted's choir sing in small venues on shore that are already on our itineraries. It's financially sound, and it would please the passengers a great deal. So we'll start small, and do it as an experiment. If it works out well, we'll see where it goes from there."

"Okay, but I still think we're the best team to implement the project," Marty told her.

"And I agree," said the CEO. "I'm putting you in charge of the plan, Marty, and I want you to coordinate everything very carefully with Ted Rasmussen. I don't want you to ask him to do anything—he has more than enough on his plate with his usual duties and the choir on top of that. But I want you to bounce your ideas off him before you present them to me and the executive board. If Ted thinks they'll fly, then go for it. I trust his judgment and yours, too. Make us a formal presentation, as you did today."

"I'll do whatever you say," Marty murmured, looking down at his notes.

"Don't be disheartened, Marty," the CEO said. "And don't forget to give Ted Rasmussen the credit he deserves. After all, without him there wouldn't have been any Neptune Cruise Lines World Choir. It was just a handful of amateur passengers when it started out, but when Ted took over it grew like Topsy. Just keep that in mind when you and your team get down to the details of your advertising campaign."

"I will," Marty said, brightening. "I'll do my level best to make sure that we do everything we can to promote the NEPTUNE CRUISE LINE'S WORLD CHOIR in the best way possible."

"Just be patient and keep a positive attitude," the CEO said, giving him a pat on the shoulder. "It'll all work out."

Back in his cabin on the Cerulean Neptune, Ted Rasmussen had come to the conclusion that he was at liberty to tell the choir that the executives of the Neptune Cruise Line in Santa Marta were seriously considering the idea of approaching the Sydney Opera, or they would not have written to him about it in the first place. They had not told him where the plan stood or to what extent it had been developed, but the choir would be excited and encouraged to know that the idea had been hatched and was now in the works.

"I have something interesting to share with you," he said to the members of the choir when they met the next day for their practice. "But don't get too excited just yet," he warned them. "Nothing has been finalized."

The choir members murmured among themselves until Ted put up his hand for silence.

"Tell us what it is, then," said Piglet.

"Yes, don't keep us in suspense," Paloma pleaded.

"Out with it, Ted," Bella said, nudging Dominique.

"Is this what you people call *not* being excited?" Ted taunted them.

"We're an excitable bunch," sang a man in the tenor section, using the tune and rhythm of "I am a shining star."

"Okay, you win," Ted chuckled. "So here's the news. It looks as if there's a small chance we might just possibly be invited to sing at the Sydney Opera House next year."

The choir erupted in questions and exclamations.

"Did I just hear what I think I heard?"

"The Sydney Opera House? How can that be?"

"Aw come on, you gotta be kidding!"

"We're not good enough! We're just passengers…"

"There's a small chance, just a very *small* chance," Ted reminded them, putting the tips of his thumb and forefinger together to indicate how small the chance really was. "But there's no way of knowing exactly when that will be."

"Are we allowed to tell our friends?" somebody asked.

"I suppose so," Ted replied. "Just make sure they know that nothing is settled yet. But I was told that the bigwigs are discussing it at the corporate office in California. It would be very good publicity for both the Neptune Cruise Line and the Sydney Opera. Neptune has sent plenty of passengers to the Opera House, and the chance to perform there would attract even more passengers to the Neptune world cruises, so it's a win/win situation for everyone involved."

"But we're not even professionals," someone remarked. "How on earth can we fit into the program?"

"We wouldn't be part of the real program," Ted guessed. "We'd probably just sing at the intermission, or something like that. Anyway, it's too soon to say. I'm not sure how they'll handle it, and they probably haven't yet figured it out themselves either, so we'll just have to wait and see what comes of it. But still, I thought you'd be happy to hear that they're seriously thinking about it at corporate headquarters, and I'm sure they'll let us know as soon as they come up with a plan. But right now we have work to do. I have a new song for you this morning. Bella, could you pass these scores to the soprano section, please? And Paloma, would you give some to the rest of the choir? Thank you very much."

While Bella and Paloma were handing out the musical scores, Ted told the choir that the new song was from *Man of la Mancha*, with a book by Dale Wasserman, lyrics by Joe Darion, and music by Mitch Leigh. Piglet was one of the first choir members to receive the music, which he read while he heard the melody playing in his head:

To dream the impossible dream,
to fight the unbeatable foe,
to bear with unbearable sorrow
to run where the brave dare not go;

To right the unrightable wrong.
to love, pure and chaste, from afar,
to try, when your arms are too weary,
to reach the unreachable star!

This is my quest to follow that star,
no matter how hopeless, no matter how far,
to fight for the right without question or pause,
to be willing to march into hell for a heavenly cause!
and I know, if I'll only be true to this glorious quest,
that my heart will lie peaceful and calm
when I'm laid to my rest.

And the world will be better for this,
that one man, scorned and covered with scars,
still strove, with his last ounce of courage,
to reach the unreachable stars!

Piglet smiled as he listened to the words. He had once quietly nurtured what he thought was an impossible dream, the dream of a man who was only five feet tall and who was secretly in love with a woman who was almost six feet tall in her stocking feet. His quest was to win the heart and the hand of this fair maiden, and to lay the world at those stocking feet so his heart could lie peaceful and calm when he was laid to his rest. He followed his quest with great hope but without certainty, and with faith but not with the full assurance that he would share his life one day with this woman who was so beautiful in his eyes, both inside and out. Persistence was the key, Piglet told himself, when he looked back on those days. Persistence, coupled with a firm desire to learn what Paloma needed, and then finding ways to fulfill her yearnings.

Little by little the quest led miraculously to a conquest, although Piglet himself never saw their growing relationship exactly in those terms. He saw it as a natural development between two people who loved each other and wanted the best for each other, but Piglet was so timid in the beginning that he found it hard to believe what he thought he could see in Paloma's heart. Was it all just wishful thinking on his part, or did she have feelings for him too? There were moments when he thought she did, but those moments were quickly eradicated because he could not bring himself to believe that he was actually loved by the very woman without whom he knew for certain he could not live or breathe.

It had all boiled down to one thing, Piglet thought, as he pondered those torturous first steps. He had followed his quest because he had no choice but to do so. He strove with his last ounce of courage until finally, incredibly, he reached the unreachable Paloma and made her his bride.

Just then Ted played a chord on the piano and plunged into the introduction to *The Impossible Dream*. At just the right moment he looked up at the choir and nodded for them to begin. Everyone hit the right note for all their sections: first sopranos, sopranos, second sopranos, altos, tenors and basses. Their voices were full and strong, and the harmony was perfect right from the start, since the song itself was so familiar that nobody in the choir hit even one false note.

Bella noticed that Ted's face was shining, but what she couldn't see was that Staff Captain Lars Jensen's face was shining even brighter while he leaned against the bar at the rear of the lounge, his eyes fixed on Bella's profile.

What the staff captain didn't know was that Angel was standing behind the bar wiping glasses while he scrutinized Jensen's rapt expression with thoughtful, calculating eyes.

CHAPTER NINE

Bella awoke the next morning fully aware that she had been dreaming. She had found herself in a beautiful garden, and the colors were brightly vivid, stretching from one side of her dream to the other, like scenes from a Todd-AO movie shot on 65mm Technicolor film. She was astonished to discover that although she knew she was in her bed in her stateroom on the Cerulean Neptune, she was still able to remain in the garden dream, just as if she were in two different places simultaneously.

The garden reminded Bella of the property where she had grown up, and which her mother had wanted to develop into a park-like garden someday. In real life she had worked on it little by little, hiring gardeners now and then to give her a hand. Bella had enjoyed watching the garden develop, with golden forsythia blossoming by park benches and willow trees growing by the side of the duck pond, bending their thirsty branches toward the water.

In her dream the garden was peaceful, although in real life it was generally alive with the sound of children chasing one another and screaming with laughter and excitement. But in her dream Bella found an unexpected sense of profound and abiding happiness emanating from the perfect serenity in the garden. She couldn't see her mother, but she knew that she was nearby, occupied with the satisfying task of creating more beauty wherever she directed her efforts.

Bella had the strange feeling that Lars was there too, and that the garden was having the same effect on him. Where were they, and what could this possibly mean? Had they grown old together? She felt as if she had known him always and that the peaceful serenity in her heart was connected in some strange way to what he was feeling. Then she slowly awoke against her will, and the proximity of Lars and her mother disappeared.

It was time, Bella decided, to get her lazy bones out of bed and go to the Club Restaurant for breakfast.

Meanwhile, two decks below the Club Restaurant, Angel and Selim were huddled over a table in the crew mess hall, eating fried eggs over easy with hash browns, and washing them down with orange juice and black coffee.

"What do you mean, you don't know?" Angel said in a low voice, speaking out of the corner of his mouth so nobody else in the mess hall could read his lips. "How can you not know? It's your bloody *business* to know."

"I opened her shampoo and her perfume bottles, but they all smelled normal," Selim told him.

"It's not a liquid, you dumb jackass. It's a sort of crystal, like rock salt," Angel replied, raising his voice. "Look for a box, not a bottle. Don't you know *anything?*"

"You don't have to shout. People are looking at you."

"If you can't find it, just *ask* her for it," Angel hissed. "Maria's in on this. She'll hand it right over if you just tell her to give it to you. Did you ever think of *that?*"

"Okay, I'll ask her for it next time I go to her cabin."

"Why do I have to tell you what to do, right down to the last detail? Can't you think of anything by yourself? What are you doing to make that Bible class as big as possible, for example?"

"I didn't know I was supposed to do anything."

"Who hired you, anyway? You're totally useless."

"You're supposed to be my boss. So tell me what to do."

"You have access to all the staterooms on Deck Six. So when you see a passenger, talk up the Bible study. Tell them that everybody loves Maria's classes. Tell them they'd better sign up right away or there won't be room for them."

"They're going to wonder how I know this," Selim said dubiously. "They'll be suspicious."

"Oh, stop being such a wimp. Just say you've heard the passengers talking about the Bible study. Tell them *everyone* knows how interesting it is. Say you have insider knowledge. That'll make them perk up. If you tell people that everybody is pushing and shoving to get into the class, they'll want to join it as well. Nobody likes to miss out on something that's popular with everyone else."

"Bible studies are never popular," Selim said. "They're not cool."

"Good teachers are always popular," Angel assured him. "People just *love* to be entertained. Don't you get it? That's what the world cruise is all about. Entertainment. So get your ass in gear and go round up all the Christians and would-be Christians you can find, and get them to sign up. We'll give them a welcome party they'll never forget."

"They'll forget it soon enough," Selim corrected him.

"You're right," Angel chuckled. "Maybe I haven't been giving you enough credit for subtlety, my friend."

"Am I the only recruiter?" Selim asked.

"Of course not. I have stateroom attendants working on all the decks. But that's none of your business. You're on a need-to-know basis. That way you can't spill the beans to the wrong people."

"I wouldn't do that," Selim said indignantly.

"Who the hell knows *what* you might do? I'm not taking any chances."

Just as Selim was attempting to think of an appropriate response to this insult, Angel's face suddenly lit up as a new thought struck him.

"Hey, I've got an idea. Listen to this. I was cleaning up the bar in the Neptune Lounge this morning when the choir was practicing, and Staff Captain Lars Jensen was leaning against the counter staring at some babe in the front row. He couldn't take his eyes off her. I want you to go to him and tell him that since the welcome party for the Bible study will be given in the Neptune Lounge immediately after the choir rehearsal, it would be nice to invite the whole choir to attend the party as well. That way, see, we'll have a whole lot more Christians rounded up all in one place."

"What makes you think the people who sing in the choir are necessarily Christians?"

"They're old, dumbbell. Most of them were brought up in the fifties, in the Beaver Cleaver days. Everybody went to church back then, and no doubt they still do today. Old folks are set in their ways."

"There's probably more to it than that," Selim said.

"Maybe some of them live by what they believe, what do I know? Perhaps it's not just a habit for them. But who cares? It doesn't make any difference to me."

"What if there are some Muslims among them?"

"There won't be."

"But what if there are?"

"Then they'll be martyrs and go right to heaven. We'll be doing them a favor."

"I hope they see it that way."

"Don't worry, Selim. There won't be any Muslims at the welcome party."

"Really? Why do you say that?"

"Because Muslims don't drink alcohol, stupid."

"Okay, but answer me *this*, then. How are you going to get all the people at the party to drink at the exact same time? Are you going to expect Ted Rasmussen to orchestrate the Christian and non-Muslim drinking spree with a baton?"

"You're on the right track, Selim. First I'm going to get Maria Morgan to give the welcome speech, then I'll ask Ted Rasmussen to introduce the choir and maybe have them sing something sweet and romantic, and then I'll step forward and propose a toast. They'll raise their glasses when I'm finished, then they'll drink their wine all at the same time. How's *that* for a plan?"

"What makes you think *you* should be giving a toast? You're only a bartender."

"I'll just do it, that's all. Nobody will want to shut me up and spoil the party. I'll say the stuff I'm going to say before anyone figures out how to stop me."

"I gotta hand it to you. You've thought of everything, Angel. You're a genius."

"That's why I'm the boss and you're the lackey, pal," Angel replied, with a smug little smile.

Later that morning, as the choir members were busily pulling their chairs onto the dance floor to make three semicircular rows around the piano, Angel went up to Ted Rasmussen as he was going through the new musical scores that he was about to hand out to the choir.

"Can I have a word with you?" Angel asked him.

"Of course. What can I do for you, Ahmad?"

"Just call me Angel. I'm more comfortable with that."

"I keep forgetting," Ted said apologetically.

"It's a Muslim thing. With me being a bartender and all, it gives the wrong impression."

"I understand, Angel. You don't have to explain."

"So Maria Morgan is planning to throw a welcome party after your choir practice tomorrow for the passengers in her Bible study, and she thought it would be nice to invite you and the choir too, since you'll all be here anyway. What do you say?"

"Maria's not here today?" Ted said, looking around. He spotted her in the soprano section, with her head buried in her choir folder. "Why doesn't she ask me herself?"

"She thought I should approach you, since it involves both the choir *and* the Bible study, and I have to know how much wine to order. But if you want me to get her…"

"No, no. That's okay. Don't bother. Of course we'd be happy to join you. Tomorrow, did you say?"

"Yes, right after choir practice, before you go to lunch."

"No problem. I'll make an announcement right now, as soon as they get settled."

"I'd appreciate it. Thanks for your help."

"My pleasure, Angel. Thank *you,*" Ted said, walking to the left flank of the choir and handing the woman at the end of the row some sheet music to pass along.

Dominique had been watching Angel as he spoke with Ted, knowing he was asking him to announce the welcome party that would take place the next day after the rehearsal. She couldn't believe she had felt too shy to ask him herself. What was wrong with her? Why did she feel nervous about approaching a perfectly nice man like Ted? After all, she was a woman of a certain age, and she was accustomed to taking charge when it was appropriate to do so. Was it because she was ashamed of being a stowaway and fearful that she might be caught, or was it Ted himself who made her feel tongue-tied when she was around him? Why did he have such a profound effect on her? She felt bewitched, bothered, and bewildered by him, and annoyed with herself for being so foolish. She hoped he wouldn't notice how flustered she felt.

"Okay everyone," Ted said, after the warm-up exercises. "Do you have the new sheet music? Yes? Good. Let's take a run through it and see how it goes. I'm sure you all know it very well, so it shouldn't be hard at all. Oh, and by the way, there's going to be a welcome party for Maria's Bible study tomorrow after choir practice, and she wants you to know you're all invited. Isn't that right, Maria? Is there anything else you'd like to add?"

Dominique smiled and shook her head.

"Well, there it is. Thank you, Maria. It's always nice to get together and have a good time. We're happy that you've offered us the opportunity to welcome your Bible class. I'm sure it will go very well for you."

"Thanks, Ted," Dominique said gratefully.

"Ted, I didn't get my music," someone remarked. "Do you have an extra copy for me?"

"No, I'm sorry. I'm one short, then. I'll print some more copies when I get a chance. I'll leave them on the piano, and you can pick them up tomorrow. Okay now, here we go."

Ted played a chord for every section, then he played the introduction to *Some Enchanted Evening,* nodding his chin at the choir when it was time for them to sing.

> *Some enchanted evening, you may see a stranger,*
> *you may see a stranger across a crowded room,*
> *and somehow you know, you know even then,*
> *that somehow you'll see her again and again.*
>
> *Some enchanted evening, someone may be laughing,*
> *you may hear her laughing across a crowded room,*
> *and night after night, as strange as it seems,*
> *the sound of her laughter will sing in your dreams.*
> *Who can explain it, who can tell you why?*
> *Fools give you reasons, wise men never try.*
>
> *Some enchanted evening, when you find your true love,*
> *when you hear her call you across a crowded room,*
> *then fly to her side and make her your own,*
> *or all through your life you may dream all alone.*
> *Once you have found her, never let her go.*
> *Once you have found her, never let her go!*

"How appropriate," Dominique thought when they had finished singing the popular Rodgers and Hammerstein song. She was looking at Ted across the crowded room from her position in the soprano section. There she was, hearing him laughing as he chatted with somebody who had approached him at the piano. Would the sound of his laughter sing in her dreams? She couldn't even begin to explain her feelings, so she decided to emulate the wise men in the song and not look for reasons. Even so, she thought, people don't usually relish the idea of dreaming all alone for the rest of their lives.

Dominique gazed at Ted for a long time as he interacted with various members of the choir. He smiled and chatted with them as they approached him with their questions, and they were responding with affection, animation, and delight. She was suddenly reminded of an observation she had once heard many years before: *People will forget what you said, and people will forget what you did. But they'll never forget how you made them feel.*

CHAPTER TEN

Dominique was in her stateroom again, with library books and written notes spread out on her bed as she prepared her next class. She was almost finished, and it was time for a little break. She got up, stretched, and went over to the small refrigerator under the desk to look for something to drink.

The first thing she saw was the bottle of red wine that Angel had left next to the fridge the day before. She picked it up and saw that the label read *1971 Château Apollyon Belial 1er Grand Cru Classe Pauillac Bordeaux*. She looked at it for a moment, thinking how nice it would be to enjoy a few sips of it without having to open a whole bottle of her own. She wasn't fond of wine, and never drank it except when she had to be sociable at a dinner party or similar occasion, but Angel had piqued her curiosity when he told her not to taste it or even touch it. He wanted it for "back-up," he said, so he must have meant that it was an expensive vintage and that he wasn't intending to use it except as a last resort if the regular wine, provided by the Cerulean Neptune, ran out before the end of the welcome celebration.

Dominique looked at the label again, wondering what in the world made people rave so much about expensive wine. Judging from the missing seal over the cork, Angel had no doubt tasted it already and wanted to keep the rest of it for himself. He must have thought that people wouldn't notice if he didn't remove the seal right in front of their eyes.

What was good for Angel was good for her, Dominique thought. Feeling like Eve in the Garden, she took the bottle into the bathroom and held it over the sink, trying to pull out the cork that was sticking up from the top of the bottle. After struggling with it for a while, the cork suddenly popped out and red wine splashed into the sink. Dominique stood there for a moment, staring at the red stain and wishing she had never messed with the bottle. The remaining wine was about three or four inches down from the top now, so the amount that was missing would definitely be noticeable to Angel. She had no choice but to open one of her own wine bottles and top off Angel's bottle before replacing the cork. Then, just as she turned to leave the head, she noticed a peculiar, acrid odor coming from the sink.

"What's that horrible smell?" she asked herself out loud, flaring her nostrils and turning back to the sink. "Phew! It smells like bitter almonds. I don't know how the wineries ever manage to sell so much of that stuff, and I can't imagine how people can convince themselves that they're enjoying a marvelous gustatory experience when they sip fine wine."

She looked around for some kind of cleaning agent to use on the sink, but the bottles containing liquid soap were attached to the bulkhead, and she didn't think she would be able to extract enough to do the job properly unless she put a lot of effort into pumping them. She checked the cabinet to the left of the sink, and at first glance she saw nothing there that looked as if it would serve as a suitable cleaning agent. Then she saw the tubular container of *Natural Rock Salt* that she had unpacked from the real Maria Morgan's suitcase on the first day of the cruise.

"Aha! This should do the trick!" she exclaimed out loud, twisting the plastic wheel on the top of the container so that the large opening matched the scored lines on the cardboard underneath. She broke the cardboard with the tip of her tooth brush and poured some salt into the sink, vigorously rubbing the wine stain with a face cloth. By the time she was finished she had wasted quite a bit of water and most of the salt.

"At least the wine stain is gone," she muttered, throwing the stained face cloth into a pile of used towels.

Just as she turned to leave the head, she knocked the wine bottle into the sink with her elbow. Fortunately it didn't break, for the sink was made of plastic rather than porcelain. She let out a sigh of both relief and frustration, and began to scrub the wine stain with the salt again. When she finished the job she pushed the library books to one side of her bed and flopped down, ready to take a nice, long nap.

But sleep wouldn't come, since thoughts of wine and salt were spinning around in her mind. About half the wine had swirled down the drain, and most of the salt was gone. She couldn't ask Angel or Selim for replacements, for she knew there'd be trouble if she admitted she had been sticking her nose where it didn't belong. Maybe she could ask the server in the Club Restaurant to bring her a box of salt, or perhaps she could ask Piglet to do it, since he was a chef himself and had become friendly with Chef Giudicini and some of the galley crew.

As for the wine, that was an even bigger problem. She couldn't possibly admit to Angel that she'd opened the wine and spilled most of it down the drain. There was nothing she could do, she decided, but dump the rest, clean out the bottle, and fill it up with another bottle of wine. There was no way Angel could prove that she was the one who had tampered with it, since there had been no seal over the cork. He would suspect her, of course, but she'd stick to her story.

As she lay on her bed trying to take her nap, she began to think about the wine again. Why did such an expensive wine have such an unpleasant bouquet? It had a pungent odor, mixed with those bitter almonds. But what did almonds have to do with wine?

"People will drink any kind of wine," she thought, "just as long as it has a fancy label and a well-known vintage."

She remembered from the label that it was a Bordeaux from Château Apollyon Belial, but where had she heard that name before? She was surprised the label was familiar to her, since she was definitely not a discerning judge of fine wine.

Yet she was quite sure she had heard the name very recently in connection with something else. But what was it? The only material she had been studying since she boarded the cruise ship was the Bible and some reference books about the Bible that she had borrowed from the ship's library.

"Wine was popular back in Biblical times, just as it is today," she mused. "Jesus even turned some water into wine at the wedding in Cana, but obviously it wasn't a Bordeaux, and it wasn't from Château Apollyon Belial. So what's the connection? Where have I seen that name before? Why have I read it so recently?

"Weird name," she thought, as she started to fall asleep. "Sounds like *Napoleon*, only without the N."

Piglet and Paloma were sitting at their assigned table in the Club Restaurant, scrutinizing the dinner menu and trying to decide how to divide up their favorite dishes so they could each have a portion of what they loved most.

"If you order the Lobster Thermidor, *chata*," Piglet was saying, "I'll get the Steak au Poivre, then I'll give you half of mine and you can give me half of yours."

"It sounds like true love to me," Paloma said, bending down to nuzzle his shoulder. "*While I give to you and you give to me…*"

"*True love, true love,*" Piglet sang quietly.

"*So on and on it will always be,*" Paloma answered, singing a little louder.

"*True love, true love!*" Piglet sang back, tilting his head toward the ceiling.

"*For you and I have a guardian angel on high with nothing to do…*" they sang in harmony with each other, "*but to give to you and to give to me, love forever true!*"

"Good ol' Elvis Presley," said Paloma.

"And good for Delonge, the songwriter," Piglet replied.

"Everybody remembers performers," Paloma remarked. "But hardly anyone ever knows the writers who create their material."

The people sitting at the next table began to clap for the two singers, and soon everybody in the whole dining room was applauding them, too. Paloma covered her face with her napkin, while Piglet just sat there, looking mortified.

"Don't be embarrassed," said the man at the next table. "You have beautiful voices."

"That's right," said the woman sitting next to him. "You have nothing to be ashamed of. Nothing at all."

"Where did you learn to sing?" the man wanted to know. "You sound like professionals."

"Nowhere," Piglet said. "We just like to sing, that's all. It makes us feel happy."

"You should join the choir," someone called out from a table a little further away.

"We're in the choir already," Bella said, taking her place opposite Piglet and Paloma. "But *you* should join the choir. Everybody's welcome."

"No, no, no," said the man emphatically. "I can't sing a note. I sound like a cat on a hot tin roof."

"Oh, don't be silly," said the woman next to him. "I've heard you sing at parties. Just give him a little wine and he's good to go."

"You should join the choir, really you should," Bella told them again. "We're all just amateurs, and many of us don't even know how to read music. But Ted Rasmussen, the choir director, he has no problem with that. He's completely cool with it. Believe me! Really, you should come and find out for yourself. We sing all the old favorites—songs from the fifties and sixties, and songs from Broadway musicals such as *Les Misérables*, and *Man of la Mancha,* and *The Phantom of the Opera*, and *South Pacific.* Ted is the best choir director there ever was. I don't know how he does it. He believes in us, I guess, and it all turns out great."

"Sounds tempting," said the man at the next table.

Just then Dominique arrived and sat down next to Bella. The people at the other table turned away, for their server had come with a tray piled high with covered dishes that she deftly lowered onto the serving table as though they weighed nothing at all.

"I'm in big trouble," Dominique said, looking around to make sure nobody was listening.

"What's going on?" Bella asked.

"Tell us," Paloma urged her. "Maybe we can help."

"Well, someone called Angel came to my stateroom to take inventory of my refrigerator, saying he needed to do it so he could have permission to enter my cabin. He left some wine by the fridge and told me not to touch it or even taste it. It was very expensive, I suppose, because he told me to take good care of it."

"Who sent it?" Bella wanted to know.

Dominique stared at her for a while. "You know what? I never thought to ask."

"Maybe Ted sent it," Paloma said. "I talked to him about the welcome party after choir practice."

"Or perhaps Lars Jensen sent it," Bella declared. "He's the staff captain and a friend of mine. I told him about the welcome party, too. Maybe it's a gift from him."

"Or it could be from Chef Giancarlo Giudicini," Piglet suggested. "I got to know him at a cooking demonstration. I told him about the welcome party as well. They have quite a good stock of wine in the galley."

"So it could be from Ted, or Lars, or Chef Giudicini," Dominique said thoughtfully.

"Why did Angel the bartender deliver it to you?" Bella asked. "What's *he* got to do with it? Why didn't Selim bring it to you?"

"I have no idea."

"Well, why didn't he at least tell you who it was from?" said Paloma, looking baffled.

"He seemed to take it for granted that I knew. He acted as though we were in cahoots with each other, so I thought I should play along with him till I figured out what was going on. I didn't like it, though. He called me by my first name. He acted as if I had a subservient role to him."

"Maybe it's a cultural thing, Maria," Bella suggested. "You know how it is in the Middle East."

"Yes, but there are men serving on this ship from all over the world," Dominique replied, "including countries where the men make no bones about controlling the women. But on the ship, the crew is supposed to serve the passengers. That's all there is to it. They shouldn't talk down to us."

"He talked *down* to you?" Bella said, taken aback.

"Well, maybe I'm just being too sensitive," Dominique admitted, "but I'd say he was pretty rude to me, yes."

"Like what, for example?" Paloma asked. "What exactly did he say that was rude, Maria?"

"He was unpleasantly bossy, mainly," Dominique said. "He put the bottle of wine next to my fridge and then he told me not to taste it or even touch it, and then when I asked him about it he told me not to play dumb with him."

"The nerve!" Bella exclaimed.

"Did he tell you it was for the welcome party?" Piglet asked her.

"No, he didn't say either who it was from or what it was for," Dominique said, looking just as puzzled as Piglet.

"There's something fishy going on here," said Bella.

"That's what I think, too," Paloma agreed.

"He told me the wine was back-up," Dominique said, "and he assumed I knew what he meant. But of course I have no idea what he was talking about. In fact, I have the feeling that the label on the bottle was replaced by a fake one."

"What makes you think that?" Piglet asked.

"Something very strange is going on here," Dominique declared.

"So tell us about it, then," Paloma urged her.

"What does the fake label say?" Bella wanted to know.

"It says *1971 Château Apollyon Belial Bordeaux*."

"I've never heard of that one," Piglet remarked, "and I have dealt with a lot of labels in my life."

"My point exactly," Dominique declared. "Yet for some reason or other the names sounded familiar to me. Then I remembered I'd seen them somewhere as I was preparing my Bible class. So I looked them up in *Strong's Concordance* in the library, and there they were!"

"So what do they mean?" Paloma asked. "Don't keep us in suspense, Maria!"

"The name *Apollyon* is mentioned in Revelation, and it derives from a Greek word meaning *destroyer,*" Dominique explained. "*Belial* is mentioned in Second Corinthians, and refers to the prince of darkness."

"Wow!" Bella exclaimed. "I see you've really done your homework! But how would someone like Angel know about that? I mean, it's far too scholarly for most people. Who'd be interested in that sort of thing? No offense, Maria."

"None taken," Dominique said. "But that's exactly my point. I think there's someone else behind it. Or a whole lot of people, more likely."

"So you think Angel believes you're one of them? Is that what you said a while ago?" Paloma asked her.

"Well, that's the impression I got," Dominique admitted.

"Why would he think that?" Piglet wondered.

"I have no idea," Dominique said. "I could have been imagining things, but why else would he have told me not to play dumb? Oh, that reminds me. I meant to ask you, Piglet, if you could possibly find me a box of rock salt."

"Rock salt?" Piglet repeated, looking surprised.

"Yes. I brought some with me, but I spilled it. I made a dreadful mess with it. But anyway, I was wondering if you could ask your friends in the galley if they happen to have any that they could give me. It's a stupid request, I know, but if it's not too much trouble…"

"No trouble at all," Piglet said gallantly. "Did you want a whole box? Is that what you said?"

"Yes, please and thank you," Dominique said. "I'm very grateful, Piglet."

Just at that moment the server appeared at their table with their orders, and the conversation turned to other topics. Dominique was relieved that nobody asked her why she had brought a box of salt with her. Only Piglet wondered about it, but he trusted her judgment on matters of that sort.

Dominique excused herself and left the dinner table early, as she wanted to get back to her cabin and continue preparing for her Bible class. She realized she was probably putting more work into it than was strictly necessary, but she had never taught the Bible except in terms of English literature. She wanted to develop a deeper, more subtle understanding of its purpose and continuity.

As she passed into the Casino Lounge, she was surprised to see that Ted Rasmussen was still at the piano, shuffling through his sheet music in search of a new song. He looked up and smiled at her as she walked toward him, heading for the grand staircase at the other end of the lounge. Just as she was about to pass him, he found the sheet music that he was looking for and began to play again. She recognized the song from *Les Misérables* as soon as he played the first notes.

On my own, pretending she's beside me.
All alone, I walk with her till morning.
Without her I feel her arms around me,
and when I lose my way I close my eyes
and she has found me.

In the rain the pavement shines like silver.
All the lights are misty in the river.
In the darkness the trees are full of starlight,
and all I see is her and me forever and forever.
And I know it's only in my mind

that I'm talking to myself and not to her,
and although I know she isn't mine,
still I say there's a way for us...
I love her, but when the night is over
she is gone, the river's just a river.
Without her the world around me changes,
the trees are bare and everywhere
the streets are full of strangers.

I love her, but every day I'm learning
all my life I've only been pretending.
Without me this world will go on turning,
a world that's full of happiness that I have never known.

I love her, I love her, I love her, but only on my own.

Dominique noticed at once that Ted had changed all the masculine pronouns to feminine ones. Was she imagining it, or was he singing that song especially for her? She scolded herself for being so presumptuous as to think in terms of such a possibility. He doubtless changed the gender of the third person pronouns simply because he was a man, and for no other reason. As for the song, Dominique could identify with it more fully in its original form, when Eponine sang alone on the stage about her poignant, unrequited love for Marius—the masculine form, oddly enough, for Maria. The words of the song took her back to her student days in Paris when she, too, had walked along the banks of the Seine in the midnight rain. Such a promenade, she thought ruefully, would almost surely be an impossible undertaking nowadays without one's getting mugged, or robbed, or worse.

Dominique had experienced her share of loneliness in her life, just like Eponine. Her father had deserted the family when she was a baby, although he had been kind enough to leave them the house in Mayfair and a decent allowance. But her mother had later developed heart trouble, so Dominique had cared for her until she finally died in her early sixties. Later she lived all alone in the West End London townhouse that her mother had left her, but her daily routine and her arduous teaching responsibilities at the University of London had slowly enveloped her, so that she ended up living almost entirely in her head instead of vibrantly and joyfully with all her heart and soul.

Now here was Ted Rasmussen, who showed her what it meant to reach deep inside himself and perform with feeling, sincere feeling—so Dominique took every opportunity to listen to him sing. As for the choir, she looked forward to the rehearsals every day. The music was precisely her cup of tea, so to speak, and getting to know Ted was as delightful for her as it had been for Anna when she was getting to know the King of Siam.

Let the cards fall where they may, Dominique thought. She would let herself go and revel in the music Ted played and the songs he sang until it was time to leave the lounge. She noticed with pleasure that he was still smiling at her as she stood there listening to him in the Casino Lounge. What could be wrong with feeling the special delight of getting to know someone? Ted seemed to read her mind as he sang Lerner and Loewe's *On the Street Where You Live* from *My Fair Lady:*

> *I have often walked down this street before,*
> *but the pavement always stayed beneath my feet before,*
> *all at once am I several stories high,*
> *knowing I'm on the street where you live.*
>
> *Are there lilac trees in the heart of town?*
> *Can you hear a lark in any other part of town?*
> *Does enchantment pour out of every door?*
> *No, it's just on the street where you live.*
>
> *And oh, the towering feeling,*
> *just to know somehow you are near!*

The overpowering feeling
that any moment you may suddenly appear!

People stop and stare, they don't bother me,
for there's nowhere else on earth
where I would rather be.
Let the time go by, I don't care if I
can be here on the street where you live!

For Dominique the street where Ted Rasmussen lived was the starboard hallway on the Cerulean Neptune which led to his stateroom on Deck Six. There were no larks or lilac tress on this shipboard street, and the floor didn't always stay firmly beneath her feet when the sea was rough, but she had to admit that enchantment did seem to pour out of Ted's door when he suddenly opened it as she was passing by, or when he happened to step off the elevator at moments when she least expected it. She experienced an overpowering feeling just to think he might be somewhere nearby as she sat in her cabin, preparing her Bible class.

On the other hand, she thought with a shudder, some of the overpowering feelings were also connected to the worry and concern she felt about the mysterious plans that Angel the bartender seemed to be concocting.

CHAPTER ELEVEN

It was almost five o'clock in the afternoon, and the streets of London were glistening in the rain. Even the residents of the Mayfair district, who were accustomed to the best of everything, were not spared from the terrible weather that hung drearily over the city. The mirrored reflections of moist pedestrians could be seen hurrying along the pavements as they looked for temporary shelter beneath the awnings of various hotels and boutiques.

A group of weary, impatient people stood on the corner of one of the major thoroughfares waiting for the lights to change, when suddenly a heavy-set, dark-haired man in a tan mackintosh approached one of the women in the group and grabbed her from behind, covering her mouth with his strong fingers. He pushed her forward toward the street, jostling the indignant pedestrians standing in front of her, and then he shoved her violently through the open door of a car that had stopped briefly just under the traffic lights. The cars behind the vehicle immediately began tooting their horns, creating a cacophony of unharmonious sounds that grated unpleasantly on the ears of everyone in the vicinity.

"Help me!" the woman cried through the partially open window as she was carried away in the black car that wove quickly through the traffic. The vehicle disappeared into the driving rain before anyone could come to her rescue or make note of the details of the kidnapping. When the bobbies questioned them later on, not one of the witnesses was able to give any useful information about the abduction that had taken place right before their startled, unblinking eyes.

Later, in a gloomy garret somewhere in North London, the abducted woman sat tied to a chair while the heavy-set, dark-haired man questioned her by the lamplight that shone through a dusty, cracked window under the eaves.

"You were meant to be on the Cerulean Neptune when it left Southampton," he was saying. "So what happened? Give it to me straight."

"I've already told you a dozen times," replied the real Maria Morgan. "What's the matter with you? Are you deaf?"

"You think you're so clever," he growled, slapping her in the face.

Maria let out a sharp cry of pain. "*That's* not going to do you any good!" she exclaimed. "What do you want from me? Do you actually expect me to change my story just because you *slapped* me? We're on the same team, you know."

"We'll see about that. I contacted the ship, and they told me you were on board. Now I find out that you're right here in London, and you're not on your mission after all. So what are you up to? Are you trying to pull a double deal here?"

"Of course not. I know it looks funny, but I can't help that. I already told you I lost my cruise card, so somebody else must have found it and used it to get on the ship."

"That's impossible. Your photo is embedded in the card. They'd see right away that the photo didn't match the face of the other woman. That is, if there *was* another woman."

"She obviously must have looked something like me if they let her board the cruise ship," she said, remembering that she had only seen the back of the woman's head as she kneeled down to help her gather her belongings.

"How can she look enough like you to fool anyone?"

"How should I know? Lots of people look like me. Short gray hair, blue eyes, long nose, thin lips…"

"Shut up! I *know* what you look like."

"All right, so then you obviously know what *she* looks like, too."

"You'd better not get cheeky with me," the real Maria's abductor said, slapping her in the face again. "I was sent by the imam."

"Even so, why do you have to *slap* me?" Maria shouted at him. "That *hurts!*"

"Well, it'll hurt a lot more if you don't come clean with me. It'll be much worse for you if the imam questions you himself. So you better tell me what your game is. And you better do it now, because I'm going to find out anyway."

"I told you, I went to Southampton early in the morning to avoid the crowds, and I gave them all the information they needed to let me board the ship. They took my picture and they issued me a cruise card, then I turned around and took a train back to London."

"Without going aboard the cruise ship?"

"That's right."

"Why didn't you?"

"I had plenty of time left, so I decided to go shopping."

"Why didn't you stay in Southampton to shop? Why did you have to go all the way back to London?"

"Do you actually believe that they sell the latest styles of clothing in *Southampton*?" Maria said, with a scoffing laugh. "You must be mad."

"You think you're so clever, don't you?"

"Going shopping in a lovely, upscale neighborhood has nothing to do with being clever. It's a special treat, that's all. I imagine even *you* do those things from time to time."

"Stop acting like you're so damn clever," her abductor said, slapping her in the face yet again.

"*Ow!*" she protested. "I told you to stop doing that! I'm not going to talk to you if you keep slapping me in the face every time I open my mouth!"

"I'm not asking you if you want to talk or not. I'm under strict orders from the imam, and he wants to know what the hell you're up to. Where did you meet the woman you gave your cruise card to?"

"I didn't meet her anywhere, and I certainly didn't *give* her my cruise card, either. I never even *saw* her."

"So how did she get hold of your cruise card, then?"

"I was in a hurry and I grabbed my open handbag by only one strap, so the whole thing tipped onto the floor."

"And you bent over and picked them all up, right?"

"Right."

"So why didn't you pick up the cruise card, too?"

"I didn't see it. Maybe I kicked it or something before I bent down to pick up the rest of my belongings."

"Then how was the other woman able to see it when you couldn't?"

"I have no idea. All I know is that if I had seen it lying there on the floor myself, I would have picked it up."

"So that means you must have gone all the way back to Southampton without your cruise card."

"That's right."

"How did you think you were going to board the ship?"

"I didn't notice that the cruise card was missing."

"Why not? Are you blind?"

"I don't usually carry an inventory sheet with me," the real Maria said sarcastically. "Otherwise I could have ticked off the items as I put them back in my handbag."

"So what do you intend to do about that woman who's posing as you? She's getting a free trip around the world, and the imam is paying for it. Be glad he didn't call you in to talk to you about it himself. You're lucky he asked *me* to get you to tell me what the hell you're up to."

"Well, my counterpart must be doing a very good job of pretending she's me, because if she weren't, the authorities on board would have found out she was conning them and they would have kicked her off the ship by now."

"She'll mess up our whole plan. She's bound to. She has no idea what's going down, and she'll get everything wrong. She'll make Angel and Selim look like damn fools. She'll botch the whole thing and we'll all end up in jail."

"Let's not panic yet," the real Maria said. "Think about it for a moment. It's in her best interest not to get caught, so she'll be friendly with the other passengers, and she'll do everything that our contacts on the ship tell her to do. She'll want to keep a low profile so she won't lose her free trip."

"What does that mean?" the abductor asked. "What was your job supposed to be? Nobody ever tells me anything."

Maria realized he was just a low-level goon sent to do the dirty job of forcing her to confess what she was up to.

"We're all on a need-to-know basis," she said finally. "It's better that way."

"Just tell me what you were supposed to do on the damn ship, and shut up about the rest."

"The imam knows all about that. It's *his* plan, after all."

"He wants to know if you're on the same page."

"Well, for one thing a contact over at the mosque gave me a tubular container with rock salt in it. *Natural Rock Salt,* it's called. I had it in my suitcase, so Selim or someone must have dropped it off in my look-alike's cabin. I don't know what she's done with it, but I'm sure they'll have no trouble getting it from her when the time comes."

"What if she decides to use some of it herself?"

"What, to flavor her own food, you mean?"

"Whatever."

"Well, you can easily guess what would happen then."

"That's my point. We don't need her dropping dead in her soup at dinner time, and messing up the whole plan. If that happens, you might as well consider yourself dead, too. The imam doesn't like it when people screw up."

"I know that only too well."

"So what else were you supposed to do?"

"They told me I'd be given some wine to bring to a welcome party on Wednesday. It serves the same purpose as the package of salt, so we'll have two weapons to use against the Christians."

"What makes you think they'll be Christians?"

"I was supposed to give them a Bible class so they'd all be gathered together in one place."

"*You* were going to teach *them* about Jesus Christ?" he snorted. "That's a laugh. If they call themselves Christians, why do they have to be taught about their own religion?"

"Don't ask *me!* I expect they're not very clever."

"You got that right. Christians are as dumb as a box of rocks. Even the stupid Americans say so—the ones who aren't Christians themselves, that is."

"So are you satisfied now?" the real Maria asked him. "How about untying me, then? My hands are going numb."

"Oh, all right," he said, undoing the knots. "But if you were really as clever as you think, you would have been able to wiggle out of these cords. I tied them with slip knots."

"Really? Where did you learn that trick?" Maria asked.

"From a magician who works the cruise ships."

"So how did you find out his secret?"

"One of the passengers—a chap by the name of Rick—he showed me how it was done," her abductor said.

"I've got a better slip knot trick. Want me to show you?"

"Sure. It can't be better than mine, though."

"Just sit down and I'll tie your wrists behind you."

"Go ahead, then," her abductor said.

"Okay. Now try to get loose."

Maria let him struggle for a while, then she slapped him smartly in the face and turned toward the door.

"Hey," he shouted. "You can't just leave me here. You have to untie the cord!"

"Now who's dumb as a box of rocks? Figure it out for yourself," she said, as she walked toward the door leading to the stairs that went down to the street.

"Wait!" her abductor yelled. "Where are you going?"

"None of your business," Maria snapped. "But I do have a question for you, come to think of it."

"Untie me first."

"Are you mad? And get slapped in the face again?"

"I won't slap you anymore. I was just following orders."

"That's what they all say."

"Ask me your question, then."

"How did you know I was still in London, and not going around the world on a cruise ship?"

"The imam traced your calls on the cell phone towers. He keeps track of everybody's calls. Imagine how surprised he was when he found out that you were still mucking about in London, making calls every day, even after the ship left port! So he told me to track you and get you to talk, and then give him a full report. You should have made your calls from a public phone box."

"Right. I haven't used a phone box in years."

"Listen," said her abductor. "I have another question. You said you didn't know that your cruise card was missing, remember? You told me you didn't have a list of the stuff that was in your handbag."

"So?"

"So why didn't you go back to Southampton after you did your shopping in London? As far as you were concerned, you were good to go. You must have thought you could go up the gangplank, show the blokes your cruise card, and go straight to your stateroom. So why didn't you do that?"

"I never said I didn't go back to Southampton. I did go back and I did go up the gangplank, but when I discovered that I didn't have my cruise card with me, I told the security guards I must have left it on the counter in the registration hall. I told them I would come right back, then I pushed my way down the gangplank against the crowd till I got to the dock. Then all at once it dawned on me that I had the perfect excuse for not boarding the Ship of the Damned. I didn't want any part of it, as a matter of fact. I knew I'd feel guilty for the rest of my life. I feel guilty enough as it is now. I wish there were something I could do to stop the plan from going forward."

"I can tell you something you could do."

"Really? What?"

"You could untie my hands."

"Dream on."

"I could drive you home. If you leave here, you'll never find a taxi in this rain, and there's no tube nearby, either."

"I'll find my way home, don't worry. Meanwhile you can work out how to untie your hands yourself," she snorted, heading for the door.

"Oy! Come back here! You have to untie me."

"No I don't. I want you to get the knots undone yourself so I'll have time to get as far away from you as I can. I don't need any more slaps in the face."

"I'm sorry. I told you, the imam made me do it. He said it was the quickest way to get you to talk."

"Well, now you can figure out the quickest way to untie those cords. Would you like me to slap you in the face? Maybe that would help you work it out a little faster."

"Come on, have a heart!"

"Let's see," said Maria, holding her chin and pretending to think about it. "No, I don't think I'll untie you. It's better for you to untie the cords yourself. It'll be good for you. It'll teach you self-reliance."

"Damn you, anyway," he said angrily, as the real Maria Morgan flounced through the doorway and started down the stairs. "Come back here! I have to take you to Heathrow!"

Maria stopped in her tracks and looked at him.

"What? Why should you take me to the airport?"

"That's what the imam wants. He told me to bring you here where nobody could overhear me while I questioned you and found out what was going on, and then he told me to take you to Heathrow and put you on a flight to Rome, where you'll board the Cerulean Neptune in Civitavecchia. Those are my orders, and he'll kill me if I don't do exactly what he says. You know that's true."

"Yes, but I can't get on the ship in Civitavecchia. You can only board at the beginning of a new segment, and the segments are much longer than just from London to Rome. I think they only have four segments altogether on the whole world cruise."

"Save your breath. The imam knows what he's doing."

"Didn't you hear what I just said?" Maria asked him.

"Shut up and listen to me! When the imposter gets off the ship to goes to Rome for her shore excursion, our Italian contact will waylay her there and mug her. Then he'll grab that cruise card she's been using for her free trip, and he'll give it back to *you* so you can use it to board the ship."

"What makes you think she'll want to go sightseeing?"

"Angel will offer her a free pass for the tour bus into Rome. She won't be able to resist a freebie like that."

"Who's Angel?"

"A bartender on board. One of the imam's men."

"It's not going to work," the real Maria protested. "Why don't they just leave well enough alone?"

"Quit trying to take charge, will you? You better not let the imam know you're trying to do his thinking for him. Just follow orders and shut up. You'll live longer."

"Don't you get it?" she said, exasperated. "That woman who's posing as me will have friends on the ship by now. If she disappears and I take her place, they'll know right away that we're not the same people."

"What are you talking about? You look enough alike to fool the security guard who checked your photo ID. Nobody will know the difference."

"Even if I look *exactly* like her, I don't know anything about her friends. They'll think I've forgotten every single one of the conversations we've supposedly had so far, and which I wasn't privy to. I'm bound to seem like someone with Alzheimer's. I don't want to do this. It's not going to work, and I'll feel like a damn fool."

"Which is better, you stupid woman, being a damn fool or a damn corpse?"

"You don't give me much choice, do you?"

"*Choice* isn't a word that the imam understands," said the real Maria's abductor, with a hollow laugh. "Now come over here and untie my hands. We've got work to do."

Meanwhile, back on the cruise ship, Dominique Perdue was enjoying the early evening hours with Bella Boorsma and the Casablancas—Piglet and Paloma—in the Casino Lounge, listening to Ted Rasmussen singing and playing the piano. Ted was glad that Bella, Piglet, and Paloma had taken Maria under their wings. He would often sit and chat with them at their table in the Casino Lounge after he finished his gig at ten o'clock, so he saw it as a perfect opportunity for him to talk to Maria occasionally. He had heard via the grapevine that she wasn't all that easy to approach. People found her to be rather shy—almost excessively so at first, but she turned out to be quite friendly when she got to know people better.

Her retiring nature was not so surprising, since she never married and had no family, and spent the majority of her time reading and writing books. She probably lived mainly in her head, Ted supposed, which was not all that unusual for scholarly, thoughtful individuals. Still, he was attracted to this shy, quiet woman, since in many ways they were polar opposites. She was an introvert, he was an extrovert. She was reserved, he was gregarious. She was an author, and he was a performer.

Ted smiled to himself as he thought about the old saying that opposites attract. They fill the empty spaces in our hearts that cause the constant loneliness, the ineffable yearning, and the feeling of incompleteness that follows us doggedly as we make our way through a life that is often filled with hurt and disappointment. He remembered the evening when they were sitting together while he was taking a break from singing and playing the piano in the Casino Lounge. He was looking at her as she sat chatting with Bella, when suddenly she turned to him as though she had been meaning to say something for quite some time.

"Do you see this ring?" she said, holding out her right hand to show it to him. "It's my mother's engagement ring. It's her anniversary today, and I'm thinking of her. She died many years ago, but I miss her just as much as ever."

"I'm sure she'd be pleased to know you're thinking of her today."

"I've never taken her ring off my finger," Dominique told him. "I've promised myself I'll never take it off for as long as I live, and I never, ever break my promises."

She held out her hand so he could see her mother's ruby and diamond ring.

"Even though my father left her," Dominique continued, "she held her head up high and kept on going. She was very brave, and we were very close. Now whenever I think I can't go on—that life is too hard to deal with—I look at this ring and I remember what she had to face. It gives me courage, just like the song we sang this morning in your choir, the one that tells us that at the end of the storm there's a golden sky and the sweet silver song of a lark. I love the songs you've chosen for us, you know."

"I'll sing another one for you that you might like," Ted said, getting up from his chair and wending his way back to the piano. He flipped through his collection of music and found a song from *Les Misérables* which he began to sing in the beautiful tenor voice of Marius when he thanks Eponine for helping him to rendezvous with Cosette, the girl he loves:

> *In my life she has burst like the music of angels,*
> *   the light of the sun.*
> *And my life seems to stop as if something is over*
> *   and something has scarcely begun.*
> *Eponine, you're the friend who has brought me here.*
> *   Thanks to you I am one with the gods*
> *   and heaven is near!*
> *And I soar through a world that is new, that is free.*

In my life there is someone who touches my life,
  Waiting near, waiting here.

A heart full of love, a heart full of song,
  I'm doing everything all wrong!
Oh God, for shame! I do not even know your name!
  Dear mademoiselle, won't you say? Will you tell?

Dominique sat completely still, unable to take a breath as she realized that Ted, in fact, really didn't know her name. Then she recalled the words that Marius sang soon afterward in a beautiful duet with Cosette when he told her, *I am lost,* and Cosette replied, *I am found.* In that moment Dominique Perdue became Maria Trouvée all over again.

CHAPTER TWELVE

It was just seven o'clock in the morning, and the Cerulean Neptune had docked in Civitavecchia right on schedule. By eight o'clock the passengers who were scheduled to take a bus tour to the Vatican were gathered in the Cabaret Lounge, waiting for their numbers to be called. Dominique Perdue—the fake Maria Morgan—couldn't believe her good fortune, for she had won a free pass for a shore excursion to the Vatican. She had just arrived in the Cabaret Lounge and was standing stock still, frozen in place by the overpowering feeling of suddenly seeing Ted Rasmussen facing her behind a table, holding up a yellow sticker with a number 2 printed on it. She stood there staring at him, unable to say a single word.

"Good morning, Maria," he said cheerily, without the slightest suggestion of having been struck dumb himself. "Are you having a good day so far?"

"Yes, thank you," she heard her voice say. "And you?"

"I'm having an excellent day, thanks," he replied, firmly sticking the number 2 onto the front of her shirt by her left shoulder. "Enjoy your tour of the Vatican, and say hello to Adam and God for me in the Sistine Chapel, okay?"

"I'll do that," she smiled, pointing her forefinger in the air in imitation of the famous painting by Michelangelo. Ted understood what she was doing, and immediately touched the tip of her forefinger with his own.

"Goodbye, then," was all Dominique could say.

"See you later," Ted smiled. "And have a great day."

I hear singing and there's no one there, Maria thought, recalling the words that the love-struck press attaché sang in Irving Berlin's "Call Me Madam." *I smell blossoms and the trees are bare. All day long I seem to walk on air, I wonder why, I wonder why.* The words were ringing in her head as she made her way down the gangplank toward the waiting tour bus. *I keep tossing in my sleep at night,* she sang to herself as she took her seat at the back of the bus. *And what's more I've lost my appetite...*

She suddenly felt mortified as she recalled that the love-sick press attaché in *Call Me Madam* was seen as a rather pathetic figure by the other characters in the musical. What was it about love, she asked herself, that makes such fools of us? Hasn't everyone been in love at least once in a lifetime, and can't they feel just a little sympathy for folks who are in the same boat? Everyone knows *there's nothing you can take to relieve that pleasant ache,* so surely the passengers on the Cerulean Neptune could show a little understanding for their pleasantly aching fellow passengers who are routinely turned away from the Medical Center without a prescription.

"Oh well," Dominique thought, "they can stop and stare as much as they like. It doesn't bother me at all, as long as Ted himself doesn't think I'm pathetic."

Both Dominique Perdue and the real Maria Morgan found themselves in the Eternal City at exactly the same time, each with her own purpose and mission, but neither one knew that their destinies had been intertwined from the moment they were born. The stress and tension of the Second World War had not only brought people together to share their various hardships, but others had been driven apart just as often by fear, want, and relentless strife. Thus Mr. Morgan announced to his horrified wife one night that he had filed for divorce and that he was taking little Maria and moving out the next morning. There were many tears and much cajoling on the part of Mrs. Morgan, who pleaded with her husband not to make any rash decisions, but he had been thinking about this for quite some time and there was no changing his mind. He had solidified his plans, and there was no turning back.

"I'm taking Maria, and that's the end of it," he had said firmly. "I'll leave Dominique with you, so at least you'll have one of the twins. There, that's not so bad, is it?" he had added, firmly peeling her arms off his neck and shoulders.

"Geoffrey, don't do this," Mrs. Morgan had begged him. "You can't separate those two little baby girls. It's heartless. They're identical twins. They need each other. I need them too. I need all three of you. Please don't do this!"

"Your parents will give you the townhouse when they pass on, Penelope. They've already promised you that. You and Dominique will both live very well here in Mayfair. You'll be fine. You'll be just fine."

"You have it all worked out!" Penelope had exclaimed, attempting unsuccessfully to control her trembling lower lip. "You must have been planning this for a long time."

"You know I always plan things very carefully, Penny. That's the secret of my success. So just try to look on the bright side. We're hedging our bets with the children, don't you see? You'll be keeping one in London, and I'm taking the other to the country. You never know where the Germans will strike next."

"You're moving to the *country?*" Penelope said in shrill tones. "Where in the country?"

"I think it's better for me not to discuss that with you for the time being. You're feeling a bit excited, Penelope. I don't want you going to the country and making scenes. You must try to get hold of yourself and calm down. Just calm down for the sake of the children. Put the children first. I'm only thinking of their safety."

"Well, who's going to take care of Maria while you're at work?"

"I've hired a nanny, Penelope. She's a delightful young woman, and Maria will love her. Have no fear."

"A *young* woman?" Penelope said, looking alarmed.

"Well, maybe not so young. She looks young to me, of course, because I'm much older than she is. Isn't that right, my dear? I'm an old codger, that's what I've become with all this hard work and the constant, nagging worries."

"Geoffrey, you *can't* be serious. This is all just a terrible nightmare. I must be dreaming. I *know* I'm dreaming. Where are you going to work? Who's going to hire you? You don't have a job in the country. What are you going to do? How will you support yourself and Maria and the nanny?"

"Don't worry about any of those details, my dear. I have it all worked out. I'll write you and tell you how we're doing as soon as I get settled. You'll hear from me shortly, I give you my word. Now, I have the car all packed, and I've put Maria's things in the boot. All I need is Maria herself. Would you fetch her for me please, there's a dear."

"*Fetch* her for you? Over my dead body! You must be mad! I'm not going to hand over one of my twin daughters just because you say so!"

"Penelope, stop and listen to yourself! You'll frighten the children if you go on like this. You'll wake them both up. Have a heart! You sound hysterical. What will they think if they see their mummy behaving this way?"

Just then the sirens sounded, and soon afterward a bomb exploded somewhere in the neighborhood. Mr. Morgan ran to the nursery and lifted Maria out of her cot. He looked over his shoulder and saw that Penny was taking baby Dominique out of the other cot and bundling her into her blanket. They both ran down the stairs clutching the two babies, bursting out of the front door and into the street. Penelope was used to dashing to the shelter when the sirens sounded, so she rushed off in that direction with Dominique in her arms. Geoffrey ran across the street to his parked car and put Maria down on the front seat. By the time Penny realized he wasn't behind her, he had already skirted Berkeley Square and was heading out of the city.

Penelope Morgan never saw her husband or little Maria again. Geoffrey managed to disappear during the chaos of the Blitz and the general confusion of the war, and was never seen again. Some thought he had gone to America with the nanny, while others said they had heard rumors that he had fled to South Africa and was working in the diamond mines. It never occurred to anyone that real life is usually far less mysterious than most people think.

The truth is that Geoffrey Morgan remained in London, where nobody thought to look for him. He joined a splinter group of radical Muslim activists in North London, grew a thick beard, donned an ankle-length thawb and a traditional keffiyeh, and settled down with the woman who had been the catalyst for all the frantic activity that had taken place on that sad, unforgettable night when Penelope Morgan lost one of her twin daughters to her domineering husband.

After years of seeking fruitlessly in a pre-computerized world for her runaway husband and her missing daughter, Penelope decided to take back her maiden name, Perdue, instead of remaining vaguely attached to a husband who was slowly becoming more and more unreal to her as time went by. Besides, she was beginning to suspect that her ongoing search for her daughter Maria was possibly being blocked, or at least being made more difficult by the fact that she was using the name "Morgan" in her inquiries. If Geoffrey didn't want to be found, he had probably warned all his friends in administrative positions to ignore any questions coming from a woman whose surname was Morgan.

In any event, Penelope had concluded that it was better for Dominique to think that her father had been killed in the Blitz, rather than letting her find out that he had chosen to abandon her. No little child, Penelope thought, should grow up believing that her own father had not loved her enough to stay with her and take care of her the way a father should.

Whether Penelope's decision was right or wrong, well thought out or ill conceived, the results were still the same: Dominique Perdue never knew her father, and Maria Morgan never knew her mother. Her father gave her a new life in a section of London where they had been promptly swallowed up by the anonymous crowds. As a result, the sisters ended up living separate lives, without either one knowing anything about the existence of the other.

Financially the twin sisters did very well in the long run. When Penny Perdue's parents died, they left her the property in Mayfair, where she lived with Dominique until she, too, eventually passed away, leaving her daughter the townhouse. Dominique had always been an excellent student, so nobody was surprised when she won a full scholarship to Oxford and later a professorship in English at the University of London.

As for Maria, she gladly followed her father's example, becoming a devoted member of the radical Muslim activists in a North London mosque, and working alongside him to achieve the many goals he shared with the other leaders in the mosque.

The Neptune Cruise Line's tour bus number two arrived at Vatican City at twenty past nine in the morning, disgorging its passengers in an orderly fashion near Saint Peter's Square to listen to the guide's description of the upcoming activities.

"You follow me now into the Vatican grounds," she said after a brief introduction, "where you will see the famous Swiss Guards who are protecting the Pope. They wear the colorful uniforms based on those worn by the Renaissance soldiers and modeled, against popular belief, from the colors of the Medici family and not from the famous Michelangelo. So, we proceed this way now, yes? Follow me. Your tour of the Vatican will end at eleven o'clock," she reminded them. "We meet your bus on the Via della Conciliazione, behind Saint Peter's piazza. This bus will then take you back to your ship, where you can have a nice buffet lunch served outside on the upper deck, yes?"

When they had finished contemplating the impressive colonnade and the awe-inspiring dome by Michelangelo, the Neptune group was led through the Vatican museums and the Raphael rooms until they arrived at the Sistine Chapel.

Everyone was delighted to see the finger of God touching the finger of Adam high above them on the ceiling.

After taking a tour through the gardens, the Cerulean Neptune passengers were tired and ready to go back to the ship for lunch. The guide gathered them in St Peter's Square where she counted them carefully.

"We're missing one person," she said, looking worried. "I am doing a name count," she added, taking out a list.

It turned out the fake Maria, Dominique Perdue, was lost or missing, or perhaps still waiting in line for the WC.

"Do you want me to go check?" one woman asked.

"Thank you, but the bus is waiting," the guide replied. "We cannot be late to go back to the ship. I will have another look for Mrs. Morgan when you will be safely on the bus. I'm sure *La Perduta* will soon become *La Trovata.*"

The big question in the mind of Federico Carpaggio, the Italian contact, was whether to kill the fake Maria or whether merely to incapacitate her until the Cerulean Neptune had set sail and the real Maria Morgan was on board and functioning well in her capacity as Angel's helper and subordinate.

But killing people was a big nuisance, Federico said to himself, in that the Italian police tended to take murder rather seriously and would probably not stop until they found the killer and saw to it that he paid for his crime. It would be more convenient, therefore, to knock out the Perdue woman and hide her until the real Maria Morgan completed the work that the imam had assigned to her.

The only problem with that approach, Federico thought, was that British women had no conception of the meaning of submissive obedience. A Muslim woman wouldn't need to be knocked out. She would have the good sense to obey any orders that he might give her, since it would be pleasing to the imam in the North London mosque. But a British woman definitely couldn't be counted on to behave in a cooperative, understanding manner if he simply ordered her not to board the Cerulean Neptune, especially if he tried to use brute force to bend her to his will. British women, he said to himself, and above all American women, had a tendency to question the obvious superiority of men, and wouldn't hesitate to seek redress for any form of physical violence.

"F---in' jerk," he muttered resentfully. "I'll have to gag her, knock her out, get her cruise card away from her, give it back to the real Maria Morgan, and then keep the imposter hidden somewhere long enough to prevent her from goin' back to the cruise ship. I can't allow both of 'em to show up at the ship at the same time—that'd be a disaster. I suppose I'll have to take her to my apartment and tie her up. I can't think of anything better. Why do the Brits always have to make life so f---in' difficult?"

CHAPTER THIRTEEN

Dominique Perdue slowly regained consciousness, only to find herself tied to a chair in a drab, stuffy living room and suffering from a dreadful headache. Her first reaction was to cry out for help, but for some reason she couldn't make any sound at all. Her tongue and throat were as dry as cotton, and she could only breathe through her nose. As soon as her mind cleared, she realized that someone had stuffed some kind of a dirty rag into her mouth and then gagged her to keep it in place. It smelled like a combination of dirty feet and furniture polish. She felt like throwing up, but she struggled against the urge so as not to choke herself. Instead, she tried to inch herself over to the window so she could break it with the back of her chair and then hope that someone would notice her plight and come to her rescue. She was almost halfway there when Federico Carpaggio, looking rumpled and unshaven, staggered out of the bedroom.

"What the hell is all this noise?" he shouted, looking at her in confusion. "Can't a guy take a nap without all this racket goin' on? Hey! What are you up to? What the f--- do you think you're doin'?"

He grabbed the chair and dragged Dominique to the middle of the room again, making as much noise by pulling the chair over the wooden floor as Dominique had made by hopping with it to the window. Somebody in the apartment below banged on his ceiling to protest the noise that was coming from above.

"Now look what you've done, you f---in' idiot," he yelled, smacking her on the back of the head. "You've pissed off the neighbors downstairs. Do that again and you're *dead.* You got that?"

Dominique gave him a baleful stare.

"You cause any more trouble for me and I'll knock you out again, and it'll be your own damn fault," he warned her. "I've just about *had* it with you."

Dominique mumbled something incomprehensible into her gag.

"If you scream when I take your gag off, I'll hit ya on the head with a *hammer* this time. Ya get it?"

She widened her eyes and nodded.

"Because if ya make noise or give me any trouble I *will* kill ya, and I mean it. I know people who are damn good at gettin' ridda bodies. In fact, maybe I'll kill ya anyways. Nobody asked ya to show up and grab that cruise card and get yourself onto the ship illegally and take a world cruise at our expense. That's *stealin'*, in case ya didn't know. It's worse than stealin', matter of fact. You've made a *huge* mess of things for us, and you're gonna pay for it big time. You've pissed off some people in high places, and they don't put up with that sorta thing, ya know. So ya better behave yourself now if ya know what's good for ya. Ya get my drift?"

Dominique nodded again.

"I'm gonna take this gag off ya, then, and you're gonna answer all my questions. And don't gimme no lies, or I'll whack ya. You're more trouble than you're worth, anyways. You're lucky I let ya live this long. In fact you're lucky I let ya live *at all.*"

Dominique raised her eyebrows as an indication of the anxiety she felt on hearing this news.

"That got your attention, didn't it?" Carpaggio sneered, undoing the gag with one hand and pulling a 9mm Smith and Wesson hand gun out of his shoulder holster with the other. Dominique spat the dirty stuffing out of her mouth, and then looked up at him with an expression of fear and defiance.

"Okay, ya gonna talk?"

"I need some water."

"Whadda ya think this is, the Hotel Ritz?"

"My mouth is dry."

"Who d'ya think I am, room service?"

"Who do *you* say you are?"

"*I'm* askin' the questions here, Sis, and *you're* gonna gimme the answers I'm lookin' for. Now, let's get down to the nitty gritty. Who the f--- *are* you, anyways? Are you Maria's identical twin, or what?"

"I've never met Maria in my life."

"Don't give me that b--- s---. Do that again and you're *toast,* ya got that?"

"You told me to tell you the truth, so I told you the truth. What do you want from me?"

"You can't be the identical twin of some broad and not know who she is. I'm not stoopid! So spill it, and make it fast, or you're *finished!*"

"I can't tell you anything, because I don't know who she is, no matter how much you threaten me."

"You can't make me believe you don't know the woman who's the spittin' image of you. People can't be identical twins unless they've got the same muthah. Unless, of course, you've got some other explanation that I don't know about. Maybe you're a clone, who knows?"

"There are over seven billion people in the world. That's a lot of faces. So if two of the faces look similar, it's not all that surprising, wouldn't you say?"

"Knock it off, will ya?" said Carpaggio, giving her a rough push. "I'm not interested in your fancy statistics. Just tell me how ya got Maria Morgan's cruise card, and why you thought ya could get away with posin' as her. You must have had some reason for pullin' a trick like that. So spit it out and make it quick. I haven't got all day."

"All right! Just hold your horses."

"Forget the horses and get to the point."

"I was at the pharmacy, waiting to get my prescription filled. Right in front of me in the queue was this woman who looked just like me, and I was as surprised as you are that we both looked so much alike."

"Not so fast, Sis. How didja know what she looked like if she was standin' in *fronta* ya? Answer me *that* if you can!"

"There was a mirror right behind the pharmacist. I could see her clearly."

"I'm gonna check this out before I letcha go, so you better be tellin' the truth."

"I am."

"Maybe, maybe not. Well, go on."

"So when she opened her handbag to pay for her stuff, she spilled the contents onto the floor."

"She spilled it all on the floor? That was pretty dumb. You expect me to believe *that?*"

"She grabbed the handbag by one strap instead of both of them, so it tipped, that's how it happened. She was in a hurry, I suppose. She must have been rattled."

"I'll rattle *you* if ya don't give it to me straight."

"I *am* giving it to you straight, as you put it. You must be from Brooklyn."

"How the f--- did you know that?"

"Three guesses."

"Ya better watch whatcha say, if you know what's good for ya. You're startin' to make me think you're too smart for your own good."

"It takes one to know one."

"What's that supposed to mean? Is that a compliment, or what?"

"That's for *you* to decide."

"Just keep on with your story, and no funny business."

"So when she tipped all the contents out of her handbag onto the floor, I bent down and helped her pick it all up. Then she ran out of the pharmacy in a hurry."

"Okay, so the broad who looks just like you, she ran out of the drugstore. So then what happened?

"Then I noticed a plastic card on the floor. I picked it up and saw it was a cruise card for the Cerulean Neptune cruise ship. I ran out into the street to see if I could find her, but she had already disappeared in the crowd."

"Why didja look for her? Do ya expect me to believe you were a good Samaritan and ya wanted to give it *back* to her? Ya think I'm *nuts*?"

"You told me to tell you the truth, so I'm telling you the truth."

"All right, already. How didja find her, then?"

"I didn't find her. I went all the way to Southampton to give it back to the people who were registering passengers so they'd have it for her when she found out it was missing."

"Yeah, right. That's rich."

"But she never showed up. She must have realized her card was missing and assumed she wouldn't be allowed on board without it."

"Geez, why am I not surprised?"

"How should *I* know?"

"Nobody fools me. I've been around the block a coupla times. Right away when you saw the card on the floor of the drugstore, that's when you decided to steal it and go on a sweet little ol' world cruise at her expense."

"That's not how it was at all. I boarded the ship with her cruise card because it was too crowded in the registration hall for me to hand it in to an official at a desk. The queues were a block long. So I decided to go aboard and give it to the purser so they could get in touch with her and tell her they had her cruise card."

"Yeah? So what went wrong *this* time? And you better make it good."

"Even the purser's desk had a really long queue, so I thought I'd take a look around the ship for a little while. I've never been on a cruise ship, you see…"

"Cut the crap and just get on with it," Carpaggio said impatiently.

"Well, the next thing I knew I heard a huge blast on the ship's horn. I ran to the balcony and looked down, and I was horrified. They'd taken up the gangplank and I saw we were underway. What could I do? It all happened so quickly!"

"Those guys, they *never* pull up the gangplank unless they make a public announcement over the loudspeaker so all the passengers will know what's goin' on."

"Well, I didn't hear any announcements."

"Of course you didn't! Why am I not surprised?"

"Listen, how am I supposed to tell you my story if you keep on saying that you don't believe a word of it?"

"You're breakin' my heart."

"Anyway, there I was, a sort of stowaway, you might say. So I decided the best thing for me to do was to enjoy the journey until something happened next."

"What's *that* supposed to mean?"

"It means that I thought it was better just to leave well enough alone. Why cause a stir if there's no need for it? The truth is, I felt a bit worried that I'd get into some sort of really bad trouble if the authorities on the ship found out I was a stowaway. Isn't that supposed to be a serious crime?"

"How should I know? I've never been a stowaway, and I've never met a stowaway, neither."

"Well, now you have, I suppose. You've met *me*."

"Just get on with your f---in' story."

"Well, there's not that much more to say. The trip was very pleasant, and I met some nice passengers, too."

"Good. *Now* we're gettin' somewheres," Carpaggio said. "What's their names?"

"You really want to know their names? Why?"

"Just gimme their names."

"They're my dinner companions, that's all."

"Their names," said Carpaggio, looming over her and staring at her with a menacing look. "Tell me their *names*," he shouted, pointing the Smith and Wesson at her head.

"Okay! Take it easy! One is called Bella Boorsma. And then there's a couple called Paloma and Carlos Casablanca."

"Piglet, right?"

"How did *you* know that? said Dominique, taken aback. "How could you possibly *know* that?"

Carpaggio bit his lip, knowing he'd made a slip.

"Word gets around," he said vaguely.

"Really? So do you know *all* the passengers' names, and their nicknames as well?"

"Nah. Just Piglet. The crew's laughin' about it."

"You know the *crew*?"

"I have a friend on the ship, yeah. He gets all the skinny on the passengers. What else can ya talk about when you're bored on board?" He cackled suddenly at his unintended play on words.

"Look, I've told you everything I can," Dominique said. "It's been nice knowing you, whatever your name is, but it's time for me to leave now. Since I'm obviously not going on a world cruise any more, I'd really like to get home. I have lots of things to do."

"Not so fast, Sis! You're not goin' nowheres."

"What reason could you possibly have for holding me? Are you *kidnapping* me?"

"I have people I report to. I'm not lettin' ya go till I get the green light."

"I have nothing more to say."

"Yes you do. I want you to tell me everything you know about the people who sit at your table. Not just their names, but everything about them. Where they're from, what they do, who they are, who they know…"

"Are you mad? Why on earth would you want to know things like that about people you've never even met?"

Carpaggio took out an Olympus digital audio recording device and slammed it down on the table.

"I'm f---in' sick and tired of your f---in' attitude. Just do what I say and quit askin' questions. Now start talkin' and make it good. I wanna know all the details. I wanna know everythin' you talked about at every meal you had together, startin' with the first dinner. And gimme their names again, too. Go!"

He turned on the recorder and sat back to listen to her, his arms folded over his chest.

Later that afternoon a limousine pulled up to the gangway of the Cerulean Neptune and deposited one last passenger.

"Welcome back, Mrs. Morgan," said the security officer on Deck Three, after the real Maria Morgan had placed her newly-retrieved cruise card in the slot. She headed directly to Deck Six, where she had been told she would find her cabin. She felt frazzled and tired after spending most of the day traveling from Heathrow to Rome via Milan, and all because the imam had been too cheap to book her a direct flight. At least Federico Carpaggio had met her at Fiumicino on time.

"I'll be damned!" he had exclaimed when he met her at the exit. "No wonder that look-alike imposter got away with pretendin' she was you. She's the spittin' image of you!"

"Never mind that," the real Maria had said wearily. "I don't want to hear about her. She's caused enough trouble."

"You've got a carry-on and your laptop with ya, but where's the resta your luggage?" Carpaggio had asked her. "Didn'tcha pick it up at the carousel?"

"It's on the ship in my cabin I expect," she had said. "I gave it to them in Southampton when I checked in, so they must have delivered it to my stateroom on the ship."

"Right. I shoulda thoughta that."

Carpaggio had given the real Maria the USB device that contained the audio files of his interview with Dominique so she could transfer it to her laptop and be fully briefed about everything her look-alike had remembered about her dinner companions and about their onboard activities and gossip.

"Thank God for this," the real Maria had said, putting it in her coin purse where it wouldn't get lost. "This will be a huge help for me. I don't want to come across as a dotty old lady who suddenly lost her memory and doesn't recognize her dinner companions anymore."

The real Maria was now looking around her stateroom, feeling as mad as a hornet. That pest of a woman who'd had the unmitigated gall to steal her world cruise, had also had the nerve to unpack her suitcase and put all her things away. She stood there with her hands on her hips, feeling violated, furious, and helpless to do anything about it. The more she looked around the cabin, the angrier she felt. She could see at a glance that the woman had worn her best cotton dress and hadn't even taken the trouble to iron it. She had used her toothbrush, too, and even her cosmetics. When Maria put her mind to it, however, she realized that the only way this fraud of a woman could have avoided using her things would have been for her to take *her* cruise card to buy cosmetics and other personal items of her own, including clothes, from the boutique. That would have meant that she, Maria, would have ended up with some hefty charges on her MasterCard. Either way it was infuriating, intolerable, and...

Just then there came a knock on her cabin door. When she looked through the peephole there was nobody there, so she assumed it was a mistake. But then just as she began to unpack her laptop, she heard yet another knock. When she opened the door she found herself face-to-face with a heavy-set little man, not much more than five feet tall, standing well below the level of the peephole. She stared down at him, not knowing quite what to do. She could see right away that he wasn't a member of the staff or crew, as he wasn't wearing any kind of a uniform. He had to be a friend of her cheeky look-alike. Who was this woman, anyway, and what kind of taste did she have in her choice of friends? She was sorry she had opened the door before she had had a chance to listen to the interview that Carpaggio had given her.

"Well," said Piglet, "may I come in?"

"Yes, of course," the real Maria replied, stepping aside.

Piglet plopped a box down onto her desk.

"Here is the box of salt that you asked to me," he said with a Spanish accent. "Chef Giudicini was most surprised, but he gave it to me anyway. This is good, yes?"

"I suppose so," Maria said, staring at the box of salt with a puzzled expression. Was salt now becoming so popular on the Cerulean Neptune that all the passengers had to have a box of their own?

"You *suppose* it is good?" Piglet said. "Was it not very important for you to achieve this salt?"

"Yes it was," Maria said, picking up the box and trying her best to look as though she cherished it greatly. "I'm very glad you brought it around."

"Maria, is there something the matter?" Piglet asked her, looking concerned. "Are you ill? Do you need help? Is there something I can do?"

"No thank you, I don't need any help. I'm just really, really tired right now. I've had a long day, and I'd like to take a nap before dinner. So, do you mind?" she said, taking Piglet by the arm and guiding him to the door.

"I will see you at dinner, yes?" said Piglet.

"I'm looking forward to it," Maria replied, closing the door firmly behind him. Then she turned around and busied herself with the task of opening all the desk drawers and the wardrobe doors and the cabinets in the head to ascertain just exactly where the imposter had put her belongings. She was still furious about the invasion of privacy.

"What's this?" she said out loud when she found the empty tubular box marked *Natural Rock Salt* in the cabinet. "Whew, what a smell! The imposter must have realized this was cyanide, and she dumped the whole thing out. Then she went and told that unappealing little man to fetch her a box of real salt to replace it with. The clever vixen!"

When she stepped into the cabin again, she caught sight of the bottle of *1971 Château Apollyon Belial Grand Cru Classe Pauillac Bordeaux* standing next to the fridge.

"That's strange," the real Maria thought. "I've never heard of that label before, and I know my wines rather well. It looks to me as if the imposter has had a taste of it already. The cork is unsealed. I think I'll give it a try."

She pulled out the cork and gave it a sniff.

"Ugh!" she exclaimed, looking at it briefly and sniffing again. "Cyanide. It has that typical smell of bitter almonds."

She picked up the bottle and sniffed the contents as well. "That's not so bad," she said to herself. "But why is there a marked difference between the wine and the cork?"

Just then there came another knock on her cabin door.

"*Now* who's coming to bother me before dinner?" she asked herself as she opened the door yet again. This time a good-looking young man was standing there smiling at her. He was wearing a uniform, she noticed, so she assumed he was her cabin attendant.

"*As salamu alaykum wa Rahmatullahi wa Barakatuh,*" he greeted her.

"May the peace of Allah descend upon you too," Maria answered, modestly refraining from extending her hand, just as she had been taught by her mudarris in the Islamic school where her father had sent her when she was a child. But how did the room steward know that she spoke and understood a certain amount of Arabic? He must be part of the plot, she decided, looking at him more closely.

"Mrs. Morgan, my name is Ahmad, but people call me Angel. I'm the bartender in the Neptune Lounge, so I don't want to use my real name, as you can probably understand."

"I know."

"It's a common Spanish name, so it's a good cover."

"Go on," Maria said impatiently.

"Anyway, I just wanted to introduce myself. The imam has told me everything there is to know about you and what your position is with us on board ship, so I'm up to date."

"I know who you are as well. The imam prepped me for this job too."

"Of course," Angel said, "but it pays to be careful. I also wanted to check to make sure that you found the container of *Natural Rock Salt* somewhere here in your cabin. Selim let me in here to make sure that everything was in order, and I noticed that the imposter unpacked your suitcase, so I think you should take a look around and find out where she put everything. I want us to be well prepared for the welcome party. I don't want any glitches."

"Well, you've already got one, I'm sorry to say. I just found the container of *Natural Rock Salt,* and it's empty. An ugly little friend of the imposter came knocking on my door about five minutes ago and gave me a box of real salt, so that other woman must have figured it out and gotten rid of the cyanide. Now we're in a real fix."

"No problem. I planned for every possible contingency," Angel said proudly. "I kept some of the cyanide and put it in a few carefully marked wine bottles to use for back-up."

"Good for you, Angel!" Maria exclaimed. "I was just going to ask you about that wine. I smelled cyanide on the cork, but the wine itself smelled all right, although I wasn't terribly impressed with the bouquet. It smelled like cheap table wine to me."

"Let me smell it. Get me some."

"Coming right up," Maria said pleasantly, all the while secretly resenting the imperious tone this young buck was using to address her, a mature woman of the world. She let it slide, however, in the interest of the final success of their common endeavor.

"I have a very good nose for wine," he said proudly, as he watched her pick up the bottle next to the fridge.

"Here, take it," she said, handing it to him. "Smell it and see what you think."

Angel carefully sniffed the cork and then the contents of the bottle.

"Just as I thought," he said. "The bitch dumped the wine I gave her and replaced it with table wine."

"Now what?" said Maria, with her hands on her hips.

"Back-up, back-up, and more back-up, that's the secret of success," Angel proclaimed. "I have more bottles of wine laced with cyanide in my cabin."

"Well, just make sure you don't get them mixed up with regular wine. You might kill the wrong people. You might even kill yourself."

"I know exactly what I'm doing. I don't need a woman to tell me what to do or to give me advice."

"How can you tell the bottles apart?" Maria asked him, controlling her anger with admirable self-discipline.

"Check out the label," Angel said, looking pleased with himself. "What does it say?"

Maria took the bottle he had in his hand and peered at it closely for a moment.

"It says *Château Apollyon Belial Grand Cru Classe Pauillac Bordeaux*," she said.

"So what does it mean to you? You're supposed to be a Bible teacher. Didn't you prepare yourself?"

"Not *that* well," Maria said, irritated by his haughty attitude. "Tell me what the words mean, then."

"They're alternate names for Satan the Devil."

"It's ironic that you call yourself Angel."

"I didn't want anyone to be surprised that a Muslim was tending bar. Not that most of the stupid infidels on board the ship would know the difference, but I didn't want to take any chances."

"That's very clever of you, Ahmad," Maria admitted. "I'll tell the imam you're doing a good job."

"So you see? I've got all the bases covered."

"Indeed. And you chose a good name for yourself, too. You're the Angel of Death."

"I thought you'd like it. Now, before I leave I wanted to check to make certain that Federico Carpaggio, our contact in Rome, has briefed you about the information he got out of the imposter who was posing as you."

"He recorded the interview for me and gave it to me on a USB device, so I'll listen to it as soon as I can. He also told me what he could remember about my dinner companions while we were in the limousine coming over here to the ship, but I still think this is going to be hard for me to pull off," Maria said, looking worried. "If I make even one mistake, they'll start asking me some pointed questions."

"Look, if you find yourself in hot water, the best thing for you to do is to pretend you're not feeling well. You can always excuse yourself from the table and have room service send something to your cabin if you think things are looking bad for you down there in the dining room. Just try to say as little as possible. Let *them* do the talking."

"That's what I was intending to do."

"Just do your best."

"If you want my opinion, I think the safest thing I can do is stay here in my cabin and order room service and then listen to the interview instead. It's better for me to be well informed about my dinner companions than to make some sort of a blunder tonight. Tomorrow it'll be all over anyway, so better safe than sorry."

"I like your way of thinking, Mrs. Morgan. The imam did well in choosing you."

"He did well to choose you too, Angel. You haven't left a stone unturned, as far as I can see."

"The important thing is to help each other to be good team players. I'm glad you'll study the interview before you meet your dinner companions in the choir tomorrow. I also think it would be a very good idea for you to explore the ship while everyone else is having dinner. That way you won't run into any people who know you while you get oriented."

"Or people who *think* they know me, better said."

"Anyway, now's the time for you to get your bearings and become familiar with the layout of the ship."

"Right you are," Maria said cheerfully, glad that what could have been a difficult meeting with Angel had turned out to be as successful as could be expected. The imam must have had a little talk with him.

"I'll see you tomorrow then," Angel said, going to the door. "If you need me for anything, just call Selim on your stateroom phone, and he'll put you in contact with me right away."

"I'll do that, Angel. You've done a good job of planning everything right down to the very last detail. We'll celebrate tomorrow, when it's all over."

"You can bet on it."

After spending a half hour listening to Federico Carpaggio's recording on her laptop computer, Maria decided it would be wise for her to take a look around the cruise ship before the dinner guests came pouring out of the dining room. As she was passing the Casino Lounge on her way to the stairwell that would take her up to the Neptune Lounge, she noticed an attractive, gray-haired man get up from the piano and put away the music he had been playing. When he turned around to leave the lounge, he spotted Maria in the hallway.

"Hey there, Maria!" he called to her. "Did you have an enjoyable day at the Vatican?" he asked, pointing his finger in the air.

"Yes, I had a very pleasant day, thank you," she said, wondering why he was pointing at the ceiling.

"How did you like the Sistine Chapel?"

Maria stared at him for a moment. Apparently the fake Maria, Dominique Perdue, hadn't said a single word about this piano player to Federico Carpaggio, or she would have known about him. She decided to play it safe and say as little as possible.

"I liked it just fine," she replied, turning away from him. "See you later. Thanks for asking."

Ted Rasmussen watched her walk briskly down the hall, wondering why she was treating him with such... well, with such indifference. Had he misinterpreted what he believed he had seen in her eyes? Had he been too obvious about his own feelings for her, and had she taken offense? When he had first seen her in the Casino Lounge she had entered his life like the music of angels, the light of the sun. But now she was treating him like a total stranger. Was she having second thoughts now? Was it going to be over before it had scarcely begun?

CHAPTER FOURTEEN

Angel and Selim were talking quietly as they ate their dinner together in the crew's mess. Not that the mess hall itself could qualify as "quiet" in any sense of the word, but they managed to find a small serving table that had been stashed temporarily in a corner. They had put a couple of chairs on one side of the serving table so they could get their heads together and have a private conversation.

"I'm glad that it'll all be over by Wednesday morning," Angel was saying. "Things are getting messy now that the imposter is out of the way."

"I thought that was what you wanted," Selim said, with a puzzled look. "Isn't it a lot better to have one of our own operatives in place here, rather than having to deal with some bird brain who took it into her head to grab a free ride on a cruise ship?"

"*You're* the bird brain, Selim," Angel remarked, taking a bite of his cinnamon roll. "The fake Maria was on board ever since Sunday, and during that time she got to know some of the passengers quite well. So now that the real Maria is here instead, sooner or later those passengers are going to notice some differences between the two of them."

"I suppose you're right," Selim agreed.

"Of *course* I'm right. Anyway, tomorrow is D-day, so it should go without a hitch if nobody makes any big mistakes before then. I'm worried, though, I gotta say. I can't exactly monitor everything Maria says and does, because as a crew member my movements are limited."

"What do you mean?"

"Well, for example I can't sit down to dinner with them.

I wish I could, then I'd be able to see to it that Maria didn't put her foot in her mouth."

"I don't know about that," Selim said. "Even *you* don't know every detail of everything they discussed at the dinner table for the last three nights. Maria will just have to pretend she has a poor memory if she messes up."

"Well, luckily she's old enough to be convincing."

"Why, how old do you think she is?"

"I dunno. Around eighty, or something like that."

"*Eighty?*" exclaimed Selim. "I don't know about that. To me she doesn't look a day over sixty."

"Oh, drop dead, Selim. What do *you* know? Are you an expert on old women now?"

"Speaking of experts, does Maria know how to handle the Bible study that the imposter was supposed to give on Wednesday morning? What would she know about the Bible, anyway?"

"Put your thinking cap on, Selim. She was going to give the Bible study anyway, before the fake Maria showed up in her place. She told me a long time ago that she was going to teach the class using a book called *Old Testament Alive!*."

"You've got everything covered, Angel. If all goes well, nobody will be complaining about the Bible study anyway."

"True enough," Angel said, with an evil chuckle.

Halfway through dinner Maria decided to excuse herself and go back to her stateroom. She never should have changed her mind and gone down to dinner in the first place, she said to herself. She hadn't yet had the chance to listen to the whole recording of the interview between Federico Carpaggio and Dominique Perdue, that cheeky thief who had tried to steal a world cruise. She could see that her dinner companions had been puzzled by some of her answers to their questions, and she had caught them glancing surreptitiously at one another with expressions that appeared to promise that they would have plenty to say about her after she left the dinner table.

She had intercepted these expressions two or three times, and had finally decided to tell them that she was coming down with something and that she thought she had a fever, so she was going to retire early.

"Oh, I'm so sorry to hear you're not feeling well," Bella said, with genuine concern.

"We have some Motrin in the cabin," Piglet mentioned. "Just let us know if you'd like some. It really helps a lot with the aches and pains that come along with the fevers."

Maria thanked them and excused herself from the table before the main course arrived. When she started walking through the Casino Lounge she noticed that Ted Rasmussen was at the piano again, finishing up a song. As soon as he caught sight of her, he began to play Lionel Richie's *Hello:*

I've been alone with you inside my mind,
and in my dreams I've kissed your lips a thousand times.
I sometimes see you pass outside my door.
Hello! Is it me you're looking for?
I can see it in your eyes, I can see it in your smile,
You're all I've ever wanted, my arms are open wide.
'Cause you know just what to say,
and you know just what to do,
and I want to tell you so much I love you.

I long to see the sunlight in your hair,
and tell you time and time again how much I care.
Sometimes I feel my heart will overflow,
Hello! I've just got to let you know!
'Cause I wonder where you are,
and I wonder what you do,
are you somewhere feeling lonely,
or is someone loving you?
Tell me how to win your heart,
for I haven't got a clue,
but let me start by saying I love you.

Maria stood there listening to him as he sang, thinking that he had presented the song beautifully in sweet, haunting tones, but Ted could see right away that the song had not moved her in a personal way. He saw nothing in her eyes and nothing in her smile to indicate that she shared his feelings in even the slightest way. Her heart was clearly not overflowing with anything at all. It seemed to him that it had been frozen instead into a block of ice.

Why, he wondered, had she changed so drastically from one day to the next? It was only yesterday that he had sat next to her in the Casino Lounge during his break, and she showed him the ruby and diamond engagement ring that her father had presented to his bride-to-be. So why were Maria's eyes so cold now? Had he done something to offend her? Yet she didn't look hurt. She looked... well, to put it bluntly, she seemed to be looking at him without any sign of recognition.

That was it, Ted thought with a stab to the heart. She was looking at him as if she didn't even know him at all. She was acting, in fact, as though he didn't even exist. What had he done to alienate her? What could he do to make amends? He couldn't start by saying he loved her. That was all right for Lionel Richie, but on the Cerulean Neptune a member of the staff could lose his job for making such an overture if the passenger complained.

Ted began playing a medley of different love songs in an effort to find one that reflected his present mood. After several attempts that seemed to lack the proper description of the pain and confusion he was feeling as a result of Maria's cold and indifferent look, he happened to find the musical score for *The Rose* in his collection. It was a song that he had liked in many ways, but which he used to think was a little too pessimistic and melancholy to capture his own generally upbeat spirit, but that night he changed his mind. The words to the song written by Amanda McBroom were the perfect description of his mood that evening. He propped the score on the piano and began playing again.

Maria walked down the hallway without looking back. If Ted had been singing any other song, it would have been hard for him to perform it with feeling as he watched Maria walk away from him. But this particular song reflected his true sentiments at that moment.

Some say love, it is a river that drowns the tender reed.
Some say love, it is a razor that leaves your soul to bleed.
Some say love, it is a hunger, an endless aching need.
I say love, it is a flower, and you its only seed.

It's the heart afraid of breaking that never learns to dance.
It's the dream afraid of waking that never takes a chance.
It's the one who won't be taken who cannot seem to give.
And the soul afraid of dying that never learns to live.

When the night has been too lonely,
    and the road has been too long,
and you think that love is only for the lucky and the strong,
just remember in the winter far beneath the bitter snow
lies the seed that with the sun's love
    in the spring becomes the rose.

That evening Ted Rasmussen connected fully with *The Rose,* for Maria's empty look and unfeeling eyes had given him the aching sensation that rejection inflicts on us all. But it was the last verse that gave him the hope he was seeking. The image of the seed of love hiding far beneath the bitter snow of a freezing cold winter reminded him of the ruby and diamond ring that Maria had shown him the evening before. At that moment she was an entirely different person, with a soft expression and a promising look in her eyes.

Ted resolved not to allow himself to assume that love is only for the lucky and the strong. He would find the courage to retrieve the ruby and diamond ring that had lain dormant under the bitter snow, and he would present it to Maria in the form of a real rose, blooming radiantly with the warmth of his love.

"This song," he said to himself as he finished playing it in the Casino Lounge that night, "this song should be sung by the choir. I'll introduce it to them tomorrow."

Meanwhile, the real Maria was in her cabin listening to the interview that Federico Carpaggio had conducted with her look-alike, Dominique Perdue, at his flat in Rome earlier that day. When she finished the task, she sat back in her chair and reviewed the information in her mind. Her dinner partners, she said to herself, weren't as pathetic as she had previously believed. Bella was a graduate of the MIT Sloan School of Management, and had become a top executive with a major advertising firm on Madison Avenue in New York before she took early retirement. The Casablancas were self-made entrepreneurs who had built two highly successful businesses from the ground up—a boutique hotel and a highly-rated restaurant—and the two of them were very well known and appreciated for their successful employment creation and for their volunteer work in the community.

During the truncated conversation she had conducted with her dinner companions, Maria had also heard some very flattering things about two Neptune employees on the cruise ship—Staff Captain Lars Jensen and Choir Director Ted Rasmussen. These two individuals had not been mentioned by Dominique in her interview. Had she forgotten to bring up their names, or was she leaving them out on purpose to protect them? Their omission from the Carpaggio interview automatically made them "persons of interest" to Maria. She had never heard anyone use the title "staff captain" before, so she decided to consult Google for more information. She was informed by a job description posted by *Just Cruisin' Recruitment Inc* that "the staff captain shall be familiar with the master's duties, responsibilities and authorities and shall be prepared to take command without notice. The staff captain shall assist the master in all service matters and keep him informed of significant events and trends pertaining to the welfare of the ship, passengers and crew."

"So," Maria thought, "this Lars Jensen who likes Bella so much is someone who might just get in the way if I'm not careful." She made a mental note to warn both Carpaggio and the imam back home about this man, then she proceeded to turn her attention to the choir master. After thinking about him for a minute or two, she decided he was not a subject of serious concern.

"What can a mere choir director do to spoil our plans?" she asked herself. "On the contrary, I think I'll use him to provide a distraction at the welcome party tomorrow so we can move forward without any unnecessary interference. His specialty seems to be Broadway musicals and songs from the fifties and sixties for the older crowd, so I'll ask him to have the choir sing one of their favorite songs while Angel makes the drinks for the special toast."

"Yes," she said aloud, rubbing her hands in anticipation. "tomorrow will be a red letter day—a day that will go down in history."

Dominique Perdue had spent the last hour struggling to untie herself while her captor was out of the apartment on some sort of nefarious errand, she supposed. Just then she felt her bonds beginning to loosen at last, and she was finally able to pull one thumb free, then the other. She managed to use her thumbs to manipulate the knot, but at first she had no success in working it loose. Eventually she found that if she pushed at the cords that lay tightly over the back of her left hand, she seemed to make some progress, so she pursued that approach for the next ten minutes. At last the the upper hand began to slide slowly through the cords, and suddenly she was able to work her way out of the knot. She stood up so quickly that the chair fell over with a resounding crash.

Dominique remained still for a little while, listening for sounds of protest from the neighbors in the apartment below, but she heard nothing. Most Italians, she said to herself, were probably never home at nine o'clock at night, which they no doubt thought was the early part of the evening. She looked around in the dark, but she couldn't see her handbag, or her coat, or any of her personal belongings, so she mustered her courage and turned on the light so she could grab her things before escaping into the street.

Once she had gathered her belongings she crept over to the door, turned off the light, and started to make her way down the stairs. She was relieved to see that the stairway was well lit so that she wouldn't trip and fall. But just as she got to the second floor, the lights suddenly went out, leaving her in pitch black darkness.

Where was the light switch? Would the lights turn on again automatically if someone came through the front door? What if it happened to be her captor, Federico Carpaggio? All of a sudden the door next to her opened and a shadowy figure, backlit by the lights in the apartment, appeared on the landing. The stairwell lights turned on right away, much to Dominique's great relief.

"*Chiedo scusa, Signora*," said the figure, which turned out to be a teen-aged boy. "*Posso essere d'aiuto?*"

"*No, grazie. Sto bene.*"

The boy smiled and dashed down the stairs, taking them two by two. Dominique followed along behind him until she reached the front door.

The traffic was horrendous, especially for that time of night, Dominique thought. She knew there were trains that could take her back to Civitavecchia, but she had no idea where she was or where the Termini Station was located. She had no desire to ask directions or to go there on foot, but by some miracle a taxi pulled over just a few yards down the street and disgorged two passengers. As she approached the taxi she realized, to her horror, that one of the passengers on the sidewalk was none other than her kidnapper, Federico Carpaggio, who at that moment was in a passionate embrace with his latest companion.

Dominique went over to the other side of the taxi where he couldn't see her, letting herself into the back seat from the street side of the cab. When the driver looked at her in his rearview mirror, she told him to go to Civitavecchia and to please recommend a hotel for her as close as possible to the cruise ship terminal.

"*Con piacere, Signora*," he said, resetting the meter and pushing his taxi into the traffic with perfect confidence while he happily tailgated the vehicle in front of him.

About an hour later the cab pulled up to a cute little bed-and-breakfast called *Il Fortunello*, located close to the cruise ship terminal. After settling with the driver and registering for a room, Dominique flopped down on her bed without even taking off her coat. She wanted to brush her teeth and comb her hair, but she only had her handbag and the coat on her back, since she had never expected to travel all the way to Italy when she had set off for Southampton the week before.

A few minutes later she looked at her watch, and seeing it was ten thirty already, she pulled out her iPod and called the main number of the Cerulean Neptune. She wanted to talk to Ted Rasmussen, and she knew he would have finished his evening performance in the Casino Lounge and would be having a lively chat with a group of passengers by then.

"Ted?" Dominique said eagerly when he finally came to the phone. "This is Maria. Maria Morgan. I'm so very glad they found you! I told them you'd be in the Casino Lounge, but I expect they knew that already."

"Maria?" Ted replied. "I'm so happy to hear from you. I missed you in the lounge tonight."

"I wish I could have been there, Ted. I have so much to tell you. I need to talk to you. Do you think we could meet for breakfast tomorrow?"

"Of course. When and where?"

"How about 7:30? Is that okay with you?"

"Perfect. Where shall we meet? In the buffet?"

"What's your schedule like in the morning?"

"Well, I was going to do some harmonies for the new songs I'll be introducing to the choir at noon, but that won't take me long. Otherwise I'm free all morning."

"I have so much to tell you, Ted, and it's very important. It's actually a matter of life or death."

"What? Are you serious?"

"I think so. I don't want to exaggerate or be panicky for nothing, but I really believe we have a big problem."

"Well, how can I help?"

"You're going to be very close to the action tomorrow, if I'm right about everything, so I'd like to tell you about my theory and prepare you for the worst. If the worst doesn't happen then we can rejoice, but if it does happen, we should try to be prepared."

"Are you talking about a problem for our security team? Is that what this is about?"

"Yes."

"Then you should contact Lars Jensen, the staff captain. He'll know exactly what to do and who to contact. Bella is very close to him. Can it wait till morning?"

"I don't think so. It's probably best to give it as much time as we can, so we can discuss in more detail what should be done. What do you think?"

"Where are you, Maria? We should sit down and talk this over calmly, and think about it carefully. If you like, I could see if Lars is available tonight."

"Would you? I really feel we should get the ball rolling, but I'd be terribly embarrassed if it turned out I was crying wolf. I'd be absolutely mortified."

"Well, it's better to be safe than sorry. So tell me where you are, Maria. If we can sit down and talk about it together, maybe I can help sort it out. Two heads are better than one. It's good to get a second opinion, too."

"You're right, Ted. You're absolutely right."

"So where can I meet you, then? Do you want to come here to the Casino Lounge? That's where I am right now, as you know. But I'll go to you right away, if you just tell me where you are."

"I'm not on the ship."

"What? Where are you, then?"

"If you walk down the wharf, keeping the ship to port, and then cross the street, you'll see a little bed-and-breakfast called *Il Fortunello*. That's where I am."

"*Il Fortunello!* I know it well. Have you had dinner?"

"Believe it or not, I haven't eaten for about twenty-four hours. I'm starving, actually. I'm totally famished."

"For God's sake, Maria. I'll be right there. I'll meet you by the reception desk in ten minutes."

"Thanks, Ted. Thank you so much."

When Dominique went to the bathroom she was pleased to see it was equipped with a cellophane package containing a toothbrush, toothpaste, and a comb, so that she could make herself presentable for Ted.

The real Maria Morgan was in her stateroom, where she had just finished writing a report for the imam. She yawned and stretched, then looked at her watch. It was getting late, and she wanted to get plenty of sleep that night because she was going to need her wits about her in the morning. Even so, she thought it wouldn't be a bad idea to go up to the Neptune Lounge and check up on Angel. She wanted to make certain that he knew the drill properly and that he had everything he needed behind the bar. It would be a good idea to make up an inventory sheet for him too, if he hadn't already done so himself. She wanted to be sure that everything went without a hitch, or there would be hell to pay in North London.

Just as the real Maria was climbing up the stairs to go to the Neptune Lounge, Ted Rasmussen was going down the stairs on his way to the gangplank to meet Dominique at *Il Fortunello* and invite her to dinner. When he came face-to-face with Maria Morgan in the stairwell, however, he was so taken aback that he was at a complete loss for words.

"What's the matter Ted? Cat got your tongue?" Maria said, with a nasty hint of sarcasm.

"Maria! What are you doing here?"

"What kind of a question is *that*? I'm a passenger on this ship, just like you. That's what I'm doing here."

"I don't understand. I thought you said you were off the ship this evening."

"You must have me mixed up with somebody else. Now if you'll excuse me," she said, trying to push past him.

"Maria, is this some kind of a game?"

"I have no idea what you're talking about," Maria said, placing her right hand on his chest to get him to move. "Now if you don't mind, I'm rather busy just now."

Ted looked down at her hand, hoping to catch a quick glimpse once again of her mother's engagement ring, but he was surprised to see that she wasn't wearing it.

Maria sashayed around him and continued up the stairs while Ted watched her go. She certainly wasn't herself that evening, he thought. It didn't make any sense for him to go to *Il Fortunello,* now that she had decided to come back on board. But why was she being so cold to him, when she had spoken to him so warmly not ten minutes ago?

Then suddenly he remembered that Maria had told him that she had never removed her mother's engagement ring in all the years that she had worn it. So what was going on? Could there be two Marias? They would have to be identical twins, in that case. Ted decided he would simply have to get to the bottom of this mystery, so he kept on going down the stairs to Deck Three, where he inserted his cruise card into the slot at the security check-out point, nodded to his friends at the check-out, then went down the gangplank for the short walk to *Il Fortunello*.

As he proceeded along the wharf in the direction of the little bed-and-breakfast where Maria had promised to wait for him, he thought about his recent encounters with her. There was no doubt in his mind that either they were two different women, or Maria had a split personality. The Maria he knew and yearned to see that night at *Il Fortunello* was an upbeat, good-natured woman with a sense of humor, albeit a little too shy for his taste. But the Maria he had just met on the stairs had a scrutinizing expression and an overbearing personality. Surely they couldn't both be one and the same person. There must be two of them—a right Maria and a wrong Maria. He didn't know how else to explain it.

He remembered the evening he had first seen the right Maria. He had been playing in the Casino Lounge as usual, and she had walked past the piano on her way to the Club Restaurant. She had stopped short when he sang the words, *Maria, I've just met a girl called Maria, and suddenly that name will never mean the same to me...* She had looked at him entranced, and listened to the song all the way to the end before she continued on to the dining room. It felt like love at first sight, although Ted had a difficult time believing that such a thing could happen to him at his age. Even so, he had never stopped thinking about her since that moment, and he hoped she felt the same way.

The wrong Maria, on the other hand, had been totally unmoved by Lionel Richie's *Hello*. He recalled her icy stare as he sang the song, which began to die in his mouth. Songs and hearts wither in the presence of a hard, judgmental gaze, and Ted had to muster all his experience and professionalism to sing it convincingly in spite of her standing in the hallway, staring coldly at him with her hands on her hips.

Just then he arrived at *Il Fortunello* and immediately spotted the right Maria standing at the reception desk waiting for him. As soon as she saw him come through the doorway she ran over to him and gave him a huge bear hug, while Ted returned it with the same warmth and enthusiasm. All his fears about how she probably didn't have feelings for him suddenly vanished.

If Ted ever had doubts about there being two Marias, they were quickly dispelled that evening, for when he took Dominique's hand to escort her into the dining room, he noticed that she was wearing her mother's ruby and diamond engagement ring.

CHAPTER FIFTEEN

Lars Jensen joined Ted Rasmussen and Dominique Perdue at *Il Fortunello* after dinner to learn what she had to say about the scheme that was developing on board his cruise ship. She told them everything she knew about the situation, beginning with how she had discovered a box of rock salt in a suitcase in her cabin, and how Angel had put a suspicious bottle of wine next to her refrigerator, bearing the ridiculous label *Château Apollyon Belial*, which are two of the names that the Bible assigns to Satan.

"It certainly sounds like Angel is thumbing his nose at us," Lars had remarked, with growing interest. "But why was someone else's suitcase in your stateroom, anyway? Did the cabin attendant make a mistake and deliver the wrong one?"

Dominique explained how she had become involved in the first place when she had encountered a woman in a queue in a pharmacy who looked exactly like herself, and how her look-alike, the real Maria Morgan, had dropped her cruise card, which eventually led her, the fake Maria, to become an accidental stowaway on the Cerulean Neptune.

"I should make a note of this," Lars had said, taking out his pen and writing something in his notebook. "We really need to install equipment that can read eye and finger prints. This sort of thing shouldn't be happening."

Dominique told them that Angel and Selim, her cabin attendant, were planning something that was meant to take place at the welcome party after choir practice the next day. The salt and the wine should no longer be of concern, since she had accidentally spilled the wine and used the rock salt to scrub up the mess.

"An accidental stowaway and an accidental spiller of suspicious wine," Lars noted. "Your mishaps have turned out to be rather effective security measures. But do go on."

"Well, I asked Piglet if he could get some salt from the galley to replace the salt that I used when I was cleaning up the spilled wine," Dominique continued.

"Excuse me," Lars said, looking up from his notes. "Did I hear you say *Piglet*?"

"His real name is Carlos Casablanca, but everyone calls him Piglet," Dominique explained. "He's short and heavyset, but he likes to be called Piglet. It's what his wife Paloma calls him, so he actually loves that name."

"I see," Lars replied, with a hint of a smile.

"I'm glad you replaced the salt, Maria," Ted said. "That way Angel and Selim won't know they've been found out. I'm sure you want them to go ahead with their plans, Lars, so you'll at least be able to nail them for attempted murder."

"You're absolutely right," Lars declared. "I'll let the staff bring the food and drink to the welcome party, but I'll step in before they can give any to the passengers. I don't want them to be exposed to anything that could harm them, but at the same time I have to prove the perpetrators' intent to commit murder."

Lars scribbled a quick memo in his notebook, reminding himself to make sure his staff did better background checks before hiring crew members.

"Is there anything I can do to help?" Dominique asked. "Should I come aboard and confront the real Maria Morgan? Is there anything to be gained by that?"

"The real Maria Morgan," Lars remarked thoughtfully. "I suppose that makes you... the *fake* Maria Morgan, is that right?"

"Quite right," Dominique smiled. "I wish it didn't have to be that way, but somehow that's who I became."

"What's your real name, then?" Ted asked her.

"My name is Dominique. Dominique Perdue."

"But you must be related somehow to Maria Morgan," Lars said. "You have to be identical twins, or at least sisters of almost the same age. There's no way, otherwise, that the two of you could look so much alike."

"I'm sure you're right," Dominique agreed. "But I don't know anything about it. My mother never said a word to me about my having a sister hidden away somewhere."

"That could be the subject of your next adventure," Ted suggested. "But I'll always think of you as Maria."

"Right now, however, we have to focus on the dangers we'll be facing tomorrow," Lars reminded them. "Ted, I'd like you to help me by keeping your eyes wide open. I'm not going to ask you to do anything special, for I have a group of well-trained security officers to help me, and I don't want any of the staff to be in danger. But you'll be standing on the platform where the piano is, so you'll have a good view of the whole room. If you see anything, just give me a signal."

"I have an iPhone," Ted said. "I could take some photos of them from the platform."

"Excellent," said Lars. "The more proof, the better."

"What can *I* do?" Dominique asked. "How can I help?"

"You can start by telling me if that salt had any odor that you could detect," Lars replied. "What did it smell like?"

"It smelled sort of like bitter almonds."

"Potassium cyanide," Lars muttered, knowing that bitter almond was an odor often associated with cyanide. "That's very bad news."

"It looks as if they're planning another Jonestown," Ted remarked.

"Yes, it looks that way," Lars agreed. "It takes very little cyanide to kill someone, and it works quickly, too. A fatal dose for humans can be as low as one and a half milligrams per kilo of body weight."

"I wish there were something I could do to help," said Dominique. "If you'd be willing to vouch for me, Lars, you could easily get me back onto the ship."

"I could, but I'm not sure how that would help matters. If anyone saw the two of you together—you and the real Maria Morgan, I mean—that would set off the alarm for the perpetrators."

"I agree with Lars," Ted said. "I think you should stay right here at *Il Fortunello,* where you'll be safe. Nothing can happen to you here."

"I suppose you're right, Ted," Dominique said. "Still, I wish I could be with you on the ship."

"I tell you what," Lars said, "once we get these bozos locked up, I'll let you have one of the mini-suites that aren't occupied right now. We would be happy to have you as our guest for the rest of the world cruise. You deserve it for all the help you've provided with the information you gathered while you were on board. You did a terrific job, Dominique, and we're very grateful."

"Well, I'm a *fortunella* to know the two of you, and I thank you, Lars, for your generous invitation."

"What did you just call yourself?" Ted asked her. "Did you say you were a… a *fortunella,* like the name of this bed-and-breakfast?"

"Yes, I did call myself a *fortunella,*" Dominique smiled. "Loosely translated, it means *lucky duck* in Italian, and that's just what I am."

After spending most of the evening carousing in the lively neighborhoods near the Pantheon, Federico Carpaggio and his girlfriend of the moment descended from a cab down the street from his apartment. He stuck a handful of *lire* through the open window on the passenger side, then he turned and embraced his girlfriend. The driver barked a gruff *grazie* and quickly moved into the traffic while Federico Carpaggio, his girlfriend draped comfortably over his shoulder, stumbled down the sidewalk in the direction of his apartment.

"When we get to my place," he said, "you'll see a dame sittin' there, gagged and tied to a chair. Pay no attention."

"I'm not into that kind of stuff," his girlfriend replied, disengaging herself from him. "You never told me nothin' about bein' a threesome, neither," she said, her anger rising.

"Don't worry. It's nothin' like that," he assured her.

"Well, what *is* it like? It sounds like sado-masochism to me. I wasn't born yesterday."

"I had to tie her to the chair to keep her from runnin' away, that's all."

"Runnin' away? What didja do? *Kidnap* her? I don't wanna get involved in anything like that. I'm not spendin' any more nights in the slammer, thank you very much."

"Lower your voice," he said, pushing ahead of her into the elevator. "You're not gonna go to jail, so just shut up."

"What's she doin' in your pad, then? I'm not goin' up there till you tell me, and it better be good."

"She's stayin' with me till tomorrow morning, then I hand her over to my boss. I had to stash her there for the time bein'. I had nowheres else to put her."

"Your boss? Who's your boss?"

"I can't tell you that."

"Why not?"

"He works under cover."

"Really? Is he a spy or somethin'?" she asked, sounding impressed.

"You could say that, I suppose. Sure, let's just say he's a spy and leave it at that."

By this time Federico Carpaggio had opened the door to his apartment and was standing there in the doorway, staring at the wooden chair that was on its side on the floor, with Dominique's cords strewn all around.

"What the f--- happened here?" he shouted, feeling both surprised and angry at the same time.

His companion leaned against his back and stared over his shoulder at the overturned chair.

"Suits me fine. I didn't wanna be a threesome anyways," she declared.

"Listen," he growled, turning to face her. "Ya better get outta here. I've got some phone calls to make, and I may have to go talk to my boss after that. So get lost, will ya?"

"Well, f--- you too!" his girlfriend shouted, turning on her heel and slamming the door behind her.

Carpaggio picked up his cell phone.

"Hey, Boss? The British broad is gone. The look-alike, yeah. I had her tied up good, but she escaped somehow... What? How should I know? She's gone, that's all... *What?* Call all the hotels in Rome? Are you *kiddin'* me? Do you know how many...? All right, already. I'll do what I can. You got a pretty good idea there, matter of fact. If the damn imposter's gonna try an' blow the whistle on us, that's where she's gonna be. *Of course* she can't be on board. I know, I know. Maria's got her cruise card back, and she's in her stateroom right now. Yeah, she heard the interview I had with Dominique Perdue. I recorded it and gave it to her on a USB device. She knows who's who on the ship now, so there won't be no problems. Yeah. I'll start with the hotels near the cruise ship terminal in Civitavecchia. *Ciao. A domani.*"

Ted Rasmussen couldn't sleep very well that night, thinking about Dominique and worrying about her safety.

"What if they find her somehow," he thought, "and get to her before I do?"

By six o'clock that morning Ted was up and dressed and marching down the gangplank, determined to make sure that nothing happened to Dominique. When he reached the bed-and-breakfast he nodded with self-assurance at the clerk at the front desk, as if he were a registered guest. The clerk nodded back, and kept on reading his morning newspaper.

"He must be one of the night staff, still on duty," Ted thought. "I'm sure I remember him from last night. He must have recognized me too. That worked out well."

Ted climbed up the stairs two at a time to get to Maria's floor as fast as he could. When he turned the corner near her room, he almost bumped into a server who was standing just outside her door with a stainless steel trolley loaded up with trays of covered dishes.

"*Mi scusi!*" Ted said to him.

"*Non c'è di che,*" replied the server, glancing at him.

Ted had the impression that this room service chap was up to no good. His furtive expression said it all. Ted kept on walking to the next corner, then watched what he was doing. He saw him take a look around to make sure he wasn't being observed, and then he removed a small envelope from his breast pocket and opened it. He looked up and down the corridor once again, then he poured some white crystals onto the scrambled eggs on one of the plates. After taking a quick look over his shoulder, he picked up a fork that was lying on the tray and gently mixed the crystals into the eggs.

Ted took out his iPhone and snapped a picture of him as he was stirring the eggs with the fork and holding the little envelope in his other hand. The room service man seemed jittery and nervous, and kept looking over his shoulder to see if he was being watched, but each time he turned his head, Ted would duck around the corner again.

When the room service man was sure that the coast was clear, he rapped smartly on Dominique's door.

"Room service!" he called out, knocking again.

When Dominique opened the door to let him in, Ted stepped forward and walked in with him, not wanting the room service man to be alone with her in her room.

"Ted!" Dominique exclaimed.

Since Ted was standing behind the server, he was able to put his finger to his lips as a signal to Dominique.

"Surprise!" he cried suddenly, startling both Dominique and the room service man as well. "I got back early from my business trip," he said, gathering Dominique into his arms.

"Well, I'm *very* surprised, you can be sure of that! I'm so happy to see you, darling!" she replied, knowing at once that Ted was putting on a show for the room service man.

"That will be all for now, thank you," Ted said, turning to the server and handing him a tip.

"Thank you, sir," he said, briefly touching his cap before leaving the room.

"Don't eat those scrambled eggs," Ted said, in an urgent tone of voice.

"Why? What's wrong with them?"

"I just saw that room service man sprinkle some white crystals on them. It might be cyanide."

"Cyanide? Good Lord, Ted! How did they know I was here? How did they find me?"

"I suppose they must have checked all the waterfront hotels in Civitavecchia. Anyway, I'm here too now, and I won't let anything happen to you."

"Thank God you came back just in time! I'm so happy you thought to check up on me. You saved my life!"

Ted put his arms around her and gave her one of the biggest hugs ever.

"I'd rather die than let anything happen to you," he said. He gave her a sweet, sweet kiss, then he held her at arm's length, contemplating her radiant smile... that certain smile he knew was for him alone. He laughed for joy and suddenly burst into song.

Maria! I've just kissed a girl named Maria,
and suddenly I've found
how wonderful a sound can be!

"But my name is actually Dominique," she said, smiling and clinging to him, never wanting to let him go. "You're getting me all confused."

"I know, but as far as I'm concerned, you'll always be Maria. *My* Maria. I'll never stop saying Maria."

"Then so be it," she said, "for as long as we have time."

"Someday we'll have all the time in the world, but right now we'll have to put this off for a while," Ted said to her tenderly. "We've got work to do this morning. We have a whole lot of lives to save, you and I. But will you give me a rain check?"

"I will," she said, smiling up at him. "But only if you promise to cash in that rain check every single time it rains."

"You've got yourself a deal."

"We'll have to go to the Himalayas, then. It rains almost every day on the eastern slope."

"How do you know that?"

"I traveled there once, ages and ages ago. I remember getting soaked on a regular basis by the monsoon winds that blew in from the south."

"I can see we're going to have a lot to talk about, Maria. A lifetime of things to talk about."

"I can't wait."

"But right now," Ted continued, "I'm going to scoop up these scrambled eggs and give them to Lars Jensen so he can get them tested. He can add that to his long list of successes as the Cerulean Neptune officer in charge of security."

"Good for you Ted. That's a nice gesture."

Ted took her in his arms and gave her one last kiss.

"Don't go anywhere, Maria," he said, holding her close. "Lock the door while I'm gone, and don't let anyone in. I'll be back right after the welcome party."

"I'll be here, waiting for you."

"And I'll be there, thinking of you."

"What if the room service man has a key?"

"I doubt that he really works here, but I'll speak to the manager on my way out. I'll ask him not to let anyone harm you or let anyone know you're here. If he does a bang-up job of protecting you, maybe I can persuade the Neptune Cruise Line to recommend this bed-and-breakfast to our passengers when they embark here in Civitavecchia for a cruise."

"Sounds like a plan. I'm sure the manager will be very happy to lodge customers from the Neptune Cruise Line on a regular basis. But Ted, please be careful, promise?"

"I will. I want to make sure I survive long enough to go to the Himalayas with you."

"We'll explore the whole world together, not just the Himalayas," she said, with a big smile. "We'll go to faraway places with strange-sounding names."

Ted looked at her thoughtfully for a moment.

"It's funny how the songs from the choir keep echoing through our lives," he remarked. "But I must go now, Maria, much as I hate to. I have some collaborating to do with Lars Jensen," he told her, giving her a long, lingering kiss before heading back to the ship.

CHAPTER SIXTEEN

Angel and Selim were in the Neptune Lounge, setting up the glasses that would be used for the welcome party. Selim didn't normally work at the bar, but he had volunteered to give up his lunch hour to help Angel get everything ready for the big moment.

"Make sure the glasses are all clean," Angel was saying. "They've got to be absolutely spotless, or you'll have Lars Jensen all over you. He's a stickler for cleanliness."

"Don't worry," Selim replied, holding a glass up to the light. "I do this all the time in the staterooms. But there's one thing I don't understand. Why do we have about twice as many glasses as we really need? There are only forty people in the choir, but we have eighty glasses standing here."

"This party is to welcome not only the members of the choir, but also the passengers who are taking Maria's Bible study. She has something like forty people in her class, so we have doubled the target."

"Really? I didn't know she had that many students."

"She's a good teacher, so they go to listen to her. That's why the imam gave her the job. He knew she would attract a large crowd."

Angel knew that Selim was not aware of the switch, so he said nothing about the other Maria.

"Eighty people. That should get us tons of publicity."

"Well, hurry up then," Angel said, trying to keep his voice down. "We don't have all day. In about half an hour or so we're going to see the choir members come straggling in, dragging those chairs over there into big semi-circles around the piano. When they're done with that, some of them will be coming here to chat with us, since they won't have a whole lot to do until Ted Rasmussen comes in and gets them started on their warm-up exercises."

"What kind of warm-up exercises?" Selim asked.

"Just wait till you hear them," Angel said with a sneer. "They sing *I am a shining star* over and over again to warm up their precious little throats, just like regular opera singers. You won't believe it. They should be in a comedy show."

"Where should I put the punch bowl?" Selim asked.

"Right on the counter, where everyone can see it."

"Are you going to put the cyanide in with the punch?"

"Shut up, you fool!" Angel hissed, *sotto voce*. "Don't say that word out loud. Do you want everyone to hear you?"

"Don't worry, nobody can hear us. Nobody's near us."

"Don't you know they have recording equipment in this lounge? There could be microphones anywhere!"

"Well, they wouldn't be turned on. Nothing's happening in here right now. What would they be recording? Glasses clinking and you yelling at me, that's all."

"You can't be too careful," Angel said.

"I didn't *have* to give up my lunch hour to help you set up, you know," Selim reminded him.

"Don't start with those dumb hints of yours," Angel said angrily. "You'll get your reward when the time comes."

"When? In heaven, with my seventy-two virgins?"

"It's not only about that, Selim. Your reward is to help establish our brotherhood under Sharia law world-wide."

"I don't understand how this is going to help, that's all."

"We're making a statement, Selim. Don't you get it? We're fighting a holy jihad. So just be patient. You'll have the conquered dhimmis serving you, and you'll have plenty of money, with all the taxes the dhimmis will be paying us."

"Sounds like tax extortion to me," Selim remarked.

"You better watch out, Selim. You've been listening to the passengers too long. You're beginning to see the world through their eyes, and that will be your downfall if you're not careful. You mustn't let yourself be contaminated by them. All they care about is their own selfish pleasures and luxuries. So take my advice and keep your distance. You'll be better off. Our time will come, you'll see."

"Our time will come? Like when we get rich because of the taxes we'll make them pay after we conquer them?"

"That's right."

"So what we're trying to do is get their money so we can enjoy our *own* selfish pleasures and luxuries, right?"

"You still don't get it, do you?" Angel said, exasperated. "They've forfeited their right to enjoy their riches, because they've used their money wrongly. They've raped the rest of the world and created misery and poverty everywhere. They must be stopped before they ruin the planet. It's up to us now to establish peace and justice in the world. You should be proud to be a part of it, Selim."

"I think we should reason with them, not kill them."

"We've already tried that, Selim. They turned up their noses at our great religious leaders and philosophers. They're beyond hope, and they need to be subdued before it's too late. So stop standing around, and get the punch ready. Then I'll make sure it packs a whacking good punch. Just wait. We'll be having our own party tonight."

The real Maria Morgan was seated in the Casino Lounge, surrounded by a group of forty passengers who had heard via the grapevine that the book she had chosen for her class had been very successful with other teachers. As Maria passed out copies of *Old Testament Alive!* she explained to the class that the book focused on a selection of the Bible characters themselves, bringing them alive and having them converse intimately with the readers or classroom students about their personal troubles, fears, dashed hopes, disappointments, and also their bright dreams for future happiness. According to the people in the Bible study who had already purchased the book at home, the author was very good at presenting these Bible characters, making them seem as real as the folks next door, while at the same time reaching into the hearts and minds of the readers. The results gave them fresh insights into human psychology and the meaning of life, which usually turned out—to the amusement of some and the astonishment of others—to be instructive and entertaining as well.

Maria began her lecture that morning with a description of the most disreputable character in the Old Testament—the world's first troublemaker and original fallen angel, Satan himself.

"Satan's name was Lucifer at first," Maria explained. "Lucifer is a name which derives from a Latin word meaning *the bearer of light.* At first all the angels were thrilled with their home in heaven, but as time went by, some of them started to flirt with sin. The word *sin* derives from a Greek word that means *to go the wrong way.*"

"Now, a little sin," she continued, "can be a dangerous thing, for it tends to make you wrongly believe that you're among the happy few who are courageous enough to choose the *right* direction. So Lucifer, *the Bearer of Light,* God's most dedicated servant, awoke one morning with a swollen head. This gave him a terrible migraine, and put him in a self-pitying mood. He looked at his Master with calculating eyes, and asked himself a question that changed everything. *Why*, he muttered, *shouldn't I have God's job?*"

"I feel that way about *my* boss, too," a man said to his wife, shoving her shoulder playfully. She shoved him back and frowned at him to pay attention to the teacher.

"So eventually," Maria went on, "Lucifer convinced a sizable number of angels that servitude is for dummies, and they rose up against their Creator. God's heart broke when His angels rebelled against Him, for He had always loved them and given them everything to make them happy. But He couldn't let them stay in heaven and spoil it for the others, so He banished Lucifer and his minions. He changed Lucifer's name to *Satan*, which means *Adversary* in Hebrew, and He called Satan's followers *demons*, which in Latin means *evil spirits*. God, of course, had foreknowledge of these classical languages," she said with a wink.

And so the lecture continued until ten minutes to one, when Maria was supposed to take her student acolytes up to the Neptune Lounge for the welcome party. But before she could leave, she found herself surrounded by passengers who had questions or comments about her talk.

"I love the way the book gives the meaning of Satan's names," said a woman called Veronica. "It's interesting how important names can be."

"I never knew the word *sin* means *to go the wrong way*," a man remarked. "Does the word *repent* have an interesting meaning too?"

"It does," Maria said. "It means *to change directions*."

"I like that," he said, looking thoughtful. "I have always sort of assumed that sinning and repenting is about behaving badly and feeling ashamed, but now I see it's about going the wrong way and getting lost, and then eventually being found and led back home."

"Anyone can get lost without a road map," declared an elderly man on the far end of the lounge.

"Or a satellite direction finder," said a younger member of the group.

Maria was glad she had chosen a book that her students enjoyed. If she had only had a few more days to teach it, she thought, the book might have attracted even more students to her class, but that was a luxury she couldn't afford. She and Angel had to get the deed done as quickly as possible, before anything could get in their way.

Ted was winding up the morning choir rehearsal with a final run-through of the new song he had introduced that morning.

"It's the theme song from *Around the World in Eighty Days*," he was saying. "It was written by Harold Anderson and Victor Young, and it's still as well-loved today as it was when it first came out. So are you ready then? Here we go."

Ted played the introduction and brought the choir in on the opening note.

Around the world I've searched for you,
I traveled on when hope was gone
to keep a rendez-vous.
I knew somewhere, sometime, somehow,
you'd look at me and I would see
the smile you're smiling now...

"That's one of the most sentimental songs I've ever heard in my life," Angel remarked, with a cynical sneer.

"Lots of people like it," Selim said.

"Then lots of people must be blithering idiots, and it's time for us to show them the joys of dhimmitude."

"Dhimmitude?"

"The subjection of Christians to Sharia law. We were just talking about that. Don't you remember anything?"

"We spoke about dhimmis, Angel, but I've never heard the word *dhimmitude.*"

"It was coined by the President of Lebanon back in the eighties. Anyway, if you want the infidels to cave in to us, all you have to do is call them Islamophobes."

"How is that going to make any difference to them?"

"They want to be good and kind and fair to everyone. So all you have to do is accuse them of everything you can think of, and they back down. Forget cyber war and missiles and drones and nuclear bombs. They fall apart if you tell them they're being unfair. They're scared of being called names."

"So then why are we putting cyanide in the punch? Why don't we just call them a few names instead?"

"Don't you remember what I said before? This is our way of making a statement that'll be remembered forever as a small version of 9/11. It doesn't hurt that it's about a cruise ship either, with all those fat, rich passengers being catered to and entertained. We're fighting a holy jihad, dummy!"

"Did you just call me a dummy or a dhimmi?"

"Take your pick," Angel said. "If the shoe fits, wear it," he added, polishing a glass and holding it up to the light.

Just then the real Maria and her Bible class trooped into the lounge and seated themselves in the first three rows of chairs that were lined up in semi-circles by the bar. The choir members turned and dragged their chairs into another three rows of semi-circles behind the Bible class. The welcome party was just about to begin, and everyone was waiting with great anticipation. Lars Jensen grabbed a mike, tapped it to make sure it was on, and began to speak to the crowd.

"Good morning everyone... or should I be saying good afternoon? At any rate, it's my pleasure to welcome you to this great party to celebrate Ted Rasmussen's latest choir. He's been conducting a choir every year for the last four years on the Cerulean Neptune, and he's been fantastically successful. We've all enjoyed the spectacular shows that his choir has put on at the end of every segment of our world cruises. The choir's productions have been as good as any of the professional performances we've booked for you, and we're extremely proud of both Ted and the choir members who've participated in these presentations.

"I'd also like to thank Maria Morgan for conducting a Bible class for the enjoyment of our passengers, all of whom, I'm told, are present here today. Those of us who are in charge of your entertainment, your safety, and your well-being on the Cerulean Neptune are delighted to have Maria and Ted with us here now to celebrate the success of their activities. They both volunteered to devote a lot of their free time to developing your minds and souls and voice boxes, so let's hear it for the two of them!"

The members of the choir and the Bible study erupted in enthusiastic applause while Angel and Selim made a show of pouring half of the bottles of wine into the fruit juice in the punch bowl. Then Selim began pouring wine from the rest of the uncorked bottles into the glasses lined up on the counter.

At this point Angel suddenly took the floor. Holding a microphone up to his mouth, he announced that those who were not fond of punch could help themselves to wine, but everyone should refrain from tasting either the punch or the wine until he, Angel, gave a toast to the leaders of the choir and the Bible study.

"We must all drink the punch and the wine at exactly the same time, so that we may honor our friends, Maria Morgan and Ted Rasmussen, without putting one above the other. I'll give the toast when it's time to drink to their health."

A murmur arose from among the guests at the welcome party as they expressed their bewilderment at the idea of the bartender offering a toast to the choir director and the Bible study leader. Wouldn't it be far more appropriate for Staff Captain Lars Jensen to give the toast?

Then suddenly all hell broke loose. After Angel and Selim poured the wine into the punch bowl and into the wine glasses lined up on the counter at the bar, Piglet Casablanca flared his nostrils and sniffed the odors that were wafting past him.

"Almonds!" he shouted in a loud voice. "I smell bitter almonds! It might be cyanide. Listen to me, everyone! Don't drink the punch or the wine!"

The word *cyanide* was being repeated by everybody in the audience as they looked at one another and tried to make sense of Piglet's unexpected warning.

Meanwhile Piglet leapt up and headed directly for the bar. When he reached the counter he put his foot on the top rung of a stool and propelled himself onto the bar, landing with his body against the punch bowl, after which he slid with it across the width of the counter and fell, along with the punch bowl, onto the floor on the other side of the bar.

While the people attending the ceremony were glued to their chairs, watching Piglet in open-mouthed astonishment, Paloma jumped up and ran to the bar as fast as she could go. Angel put his arms over his chest to protect himself from the onslaught, but Paloma ignored him and put her back to the counter, hoisting herself up onto the edge. Then she turned and slid her legs over the counter and jumped down to the floor on the other side, where she ministered to Piglet.

Veronica, one of the students who had spoken to Maria after the Bible study, suddenly got up and ran to the bar too. The people in the audience turned their attention to her to see what she was going to do, assuming she would take a look at Piglet and Paloma to see if they needed any help. But instead of leaning over the bar to check on them, she swept all the full wine glasses onto the floor, while the audience gasped and stared. Then she picked up a wine bottle and addressed the members of the choir and the Bible study.

"This morning," she said, "Maria taught us about Satan in the Bible class, and she spoke about the names that were given to him to describe who he was. We learned that two of his alternate names were Apollyon and Belial, meaning *The Destroyer,* and *The Worthless One.* So look at the ludicrous false labels that have been pasted onto the wine bottles: They say *Château Apollyon Belial.* Obviously Angel and Selim are mocking us and planning to poison us, too!"

"What? That's absurd!" Angel cried out. "She's making it all up! She's a racist! She's an Islamophobe! I demand an apology!"

"Veronica is right," Piglet said, standing up and showing his head above the bar. He was slightly bloodied, but clearly unbowed. Paloma stood up next to him, looking out over the audience. "No matter who gives the toast," Piglet continued, "there is no reason why it is important for us to raise all our glasses and drink at precisely the same time. The cyanide, it works quickly in the body. It is obvious that Angel knows it, and for this he is insisting that we have to drink the cyanide at exactly the same moment, because if one of us will sip it ahead of time, he will fall unconscious immediately, thereby warning everybody else that something is wrong with the wine and the punch."

"This is crazy!" Angel said in a loud voice. "I protest! This is defamation of character! How dare you accuse me of trying to poison you? You have no proof! I'm innocent! I'm being falsely accused of attempted murder by that man over there!" he shouted, pointing an accusing finger at Piglet.

When Angel saw that the audience was rising to their feet and moving toward him like an angry mob, he turned and started running toward the door. But Lars Jensen threw himself on him and landed him with a flying tackle, while at the same time Selim was cuffed by William, a security guard who had accompanied Lars to the celebration. Lars handed Angel over to another security guard, who put handcuffs on him and then used a second pair to cuff him to the bar rail.

During the entire uproar Ted Rasmussen was calmly standing on the raised platform by the piano, taking pictures of the disturbance from every possible angle. Bella was up there with him, pointing out various scenes that were taking place and that could be of interest to future investigators. As the tumult began to die down and the security guards were leading Selim and Angel away, Bella happened to notice that Maria Morgan was no longer in the lounge, so she brought it to Ted's attention.

Ted knew, of course, that the missing woman was not Dominique Perdue, the fake Maria Morgan and accidental stowaway who at that very moment was waiting for him in her room at *Il Fortunello*. The missing woman was the real Maria Morgan, who was involved with the terrorists and must not be allowed to escape from the ship. She was almost certainly a co-conspirator working with the Italian contact, Federico Carpaggio, whom he and Lars Jensen had discussed earlier with Dominique Perdue in her room at *Il Fortunello*.

Ted realized that Dominique Perdue was now in serious danger. After checking his watch he knew that the real Maria had left the Neptune Lounge at least ten minutes earlier, and she had doubtless been in touch by that time with Federico Carpaggio and the room service imposter at *Il Fortunello*.

She had probably texted them, and they would surely want to hold Dominique Perdue hostage so Lars Jensen would have to release Angel and Selim and any colleagues of theirs that Lars and his security guards had rounded up after the melee.

"Lars! Lars Jensen!" Ted called out, as he spotted him leaving the Neptune Lounge with one of the security guards.

"Ted, what's up?" Lars said, turning to face him.

"Dominique Perdue is in grave danger," Ted told him. "Maria Morgan left the lounge about ten minutes ago, while we were all occupied with what was going on. I'd be willing to bet that she and her cronies on the ground are going to try to get at Dominique in the bed-and-breakfast now. If they kidnap her and hold her hostage, you'll be forced to release Angel and the other perpetrators. If you don't release them, they might kill her. So let's go find her now. Right away!"

"Come with me, Ted," Lars said. "I want you to come too, William," he said to the security guard standing nearby. "We have to go find a woman called Dominique Perdue."

"Dominique Perdue?" William repeated, as he ran with them toward the gangway. "Is this woman a passenger, sir? I don't recognize the name."

"It's a long story," Lars called back over his shoulder as he ran ahead. "We'll sort it out tonight. But right now we need to find her immediately."

"Is she on board the ship, sir?" William called to him.

"No, she's staying in a place called *Il Fortunello*."

"I know that little hotel. Let me call them, sir. It might save us some time."

"Good idea, William. Find out what you can."

As the three men arrived at the gangway on Deck Three, William called *Il Fortunello* on his Blackberry. He spoke briefly to the person who answered, then he turned to Lars.

"She checked out, sir. Check-out was at one o'clock."

"Good God!" Ted exclaimed. "We've *got* to find her!"

"It won't be very easy," Lars remarked, looking gloomy. "She could be with anyone, anywhere."

"This is a case for the Italian *polizia*," William said. "I'll contact them immediately if you wish, sir."

"It can't hurt," Lars replied. "The process will probably be painfully slow, though. That's my experience, anyway."

"I'm going to the bed-and-breakfast to talk to the people at the front desk," Ted said. "I'll talk to the manager, too."

"That's fine by me, Ted," Lars said. "William and I will work on it here from my office. I'll call the police to see if they can help us find her. Have you a cell phone, Ted?"

"Yes, I have an iPhone."

"Write down the number for me then, please," Lars said, handing him his notebook. "Here's my direct number and my mobile," he added, giving him his business card.

"I'll stay in touch," Ted said, slipping the card into his pocket while he presented his laminex to the security officer by the gangplank.

"We sail for Athens at five o'clock this afternoon, Ted," Lars reminded him. "Don't be late!"

"I'm not coming back till I find Maria. I'll catch up to you in Athens if I have to."

"Her real name is Dominique Perdue. You should learn to call her Dominique, my friend," Lars said.

"Never! She's Maria to me, and always will be."

"Good luck, Ted!" Lars called after him as he galloped down the gangplank, making the whole structure shake.

"Ted must really like that woman," Lars said to William, as the two men made their way to Jensen's office. "She was an accidental stowaway on this ship. That's why you didn't know anyone by the name of Dominique Perdue."

"An *accidental* stowaway, sir? How can that be?"

"It's a long story, William. I'll tell you about it later, but right now we have to get the police to help us find her. Then we have poison to analyze and prisoners to question. So let's get moving!"

CHAPTER SEVENTEEN

Ted Rasmussen entered the security clearance building across from where the Cerulean Neptune was docked, and showed his papers to an Italian security officer. He continued past the *Forte Michelangelo*, and then ran at breakneck speed along the *Viale Garibaldi* until he reached *Il Fortunello*.

"I'm looking for one of the guests here," he said to the desk clerk, trying to catch his breath. "Could you tell me what time it was when Dominique Perdue checked out this morning, please?"

"One moment, sir," she said, clicking on the keyboard of her laptop computer. "It was… let's see… she checked out at exactly 12:33," she said, with a pleasant smile.

"Could you tell me if anyone was with her when she left?" Ted asked her.

"I'm afraid I don't know, sir. I wasn't here at the time. My shift just started at one o'clock."

"Do you know this person?" Ted asked, showing her the photo he took of the room service man on his iPhone.

"No, I don't," she said, looking surprised. "He doesn't work here, but he seems to be pushing one of our breakfast trolleys. This is strange. I think I should consult the manager. I've never seen him before in my life! He's not on our staff, that's all I can tell you."

Ted's heart began to race. The room service man tried to poison Dominique, which would soon be proven when Lars had the scrambled eggs analyzed. So the room service man must have kidnapped her somehow, because she definitely wouldn't have checked out by herself. Ted had promised her that he would come back, and he was certain she would wait for him. But then how did the room service man manage to smuggle her out of *Il Fortunello* without being seen, or force her to leave against her will, without attracting attention? Ted doubted that anybody on the hotel staff could be allied with him. It would be too much of a coincidence for that to be the case.

Perhaps Federico Carpaggio had found out that she was registered there, but how? Did he call every single one of the hotels in Rome? That seemed like a stretch—there were over two thousand hotels in Rome.

Then it suddenly occurred to Ted that Carpaggio could have zeroed in on the hotels in the immediate vicinity of the cruise ship dock in Civitavecchia, in which case it wouldn't have taken him long to find her. Dominique had said he was a sleazy type, with a crew-cut and a receding hairline, with bags under his eyes and a tough look about him. He sounded like a wharf rat to Ted. Apparently he lived in a shabby part of Rome, but Dominique hadn't mentioned his address, nor had she told him about any landmarks that could help Ted to locate his apartment.

He moved away from the receptionist at the front desk and called Lars Jensen on his iPhone.

"Dominique checked out just before the afternoon shift," he reported, "so the desk clerks who are there now didn't see her leave. They can't tell me if she was accompanied or not."

"Ah, that's terrible luck," Lars said, sounding frustrated. "That's going to make it very hard for us to find her."

"If you're busy with your own part of the investigation, I could go to the police station for you and see if they can locate the address of Federico Carpaggio, the man who held her captive at his apartment somewhere in Rome. Maybe if I could speak to the police officers personally at the station, they might be able to move a little faster. They have all their computer information at their fingertips there."

"Sounds good to me," Lars replied. "See what you can do, Ted. But don't be late getting back on board."

"I know. The ship sails for Athens at five o'clock. Is there anything else you need while I'm at the police station?"

"I don't think so, but thanks anyway. We've put Angel and Selim in the brig, and we're busy now questioning others who might be involved. We've been in touch with the police ourselves, so they're sending some officers to come on board to continue the investigation, since we're in Italian waters."

"Good," Ted said, relieved. "That should give us some peace of mind, plus a little extra breathing space."

"It looks as though the Italian police will be booking the perpetrators on intent to murder, but that's just between you and me. We want to keep this thing under wraps as long as possible until we can figure out exactly how to present it to the passengers and crew. I'm hoping we'll get a little help from headquarters on that one."

Just then the manager of *Il Fortunello* walked by. When he saw Ted, he stopped and smiled.

"Lars," Ted said. "The manager is here. I've got to go. I'll call you back."

"Okay. Keep in touch."

"I'm glad to see you here again, Ted," the manager said. "I was just coming to have a talk with the desk clerk who has arrived for the next shift. I have been busy in my office, but I have not forgotten the conversation we had yesterday."

"Yes. You promised me that you'd take good care of Dominique Perdue."

"That is true, my friend. So I left a message for our desk clerks—both the clerks of the day and the other clerks of the night—telling all of them that if anybody asks for Signora Dominique Perdue, either in person or by phone, they should be told that she checked out some time ago."

"That's what they told the staff captain on the ship, too," Ted remarked. "They said the check-out deadline was one o'clock. So can we find out where she went? The desk clerk looked up her departure time on the computer and told me she left at exactly 12:33."

"My dear friend, computers can easily be programmed to provide whatever information is required. Signora Perdue, however, did not go anywhere."

"What? I don't understand."

"I felt that she needed to take some rest. The poor lady looked exhausted. But I didn't want her enemies to know where she was. You told me yesterday that these people are very dangerous, so I did not wish to take any chances with her safety."

"So what did you do, then?"

"I will tell you. I instructed the desk personnel to inform anyone who inquired about Signora Perdue that she checked out. A man by the name of Lars Jensen called from your ship, but there was no way for the receptionist to know if he was really and truly Signor Jensen or perhaps just another member of the gang who was seeking Signora Perdue."

"That was good thinking on the part of the receptionist," Lars observed. "So then what did she do?"

"She sensibly followed my orders and did not make an exception for Signor Jensen. But to you, Ted, I shall tell you the truth. Signora Perdue is still here in *Il Fortunello,* where she is resting comfortably in her room."

"What? The same room as before?"

"That is correct. She is resting in a nice secret hideaway. Like *Hernando's Hideaway,* you know the song?"

"Yes, it's a tango from *The Pajama Game.*"

"Then you will understand that I have put her *in a dark, secluded place, a place where no one knows her face.* So, my friend, you must quickly go up and give her *a glass of wine* and *a fast embrace,* no? Perhaps you will *knock three times and whisper low that you were sent along by Joe.*"

"I'll do that. Thank you so much for giving her a safe place to stay," Ted said to the manager. "I can't begin to tell you how grateful I am."

"Think nothing of it," said the manager, smiling. "I was happy to be of the service."

Ted called Lars and told him that Dominique was safely tucked away in her room at *Il Fortunello*, and that he was going upstairs to find her and escort her back to the ship.

"I'm glad you called, Ted. I just had a word with one of the Italian policemen about this fellow Federico Carpaggio. It turns out they know him very well and they know exactly where to find him. We also have the test results from the scrambled eggs, and the room service man did indeed poison them—with cyanide, naturally. So now, thanks to the iPhone photo that you took of him *in flagrante delicto*, we have the evidence we need to arrest him."

"So I don't have to go to the police station, then?"

"No. It won't be necessary. They're here with me right now doing the investigation. The policeman I was telling you about is standing right in front of me as we speak."

"Perfect. Then I'll go to Dominique at once."

"You do that, Ted. But just don't get too tangled up with her right now. You don't have much time."

"I know. The ship leaves at five o'clock."

"By the way, Michele has found a suite for Dominique. I'm sure she'll be very comfortable."

"Really? You had the time to get that done, as well as everything else?"

"You got it."

"Thank you Lars. You're the best."

Ted dashed up the stairs and knocked on Dominique's door. He sensed that she was looking through the peephole, and he stood back so she could see him properly. Suddenly the door opened wide.

"Ted! I'm so glad you're here!" Dominique exclaimed. "I didn't know where you were, or how to contact you!"

"I was worried about you as well," Ted said, holding her tightly against his chest. "They told me you checked out. I was horrified. I wasn't sure where to look for you, but the manager said you were here, and now we're together at last," he added, stepping back and holding her away from himself so he could gaze at her face. "That's the whole story, minus a few details here and there."

"I'm so glad everything turned out well. The manager was so good to me. Is everything okay on the ship?"

"Yes, Lars Jensen has it under control. The Italian police are on board and they're rounding up the suspects. Oh, and you'll be glad to know that Lars found you that suite, just as he said he would. Michele got it for you, so you're free to take a trip around the world with us! Lars has arranged for you to have free credit for any shore excursion you want, and all the clothes and sundries you need from the boutique. You get free access to the gym and the spa as well, and unlimited computer time."

"Good heavens, Ted! That's wonderful! I can't wait to thank Lars and Michele."

"Lars remembered something else for you, too."

"He did? What was that?"

"He'll meet you at the top of the gangplank and bring you aboard, because you don't have a laminex ID. Maria used it this morning to disembark."

"That was brilliant of Lars to think of it."

"You'll have to fill out the paperwork for a laminex of your own later on, but you can do that at your leisure."

"I will, Ted. But right now I have a question."

"What is it?"

"Are you allowed to fraternize with me? You're on staff, after all, and I'm still a passenger on the ship."

"We're not on board the ship right now, Maria. We're both free agents," he said, gathering her into his arms again and giving her a lengthy kiss. Then he raised his foot behind him and pushed the door shut.

Paloma Casablanca turned out to be a very great help to Lars Jensen after the incident involving the attempted poisoning of eighty passengers on board the Cerulean Neptune. She had purchased an innovative *Cruise Ship Lawyer* app for her

Android Smart phone, which had been launched by Lipcon, Margulies, Alsina & Winkleman, an important law firm in Miami. Its state-of-the-art features made it possible for her to document the Neptune Lounge debacle in real time, so no evidence was lost and no detail went unrecorded. Paloma was thrilled with her new app, for it provided her with photo, audio, and video storage to document the scene, as well as a case evaluation form, an injury-related expense tracker, and a Skype feature so she could make calls while she was at sea.

Paloma's *Cruise Ship Lawyer* app, in combination with Ted Rasmussen's clever use of his iPhone, made it possible for Lars to get Angel and Selim fired from the Cerulean Neptune and arraigned in an Italian court, where they pled guilty to attempted murder—a plea which greatly simplified the procedure as well as reducing the legal expenses.

The real Maria Morgan, who had fled the ship when she saw that her efforts to poison the passengers had failed, was later found by the Italian *polizia* with Federico Carpaggio and the room service man in a topless bar near his apartment in Rome. They were both promptly arrested, tried, and given a lengthy jail term—Carpaggio for kidnapping and the room service man for attempted murder. The real Maria Morgan was detained as a material witness at the trial, where it was learned that she was the daughter of one Geoffrey Morgan, a respected member of a certain mosque in North London. He then became a person of interest to the London police, and the main reason why Maria was later deported to England, where she was arrested, arraigned, tried and found guilty of collusion in the plot to murder the eighty passengers on the Cerulean Neptune.

During her trial Maria implicated her father and the imam, who worked closely together for many years, along with various other members of the North London mosque.

"You're a traitor," Angel had whispered to her in the courthouse while they were waiting to be called to the dock. "Why did you teach your Bible students the names of Satan,

Apollyon and Belial? If you had kept your big mouth shut, that student of yours, Veronica, wouldn't have known there was something fishy about the labels on the wine bottles. I'm going to tell the imam what you did, and he'll order a fatwa against you. Your life won't be worth a shilling."

When this issue came up during Maria's trial in London, she was given a lighter sentence for warning her students by teaching them the meaning of the names of Satan, including those on the wine labels. Later on in the trial her father was questioned about Maria's real identity, and he admitted she was the identical twin sister of Dominique Perdue. When he divorced his wife Penelope, the mother of the twins, he took Maria to live with him, while his wife kept Dominique. The twins were only babies at the time of the divorce, so to avoid complications the couple had agreed not to reveal to their respective daughters that each had a twin sister living with the other parent. Later Penelope took back her maiden name, Perdue, and changed Dominique's name to match her own. So the twins never would have known each other had it not been for the cruise card that Dominique found on that fateful day in the Mayfair Pharmacy.

All this news had quickly leaked out of the London trial and straight into the daily rags, where it became a popular topic of conversation. Not only was the relationship between the Morgan and Perdue families analyzed ad infinitum, but a great deal of interest was showered on the passengers who had narrowly escaped death on the Cerulean Neptune. None of the passengers had been injured, however, except Piglet, who had bruised and cut his forehead when he leapt onto the bar and landed on the floor behind it. He was treated for the second time by the ship's doctor in the Cerulean Neptune Medical Center, and there the matter rested.

Lars proved to be truly gifted in the art of diplomacy, for he skillfully fielded all the passengers' questions, providing answers that calmed them down and satisfied their various concerns. Everyone agreed that a situation which could have ended in the deaths of many scores of passengers had been successfully avoided, thanks to the alert and speedy reactions of Lars Jensen, Ted Rasmussen, and Dominique Perdue, as well as the intelligent and selfless help of Bella Boorsma, along with that of Carlos and Paloma Casablanca, including Veronica, the quick-witted Bible student.

There's an old adage that says that it's an ill wind that brings no good. Although cruise ship authorities have had to deal with robberies, disappearances, sexual assaults and various forms of poor behavior traceable to the influence of drugs and alcohol, and although a few cruise ships have endured attacks by both pirates and terrorists, no cruise ship to date has faced the attempted mass murder of eighty passengers at the hands of perpetrators on board.

The executives at the Neptune headquarters in Santa Marta, California were swarmed by the news media, who were pleased with the way the situation had been handled. They gave the Neptune Cruise Line some excellent press and called the ship's officers highly professional and much to be admired for their concern for the safety of their passengers.

After a few weeks, however, the excitement began to die down, and the Neptune Cruise Line executives all felt that something should be done to keep the momentum going. The board members discussed a good number of ideas, but none of them appealed to the Chief Executive Officer.

"Hey guys," said Marty Goldbloom, the Neptune Cruise Line corporation's creative director. "Remember that woman from the Cerulean Neptune who sent us a proposal to have their ship's choir sing at the Sydney Opera House? I thought she had a pretty good idea going on there. I was impressed."

"Wasn't she the Sloanie from MIT?" someone asked.

"Yes, that's the one," Marty said. "It's a highly-regarded business school with an excellent track record for producing successful graduates. What was her name again?"

"Her name was Bella," said the woman next to him.

"Bella, that's right," said Marty. "Bella Boomer, is it?"

"Bella Boorsma," somebody corrected him.

"Right. So here's the scoop. The Cerulean Neptune has blown a lot of minds recently with their exciting story about terrorist crew members and their allies, whose schemes were foiled by fearless passengers and intelligent, capable staff members working with the Italian police, who rounded up the little buggers and threw them in the slammer. Score one for the cruise lines, and zero for the terrorists, right? So how about we build on this while we're ahead, what do you say?"

"Sounds good," said one of the board members. "What have you got in mind, Marty?"

"We take that sensational presentation that the Boorsma woman gave us, and we challenge the Sydney Opera board to give it some really serious consideration this time around. That choir director, what was his name again?"

"Ted Rasmussen," said the secretary of the board.

"That was it. Ted Rasmussen. So now's the perfect time to ratchet him up where everyone can see him, and have him come forward with his whole glorious choir to paint a sort of memorable exclamation point to commemorate the success of those heroes and heroines who dealt so bravely with this dangerous terrorist attack on the high seas."

"They were docked at the time," someone said.

"Whatever. The point is that we've got to keep up the momentum. We've had some fabulous publicity lately, so we should tie it in with that talented choir master and his choir, and get the folks at the Sydney Opera to step up to the plate. We've got a home run in the works here."

"I can't see the connection," another board member said. "How do you mix and match terrorists with a choir?"

"In principal the one has nothing to do with the other," Marty said, "except that the terrorists in this case have drawn a lot of attention to the Cerulean Neptune. So while the eyes of the world are on the Neptune Cruise Line, we'll grab the opportunity to turn the attention of those same eyes onto the

Sydney Opera. Everybody is talking about the attempted murder of those eighty innocent passengers and the quick-witted staff members who stepped right in and successfully protected them and brought the perpetrators to justice. Well, Ted Rasmussen was one of those brave staff members who responded to the call of duty, so why not give the man a big round of applause at the Sydney Opera House?"

"Ted's choir is made up of just ordinary passengers, not opera singers," one of the board members pointed out.

"That's the whole point. People will want to see those ordinary passengers who were subjected to an extraordinary adventure and who came out with flying colors. The people in the audience at the Sydney Opera are mostly just ordinary folks too, so they'll relate. That's what people want."

"Okay, Marty, you've made some good points," said the chairman of the board. "Let's put it to the vote, shall we?"

The vote passed by a narrow margin, but it was all that Marty needed to win the day. It was subsequently decided during the discussion period that Bella would be invited to send her presentation to the board of governors at the Sydney Opera. Marty and his creative team would provide all the artwork necessary for the presentation, including the oilcloth banner with the words THE SYDNEY OPERA PRESENTS THE NEPTUNE CRUISE LINE'S WORLD CHOIR.

"That banner will make their eyes pop right out of their heads," Marty said, with utmost confidence. "The Neptune Cruise Line has become a household name now, just like the Costa Concordia, but for totally different reasons, of course. It doesn't matter, though. People like a success story just as much as they like a scandal."

"They like it even more, if you ask me," somebody else remarked. "It takes much more talent to become a success in life than it does to create a mere scandal. People love stories about the little guy who beats the odds."

"Don't forget," said another board member, "Piglet and Paloma Casablanca, and Bella Boorsma, and Ted Rasmussen are household names now."

"Piglet?" someone else piped up. "Did you say *Piglet?*"

"Yes, he's short and fat and he likes to be called Piglet. He obviously has no self-image problems whatsoever."

"And speaking of household names, you've got a great story with the evil twin and the good twin: Maria Morgan the terrorist sympathizer, and Dominique Perdue, the accidental stowaway," the board member reminded her colleagues.

"I remember the accidental stowaway story," a woman remarked. "What a hoot!"

"It wasn't such a good story for us here at headquarters, though," remarked the chairman of the board. "There should never be a way for stowaways to get away with it, not even in the case of identical twins. It makes us look like jackasses. Duckworth, you're in charge of security. I want you to install equipment for reading fingerprints and eyeballs."

"I'm on it," Duckworth said, typing a memo on his iPad. "The electronic equipment will cost us plenty, though."

"I don't care," said the chairman. "Just do it."

"Those are absolutely great stories, as far as the public is concerned," Marty said excitedly. "They're all over the web. Everybody's talking about it and posting comments. They're twittering, and tweeting, and you name it."

"Yeah, they've gone viral," someone else remarked.

"Now is *exactly* the right time to approach the Sydney Opera," Marty declared. "I'll bet you twenty to one they'll accept our proposal this time around. All it takes is just a little boost from something else that puts an interesting angle on the original story, and you've got yourself a winner!"

The Cerulean Neptune had finished the Mediterranean leg of its world cruise, and had sailed down the Red Sea to India and eventually over to Malaysia. It was docked in Singapore when a Skype call came through from the Sydney Opera for Ted Rasmussen. The caller introduced herself as Olivia Ling, a scheduler for the Sydney Opera, and she invited him and his choir to sing at the Opera House when they docked in the Sydney Harbour in twelve days from then.

"Will that give you enough time to prepare a ten-minute performance, Mr. Rasmussen?" Olivia wanted to know.

"It will, certainly it will," Ted replied, trying to contain his excitement. "It should be no problem at all."

"Good, I'm glad to know we have your consent. We're slotting you into the intermission, and you'll be mentioned in the printed program too. We'll make an announcement to the spectators before the intermission, so they'll know what's going on. Then they can choose to stay or leave, just as they wish. We believe a good number of them will stay to see you direct your choir and to hear the choir sing, especially since you've been in the headlines for such a long time now."

Olivia paused just long enough to let Ted get a word in.

"This is truly a fantastic opportunity for us," he said. "The choir will be thrilled to sing even for ten minutes in the Sydney Opera House. It will be the experience of a lifetime for all of us, and I thank you on their behalf and for myself for your very kind invitation. I know it will be wonderful for us to be able to experience the acoustics in the auditorium, and to be there for your performance that night."

"We'll be presenting a program called *My Christmas,* featuring Andrea Bocelli, so I think it would be a good fit if you could prepare something appropriate for Christmas too."

"Bocelli!" Ted exclaimed. "What an incredible honor this is for us! Do you know what songs he intends to sing? I wouldn't want us to duplicate anything he's planning to do."

"As far as I know, he'll be doing some classics with our chorus such as *Adeste Fidelis,* and *O Tannenbaum,* as well as popular songs from *White Christmas* and *Santa Claus is Coming to Town.* The Muppets will be there, too, to help him with his presentation of *Jingle Bells,* and then, let me see... I have the draft of our program somewhere around here... Yes, here it is. He'll be teaming up with Mary J. Blige to sing *What Child Is This?* and with Natalie Cole for *The*

Christmas Song, and Reba McEntire for *Blue Christmas*, and fellow opera star Katherine Jenkins for *I Believe*. His solo songs will include *White Christmas, Silent Night, Angels We Have Heard On High, Caro Gesu Bambino, Cantique De Noel* and *God Bless Us Everyone*. So that should give you an idea of what the program looks like."

"I believe Andrea Bocelli put out a CD and a DVD of his presentation, didn't he?" Ted asked.

"He did, and they'll both be available in the lobby. So do you have any other questions, Mr. Rasmussen?"

"My choir is used to having me accompany them on the piano. Would that be a problem?"

"Not at all. Our Steinway grand piano will be on stage."

"That's wonderful!" Ted exclaimed. "Will Terry Harper be tuning it?"

"You know Terry?"

"Not personally, no, but he has a worldwide reputation. He's known as your piano tuner extraordinaire."

"Quite right, Mr. Rasmussen. He's been with us for over thirty years now. And yes, he'll be tuning the Steinway on the night you perform with your choir."

"How long does it take him to tune it?"

"Usually about one and a half hours or so to do all two hundred and forty strings, but it depends a lot on the amount of surrounding noise and lighting, of course. Sometimes he has to work in very trying circumstances, so it takes him longer then."

"I can't tell you how grateful I am for this opportunity," Ted said happily. "I can't wait to play the Steinway Grand and to hear my choir's voices in the best venue in the world."

After his conversation with Olivia Ling, Ted sat looking at his computer screen, thinking how wonderful his life had become now that Maria was a part of it at last.

CHAPTER EIGHTEEN

Bella Boorsma was sitting in her stateroom, wondering if she should contact her doctor in New York. The dull ache in her right femur had been getting worse with every day that went by, and her pain medication didn't seem to be working as well as before. She had consulted her gynecologic oncologist the day before she was to leave New York for her world cruise. He had agreed to let her go, but with some reservations.

"You must keep in mind, Bella," he warned her, "that your cancer was diagnosed as stage 4 UPSC, so metastasis is always a concern. You've been very fortunate that the cancer seems to have been contained so far, but you must promise me that you'll fly back to New York if you experience any symptoms elsewhere in your body, so that I can start chemo or radiation therapy if necessary."

Bella realized that there was no cure for bone cancer metastasis, so she decided to complete the world cruise. She would fly back home only if the upper leg pain became so unbearable that she required radiation treatment and stronger medication to relieve it. She knew her oncologist would be concerned about her decision to put off immediate treatment, but she also knew that he always respected her decisions.

There was one other consideration, too, that neither she nor her oncologist could have predicted before the beginning of the world cruise, and that was the fact that she and Staff Captain Lars Jensen would fall in love. There was nothing, Bella mused as she sat in her stateroom thinking about him, there was nothing in the world more glorious for her than being in love with Lars and being loved by him as well.

The situation facing her now was that she had to figure out the best way to tell Lars she had terminal cancer. It broke her heart to have to give him this crushing news, for now that the terrorism problem had been taken care of and things were going smoothly on board the Cerulean Neptune, Lars had been talking to her about making a life together. Nothing could have made her happier than sharing a future with Lars, and at the same time nothing could be more devastating to her than to have to tell him that there could be no future for them, at least in this life.

Bella looked at her watch and suddenly realized it was time for her to get ready for dinner. Lars had invited her to join him in the Steak House for a special sunset meal, and she wanted to give herself enough time to look her very best for him. She chose a bright red cocktail dress that would go well with the rosy colors of the setting sun, and she put on a pair of high heels that had been dyed to match the dress. When she had finished putting her blond hair into a French braid, she looked at herself in the full length mirror and was satisfied with the results. The red colors of her clothing made her look a little more vibrant than usual, and the rouge and bright lipstick made her look healthier than she actually felt.

"You look beautiful, Bella!" Lars exclaimed when they met that evening. "Stand back and let me see you!"

"How far back into the hallway do you want me to go?" Bella asked him, laughing.

"Take my arm and let me formally escort you into the Steak House," he said, delighted to be spending the whole evening with her at last.

The maître d' seated them at a table next to the window, where they could enjoy a full view of the sunset.

"I can't think of a more romantic moment," Bella said, with a sigh of contentment. "Having dinner on a cruise ship sailing from Singapore to Sydney, in the company of a man I've seen and spoken to for the past three years, but never really came to know until now. We owe a debt of gratitude to the terrorists, don't you think? If it hadn't been for them, we might never have known each other this way!"

"I never thought of that," Lars smiled. "I used to look at you once in a while last year, hoping you wouldn't catch me staring," he admitted. "You were the most beautiful woman on the ship. I always wanted to find ways to be near you."

"You're not so bad looking yourself," Bella said, flirting with him. "All the younger women were talking about you last year, but nobody could ever pair you up with anyone. You had the reputation of being hard to get."

"In my position you have to be careful," he chuckled. "But I only had eyes for you."

"I never would have guessed," said Bella, feeling happy that he wasn't the kind of man who wooed all the ladies.

After they finished their meal and the server had cleared all their dishes away, Lars and Bella lingered at the table, enjoying the sparkling waves, the starry night sky, and the sheer joy of each other's company.

Bella didn't want to spoil the evening by mentioning her medical situation, so she decided to leave it for another time. There was no good time, however, for news of that sort, she thought ruefully.

When the real Maria Morgan had been escorted to jail along with Angel and Selim after the unsuccessful terrorist attack, Dominique Perdue took over her Bible classes, but after the first few sessions she felt compelled to apologize to the class for not having properly prepared herself ahead of time.

"So you see," she concluded remorsefully, after having provided them with a full explanation of the circumstances leading to her presence among them, "it doesn't pay to pretend you're someone you're not. It got me into a pile of trouble, and I felt awful for presenting myself as somebody else. I was successful in my role as an accidental stowaway, but it gave me no pleasure to deceive anyone. So I hope you'll all forgive me for leading you down the garden path."

The students remained silent for a few moments, then Veronica spoke up.

"I think you did a fine job of presenting the Bible to us, no matter who you are," she declared.

"Thank you for your confidence," Dominique said. "I never went to seminary, and I'm no expert on the subject of the Bible from a purely scholarly point of view. But I did teach literature all my life, and I must say that literature and the Bible have a lot in common. They're both about people and our struggles and our destinies and the basic meaning of our short stay here in this world. If you take anything away from this class, just remember that we all have to work out our own salvation in fear and trembling, just as Kierkegaard so wisely advised us to do. Think deeply, use your brains and your best judgment, and read the Bible for yourselves. The Holy Spirit, as they say, will guide you."

At that point Dominique had picked up her notebook and walked out of the Casino Lounge. Just as she reached the hallway, Veronica jumped up and called out to her.

"Wait!" she said. "Hold on a minute, Maria!"

Dominique stopped in her tracks, touched by the sound of the name *Maria*, a name she had come to love.

"You may not have gone to seminary, but I think I speak for all of us when I say that we loved your classes, and we want you to give us more. Is that right, everybody?"

"That's right," said a man in the front row.

"Yes, keep on going," said a woman in the back row. "I've been to adult Sunday school classes before, and most of them are dull as dish water. The teachers just repeat the hum-drum material in the textbooks that are put out by the powers that be, then the teachers ask us the study questions, but it doesn't mean anything to us because we can't relate to it personally. God is above all a *personal* God, the God who invented hearts and souls."

"She's right," said the man next to her. "You made the Bible come alive for us, and as far as I'm concerned, I want to hear more. Nothing changes when it comes to human nature. The Bible characters are just the same as we are. It's a good thing that history repeats itself, because we can learn something from it that way, especially when a good teacher interprets it for us."

Dominique stood there looking at them, touched by their enthusiasm and their eagerness to explore the Bible with her in spite of her lack of theological training, or perhaps even *because* of it to some extent. She knew from her experience as a professor of literature that students usually absorb the most when the teacher leads them into the very heart of the subject, where they can expand their minds and experience the true joy of learning.

"I always look forward to your classes," someone said.

"Yes, we want more," said another.

"You inspire us, Maria," said yet another.

"Yes, when you inspire us we become like… well, like new people," said someone in the second row.

"To inspire," Dominique said thoughtfully, "to inspire comes from the Latin *inspirare,* which means *to breathe into*. So when we're inspired as students, it's as if someone breathed their spirit into us and filled us with a sense of joy... a feeling of being enthusiastically alive."

"That someone who breathes into us, isn't he what we call the Holy Spirit?" Veronica asked.

"You're right," Dominique said. "You're exactly right. That's why I try to make our classes come alive, alive with the spirit of God so that we can feel inspired by Him when we read the Bible. Only then does it make any sense…"

"Keep on going, Maria," said the man in the front row. "Just keep on going. You're doing fine."

That interchange had taken place when the Cerulean Neptune was still cruising the Mediterranean. Now they had just left Singapore, and the Bible study had been going well for all that time. Once again Dominique Perdue felt that she was no longer lost. On the contrary, she had the impression that her students had found her and had helped her reach the very pinnacle of her teaching career, even though she had been retired for well over a decade.

Ted Rasmussen walked up to the platform in the back of the Neptune Lounge and turned to face the choir. The singers all cleared their throats and looked at him expectantly, thinking he was going to lead them through their warm-up exercises.

"I have an announcement to make," he said, standing next to the piano.

There arose from the choir a hum of mutterings.

"I'll get straight to the point," he continued. "We've all been invited to sing at the Sydney Opera House."

The mutterings crescendoed into a volley of questions.

"What? Really? How did this happen?"

"But we're just amateurs! How can this be?"

Ted held up his hand for silence.

"We've been getting a lot of publicity lately because of the terrorists on board the ship who tried to poison us and the Bible students, too. Eighty of us all together. So it eventually came to the attention of the executive board at the Sydney Opera that the Neptune choir survived the terrorist attack and is still singing every day since then with renewed enthusiasm in spite of everything, so the Sydney Opera board members saw this as an opportunity to get some extra publicity both for themselves and for us as well, by giving us the chance to sing during the intermission of their forthcoming Christmas production."

Another crescendo of exclamations arose from the choir, and Ted held up his hand again.

"They invited me to send them a DVD of one of our best performances, so of course I chose the one we presented here on board after the first segment, since it's the only one we've done so far on this world cruise. They listened to it and they liked it very much, so they decided to take a chance on us and invite us to perform for them."

Squeals of excitement from the choir caused Ted to hold up both his hands for silence this time.

"As you know, this is a great honor for all of us. You're going to *love* the acoustics at the Sydney Opera House, and I'll be accompanying you on a Steinway grand piano. This will be the experience of a lifetime, and it's largely thanks to Bella Boorsma, who used her experience in marketing and advertising to develop a professional package to present to the board of executives of the Sydney Opera. They turned down the one that our own head office originally presented to them, but ironically enough, the terrorists struck just at the right time as far as the choir was concerned. So let's hear it for Bella, who is a very important part of an experience that none of us will forget for as long as we live."

Everyone turned and smiled at Bella as they burst into a round of applause, making her feel both pleased and also intensely embarrassed. She looked down at her feet until the cheers and loud clapping died down.

"As you all know," Bella said, "none of this could have happened without Ted. He's brought out the best in all of us, and now we'll try even harder with a goal like this!"

"I know you will," Ted said, "but we haven't much time. We're leaving Singapore now, so we'll be arriving in Sydney in twelve days. That gives us just enough time to prepare two songs for the Christmas program that they'll be presenting at the Sydney Opera, featuring Andrea Bocelli."

Ted's last remark was greeted by a tidal wave of *oohs* and *aahs* from the choir.

"Did he say Bocelli?" one of the singers asked the man next to him. "Wasn't he an artist who did a famous painting of a naked woman standing on a scallop shell?"

"That was Botticelli, I think," said his neighbor.

"So I've chosen two songs for us," Ted continued. "One will be the *Hallelujah Chorus* from Handel's *Messiah,* and the other one will be *Ave Maria.* We're going to start with *Ave Maria* this morning."

And so began a series of rehearsals that were the most intense and by far the most exciting ones that either Ted or the members of his choir had experienced in all their lives. The choir agreed that those twelve days of Christmas leading to their Christmas performance at the Sydney Opera would stay in their hearts and memories until their dying day.

Nobody in the choir was more aware of her dying day than Bella Boorsma herself. Its looming presence had made itself palpable to her ever since she had begun to experience a tell-tale pain in her thigh, and now she felt that she couldn't put off telling Lars Jensen the news any longer. He was waiting for her at the bar in the Neptune Lounge to take her to lunch after choir practice.

"The *Ave Maria* was beautifully done," he remarked, as he approached Bella after the rehearsal. "Here, let me do that for you," he said, taking her chair and moving it back to its original position in the lounge.

"Thanks, Lars. I appreciate your help."

"You shouldn't be dragging those chairs around, Bella. They're really quite heavy, you know."

"Well, they're beginning to feel that way to me lately," she agreed. "I'm a little tired these days."

"That's probably my fault," he admitted. "I'm not letting you get enough sleep," he declared, with a sly wink. "But today's Sunday, and the luncheon buffet is terrific, as usual. Wait till you see the roast suckling pig they have on display. Come, we'll go down right away."

When Bella saw the beautiful arrangement of food in the Club Restaurant, she almost lost what little appetite she had that day. She admired the galley crew for all the trouble they had taken to make the presentations attractive, but she found this bountiful display almost overwhelming.

"I got us a table for two by a window on the starboard side," Lars said, handing her an empty plate so that she could serve herself. "See it over there? It's the one with the chair leaning against the table, so people will know it's taken."

"Yes, I see it. The third one from the end, right?"

"Right. Now you know where to go if we get separated. So what display appeals to you? The salad bar looks good."

"All I want is raw tuna, Lars. Raw tuna with pickled ginger and soy sauce and wasabi."

"That's all?" Lars asked, looking a bit worried. "Aren't you feeling well today, Bella?"

"I think maybe it's just all the excitement of actually being invited to sing at the Sydney Opera House, you know? We've been hoping to go there for such a long time, but we never really thought it would happen."

"Well, you put a lot of work into that presentation for the Opera's executive board, Bella. A lot of work. You must be tired out from that."

"I guess that's it. But remember that Marty Goldbloom, the creative director at the Neptune head office, he put a lot of effort into his presentation too, but he did his work before the terrorists gave us so much free publicity."

"I'll remember, Bella," he said, admiring her for sharing the credit with Marty.

When Bella had finished her tuna sashimi and Lars was eating his last mouthful of strawberry cheesecake, Bella put down her chopsticks and looked at him thoughtfully.

"I have something rather important to tell you, Lars."

"That's funny," he smiled. "I have something important to tell you, too. But go ahead. You go first."

"I don't exactly know the best way to tell you this, Lars, but I was recently diagnosed with cancer, and I had to have an operation. They thought they got it all, but I'm afraid it might have metastasized to my leg. I'm feeling quite a bit of pain in my upper thigh."

"Bella!" Lars exclaimed, looking shocked. "Bella! What are you saying? Is it… are you sure? I mean, do you think it's… Let me take you to Norway. They have an excellent medical establishment there. I'll take care of you. I'll stay by your side. I'll be with you every minute…"

"Thank you, Lars," Bella said, touched by his concern. "I'd love to go to Norway with you, but I have an oncologist in New York, and he's already familiar with my case."

"Of course. I'm sure you're in good hands, but maybe a second opinion…"

"A second opinion is always good. But as far as I know, when my type of cancer metastasizes to the bone, it's pretty much always fatal."

"No, Bella, no!" Lars said, taking her hand. "Don't say things like that. Try to have a positive attitude."

"I'll try. I will, Lars, I promise. But the primary cancer was UPSC, which is a bad type to have, and it wasn't caught until it got to stage four, so that's also very bad. It's migrated to my thigh now. We must look at the facts head-on so we can deal with the situation in the best possible way."

"Well, let's just take it one step at a time," Lars said, moving his chair around to her side of the table so he could be closer to her. "Do you remember I said a little while ago that I have something important to tell you?"

"Yes, I remember."

"Bella, I love you and I want to marry you. If you accept my proposal, you'll make me the happiest man in the world."

"I accept," Bella said, with radiant eyes. "I know that I'm supposed to play hard to get and keep you in suspense, but we don't have time for that sort of thing. I hope you're not disappointed."

"I like to see you smile," Lars said. "I want to make you smile for the rest of your life, and we won't try to guess how long that might be. But Bella, I don't have a ring for you. The ones in the gift shop aren't good enough for my bride."

"Don't worry, darling. You can get me one later. Maybe you'll find just the right one in Norway."

"You called me *darling*. Let me hear you say it again."

"I love you, darling."

"Me too," Lars said, and Bella knew that he meant it.

CHAPTER NINETEEN

The next night at the dinner table, Dominique Perdue and her tablemates could talk of nothing else but the forthcoming choir performance at the Sydney Opera House. Everybody was excited and they all talked at once, interrupting one another with questions and comments.

"What a happy ending to the terrorist scare that we had on board," Dominique remarked. "I can't wait to celebrate Christmas at the Sydney Opera House!"

"Speaking of happy endings," Paloma said, "I have seen you with Lars Jensen very often these days, Bella. Have you two fallen in love?"

"I don't know if I should really say anything about that," Bella replied, looking down at her plate of uneaten food. "I don't know if Lars wants me to talk about it yet."

"Oh, don't be bashful," Piglet smiled. "We need all the happy stories we can get for the Christmas season! You just said that a moment ago, is it not so?"

"Yes, Bella, do tell us what's going on with you two," Dominique begged her. "Everyone loves a love story."

"Well, if you must know, he did ask me to marry him at lunchtime."

Cries of joy erupted among her three tablemates.

"Congratulations, Bella!" Piglet said, delighted.

"That is how I feel too," Paloma concurred. "Those are wonderful news!"

"Who is going to perform your wedding ceremony?" Dominique asked. "Are you going to ask the captain to do it? Wouldn't that be fun? A wedding at sea!"

"I don't know what we're going to do about a wedding," Bella replied softly. "We haven't really discussed that yet."

"Oh Bella, *please* consider to get married in Algeciras," Paloma said, leaning close to her. "Piglet and I, we have done much weddings for our friends. They stay in my hotel and they eat Piglet's culinary creativities, and we bring in musicians from all over Andalucía. For you we would make it, how you say, the wedding to beat all the weddings. Is this the expression?"

"Paloma," Piglet said, "Lars and Bella have probably not thought this to the end. They must discuss it first."

"You're right, Piglet. We haven't made any plans for a wedding yet," Bella said. "Lars only just asked me to marry him today. But we'll keep your invitation in mind, Paloma. And thanks so much for thinking of it. I'll talk to Lars and get back to you."

"Oh, I didn't mean to push..." Paloma began.

"It's okay, really," Bella assured her. "Lars and I will talk it over," she said, thinking how good it felt to mention his name so casually in front of her friends, as if they had already been together for years and years.

"Dominique, there's something I've been wanting to ask you for a long time," Bella continued, trying to change the subject. "How is it possible that you and Maria look so much alike? Are you identical twins?"

"Yes, we *are* identical twins, and we were separated as babies, but neither of us knew we had a twin sister tucked away somewhere until this whole terrible mess developed on board this ship..."

Dominique proceeded to tell them all about how Maria had dropped her cruise card and how she, Dominique, had been left to figure out who this woman was... this woman who looked exactly like her and who had dashed out of the pharmacy without noticing her look-alike staring at her.

"You must have been astonished!" Paloma exclaimed.

"So what did you do then?" Piglet asked.

"I used her cruise card to board this ship so I could find someone who could return it to her. Nobody noticed that I wasn't Maria, since I look exactly like her. Then suddenly they pulled up the gangplank and I became a stowaway. So I decided I might as well go on the world cruise, rather than waste a perfectly good trip that had already been paid for."

"I don't quite understand," Paloma said. "How did you not know that you had an identical twin sister?"

"When my father left my mother he took Maria and just disappeared. I was raised by my mum, and that's all I know."

"When have you learned the truth of your sister?" Piglet asked.

"When Maria was arrested and taken to court, it all came out in the trial, and the details were reported in all the daily newspapers and various magazines."

"That's really something, Dominique," said Bella.

"Where is Maria now?" Piglet wanted to know.

"She's in jail, in London, and likely to stay there for a very long time."

"And your father?" Paloma asked.

"He's in jail as well," said Dominique. "Perhaps in the cell right next to hers, for all I know."

"I don't think they'd let men and the women live in the same wing of the jail," Bella declared. "There'd be too much danger of fraternization," she added, with a wink.

The four tablemates had a good chuckle, and raised their wine goblets to toast their ever-growing friendship.

Ted held rehearsals for the choir every sea day at the usual time, knowing that it would be counterproductive to increase the number of rehearsals, as too much repetition could lead to over familiarity with the music and actually weaken the emotional response of the choir members. The next day he handed out the musical scores for the *Hallelujah Chorus* from Handel's *Messiah.* While the sheets were being passed around, Ted gave the choir a little pep talk.

"When you arrive at the Sydney Opera House tomorrow, you'll be given instructions about lining up in the wings and marching onto the stage. Please listen attentively. Above all, enjoy yourselves. You're singing hallelujahs, so you should have big, big smiles. Just remember that Jesus Christ, the Lord God Omnipotent, has taken His throne on Earth, and He reigns supreme forever and ever. So just rejoice and be happy, and sing it with lots of feeling. Don't hold anything back. Give it all you've got, but watch me carefully for the crescendos and the repetitions. Ready? Here we go."

Hallelujah, Hallelujah,
Hallelujah, Hallelujah, Hallelujah! [2x]

For the Lord God omnipotent reigneth,
Hallelujah, Hallelujah, Hallelujah, Hallelujah! [3x]

The kingdom of this world is become
The kingdom of our God and of his Christ,
and of His Christ!
And He shall reign forever and ever. [4x]

King of kings forever and ever, Hallelujah, Hallelujah!
and Lord of lords forever and ever,
Hallelujah, Hallelujah!

"You sound fabulous," Ted said, winding up the choir practice. "We can't do any more today, there's no more time. Just keep it up, and you'll be fine. And don't forget, we have our dress rehearsal tonight in the Cabaret Lounge. We'll meet in the tunnel at 6:35. Don't eat too much for dinner! I want you to have room in your lungs for nice, deep breaths, so you can sing at full volume at all the right moments."

Dominique Perdue decided that the topic of her Bible class that day should be the Hallelujah Chorus.

"What do you think the word *Hallelujah* means?" she asked her class. "Anyone have any ideas?"

Veronica raised her hand, and Dominique nodded at her.

"It means something like *Hip hip, hooray!*"

"That's true. That's exactly what we'd say in English. But the word actually derives from the ancient Hebrew *halle,* meaning *praise,* and *Ya,* or *Yaweh,* meaning *God.* So when we say *Hallelujah* we're actually saying *Praise God.* And what are we praising Him for? Does anyone know?"

"For rescuing us from our stupidity?" said a woman in the back row. "Or maybe *ignorance* would be a better word."

"Indeed. As you've all probably noticed, we humans are just a mob of hopeless bunglers. We tend to get everything wrong, often because we put our own self-interest ahead of everyone else's, which leads to things like pyramid schemes in the world of finance and business, or stuffing the ballot boxes in the political arena, and you name it, we've figured out some scheme or other to get our own way at the expense of other people. So what does it all mean? My twin sister is in jail now, where she can't harm others anymore. But is that the solution? Does it make sense for a certain portion of the world's population to languish in jail, while the rest of us run around loose, wreaking general havoc wherever we go?"

"Some people never get caught," someone observed.

"Or maybe they just don't know they've been caught," Dominique replied. "Does it ever seem to you that we're *all* in a sort of reform school while we're here on this planet? A reform school where we're given various painful experiences that teach us something about the meaning of life, things that we'd never have understood if we hadn't been subjected to these particular types of learning experiences?"

"I feel as if I'm trapped in a reform school sometimes," said another passenger. "But love teaches us a lot more than reform school does. I'm in love right now, and I feel as if I've been completely reformed from the inside out."

"That's wonderful for you now, but it doesn't last," said a man in the second row. "The truth is, we're all just human beings, and we're pretty darned imperfect, if you ask me."

"Then what we need is a perfect leader," Veronica said.

"And that's precisely what the Hallelujah Chorus is all about," Dominique said. "People are rejoicing because God, who is perfection personified and a known humanophile, has put His only begotten Son on the throne to fill the role of the perfect leader. So we say a Mass to thank God for sending the Messiah to us once again, to establish peace and justice on Earth forever and ever. We call this Mass of gratitude *Christ's Mass,* or *Christmas.*"

"But where is all this peace and justice?" asked a man in the third row. "I haven't seen any signs of it yet."

"You haven't seen the Second Coming yet, either," his wife reminded him. "You'll get your peace and justice when the Messiah returns."

"I look forward to that," he muttered *sotto voce*, casting a meaningful glance at his wife.

"Anyway," Dominique continued, "the important thing for all of you to keep in mind is that the Hallelujah Chorus in Handel's *Messiah* is deliriously happy when they hear the news of Christ's return. Christians have waited for this with bated breath for the last two thousand years, so that's what those Hallelujahs are all about. Just remember what Ted said this morning. Sing with joy, for a new world has begun."

Bella Boorsma and Lars Jensen were standing with their arms around each other by the railing of the balcony on Deck Five, watching the Cerulean Neptune approach the Sydney Harbour Bridge. It was about six o'clock in the evening, and the sun was setting behind the Sydney Opera House.

"Isn't that interesting," Bella was saying. "I've always thought of the Sydney Opera House as being like a series of big white birds with their wings spread out over the harbor. But tonight The Opera House isn't like that. It isn't white at all. It's a glowing, reddish brown color, and it has an entirely different personality."

"What does it remind *you* of this evening, Bella?"

"It looks like an imposing presence of some kind, but it's not a bird this time. It's more like... I don't know. It makes me think of the throne of God."

"The Lord God Omnipotent reigneth."

"That's right. You seem to know *The Messiah* by heart, don't you darling?" Bella said admiringly.

"Only since you've been rehearsing it in the choir," Lars admitted. "I've been listening to you every day."

"I know. I saw you in the back of the lounge, leaning against the bar."

"You saw me standing there? You have eyes in the back of your head?"

"When it comes to getting a glimpse of you, yes."

"You make me happy, Bella."

"You make me happy, too," she said, looking up at him adoringly. "In fact, I've never been happier in my life. Who would have thought I'd fall in love with the staff captain of the Cerulean Neptune?"

"Cerulean," Lars said, thoughtfully. "Do you know what that word means?"

"I'm no expert, but I took Latin in school. I know that *caelo* means *sky* or *heaven,* so it must mean something like *heavenly blue.* Does that sound right to you?"

"Heavenly blue, just like your eyes. You have cerulean blue eyes, Bella."

"So do you. And Neptune too, did you know that?"

"Neptune, the Greek god of the sea? How do you know what color his eyes were?"

"No, I mean Neptune the planet," Bella answered. "The methane gas in its atmosphere makes it look blue."

"You're starting to look a little blue yourself, darling," Lars said. "It's getting cold out here on the balcony. Do you want to go inside?"

"Wait, Lars. Look up at the sky. Do you see what I see?"

"A rainbow!" he exclaimed. "There's a rainbow over the Sydney Opera House!"

"Isn't it beautiful?"

"It is. It's like a gigantic bow, but without arrows."

"That's true," Bella agreed. "A huge, overarching bow, pointed up towards heaven. In the Bible the rainbow means that God will never again send a flood to destroy the world."

"Where did you learn that?"

"In Sunday School. I used to go to Sunday School when I was a little girl."

"I wish I'd known you then. I'd have gone to Sunday School with you, just to be near you."

"You probably would have stuck the tips of my braids into the inkwell."

"You had inkwells in Sunday School?"

"No. I was just teasing you."

"Did you learn anything else about rainbows there?"

"I remember the prophet Ezekiel had a vision of Christ on his throne in heaven, shining like a fire and surrounded by a rainbow. And I also remember that John—the disciple that Jesus loved most—he saw a similar vision of Christ on his throne, under a rainbow. So that's why I love rainbows. They remind me that God loves us so much that He'll forgive us for even the worst things we've ever done, but first we have to believe He exists before we can ask Him for anything."

"I'm glad *you* exist Bella. I love you, and I'm incredibly happy to know that you love me back."

"Is it important to you?"

"What, loving you? Of course!"

"I mean, is it important to you that I love you back?"

"Yes! Nothing is worse than unrequited love. I think I can even go so far as to say that there's no greater pain in the world than to love someone who doesn't love you back."

"That's how I'd feel too, if you didn't love me."

"What are you getting at, Bella?"

"I'm just saying that God feels the same way about *us*. It breaks His heart when we don't love Him back, and it hurts Him when we say we don't even believe He exists."

"Are you cross with me, Bella?"

"No, my darling, not at all, and I'm sorry I made you think I was. I'm just trying to say that when you happen to see a rainbow, try to think of Christ on his throne looking down on you with love and forgiveness in his heart. If only you could know how much he wants you to be his own! We can't allow ourselves to just go on being blind forever."

When he heard Bella's words, Lars was gripped with a feeling of recognition. Where had he heard that sentiment expressed before? The words started coming back to him, set to music and sung by Ted Rasmussen's choir:

And although I know that he is blind,
still I say there's a way for us…

Then suddenly Lars remembered. The words were from *Les Misérables,* when Eponine sings a heart-wrenching song about how she loves Marius and wants him to love her back. But he only has eyes for Cosette, and is blind to Eponine. A sad, poignant, song it was, about the pain of unrequited love. The only way Eponine could find relief from her suffering was to believe that in spite of everything there was a way for them, if he could open his eyes and see her as she really was.

Then he recalled an alto recitative from the Messiah:

Then shall the eyes of the blind be opened,
and the ears of the deaf unstopped.
Then shall the lame man leap as an hart,
and the tongue of the dumb shall sing.

"For although He knows that we are blind," Lars said to himself, "still He knows there's a way for us."

When Lars looked up again at the sky above the Sydney Opera House, he noticed that the rainbow over the darkened sails had disappeared. The message doesn't last forever, he thought, but it comes back, over and over again, for as many times as we need it.

"How is your leg, Bella?" Lars asked her. "I didn't want to bring the subject up again because I hate to remind you of it, but I need to know how you are and if it's hurting you still just as much."

"I'm afraid it is, Lars. It hurts quite a lot, actually, but I try to think about other things."

"Do you have all you need for pain medication? Is there anything I can do?"

"No, my Lars. There's nothing you can do. Just hold me close and tell me you love me ten thousand times."

As Lars held Bella in his arms, he heard her humming the notes of *Amazing Grace*.

"Sing it Bella," he said. "Go ahead. Sing it out loud."

Bella picked up where she had left off:

When we've been here ten thousand years
Bright shining as the sun.
We've no less days to sing God's praise
Than when we've first begun.

CHAPTER TWENTY

The choir members, all dressed in their white tops and black slacks, followed Ted Rasmussen a little self-consciously down the gangplank and past the myriad shops and outdoor eateries along the waterfront until they came to Bennelong Point, which reaches out into the Sydney Harbour. The choir turned and stood gaping at the imposing white sails that stood, one behind the other, atop the Sydney Opera House. They appeared to be filled with a powerful wind that would carry them off, when they least expected it, to *those faraway places with strange-sounding names.*

As Ted and the choir approached the Opera House, they came to the Outdoor Forecourt, located directly below the famous white sails, and known all over the world as one of the best outdoor performance spaces ever designed—a venue that has welcomed many celebrities such as Sting and Oprah Winfrey, among countless others. The wide arc of the granite Monumental Steps creates a vast, awe-inspiring amphitheater that overlooks some spectacular views of the Harbour Bridge and the Sydney skyline. The Forecourt, however, was closed to visitors and performers to permit construction personnel to build an entrance tunnel to the newly-made loading dock for the Joan Sutherland Theatre.

Lars Jensen was also walking along the pier on his way to George Street to visit his old friend Susie Lambert, the co-owner, along with her husband Jim, of a jewelry store in the Wynyard Shopping Centre. His time was somewhat limited because he didn't want to be late for the Christmas show that was soon to be performed at the Sydney Opera House, but he trusted Susie to know his taste in jewelry and to show him what he was looking for in a bridal set for Bella. He ended up buying a ten carat, two-tone gold, cerulean blue sapphire engagement ring with a matching wedding band. He thanked his friends for their help, apologized to them for not being able to stay longer, and then he hurried out of the shop. He quickened his pace when he saw the Opera House looming in the distance, hoping he wouldn't be late for the show.

When Ted Rasmussen arrived with his choir at the Sydney Opera House, he was greeted by a guide posted at the main entrance to welcome incoming ticket-holders and direct them to their seats.

"Ah, so *you're* the choir from that cruise ship where the terrorists tried to poison you! It's been on the news for a long time now. Welcome to the Sydney Opera House!"

"We're very pleased and honored to be here," Ted said, on behalf of the entire choir.

"And we're delighted to have you," the guide replied, smiling at everyone. "Now, I believe Olivia Ling is in charge of you tonight. She was the one who contacted you on the cruise ship, am I right?"

"Yes, that's right," Ted agreed.

"Wait just a minute, please. I'm going to give Miss Ling a buzz. She'll be right over."

Olivia Ling, an attractive, vivacious young woman with a friendly face and a businesslike manner, appeared almost instantly and gave Ted a warm handshake.

"This is indeed a pleasure," she said, smiling at him and the choir members. "I've heard so much about you! Please follow me. I'll take you to the Concert Hall and I'll hand you over to the stage manager, who is going to give you some *very* explicit directions for where you'll be positioned in the wings and how you'll be expected to line up, and everything else you need to know for your participation in the Christmas concert."

"*Participation* in the concert, did you say?" Ted asked, looking surprised. "I thought we were only supposed to sing during the intermission."

"Oh, didn't Bocelli's people get in touch with you?" she asked, as she marched quickly toward the Concert Hall with the choir following obediently in her wake. "When he heard you were coming, he said you shouldn't have to sing in the intermission. He wants to slide your two numbers into his own show. He wants it to be inclusive. He says that's what Christmas is all about. He's rounded up a children's choir too," she told them, beginning to pant a little with the effort of talking while walking almost at a run. "They'll be singing *Suffer Little Children to Come unto Me.* They'll do it before the intermission so the parents can get them home to bed on time if they want to. Your choir members will sing *after* the intermission, so they'll have to line up in the wings on both sides of the stage to make their entrance."

"Okay," Ted said, striding to keep up with Olivia as she trotted along. "I think we understand everything now. There shouldn't be any problems."

"Here we are in the Concert Hall," she continued. "It has 2,679 seats," she declared, pointing to them with a wide sweep of the arm.

Ted had to admit that he was awed by the size and scope of the famous Concert Hall.

"This hall is home to the Sydney Symphony Orchestra, but it's used by many other concert presenters too. And over there you can see the Sydney Opera House Grand Organ, the largest mechanical tracker action organ in the world, with over 10,000 pipes. But no worries, Ted. You can be sure we won't be using the organ when your choir is singing."

"I'm very relieved to hear that," Ted said with a smile.

Lars Jensen clutched the little box containing Bella's gold and cerulean sapphire engagement ring and the gold wedding band. As he hurried down George Street he noticed that the sun had already set and the vast night sky was filled with stars. He walked more rapidly as he headed for the Sydney Opera House, fearing he might be late for the performance. How could so much time have gone by while he was chatting with the Lamberts? He must have been carried away with the joy of describing Bella and all her many sterling qualities to Jim and Susie, and now it was later than he expected.

The first part of the Sydney Opera's Christmas extravaganza was the most beautiful, inspiring performance that Bella had ever seen or heard. Andrea Bocelli and his chorus of singers sounded like angels sent from heaven, and the piping voices of the children had almost convinced her that cherubs in the paintings of the old masters had actually come to life and had made a special appearance at the Concert Hall that night.

But where was Lars? Bella had looked around for him during the intermission, but she hadn't seen him anywhere. It wasn't surprising, she supposed, considering the Concert Hall seated almost 3,000 people. Even so, she had hoped he would turn up in the wings to wish her luck before they went on stage, but he was nowhere to be found.

"Quiet in the wings!" shouted the stage manager. "The choir will assemble in the two front wings on both sides of the stage platform. Sopranos come in from stage right, altos from stage left. Tenors from the wing behind them on stage right, basses behind the altos from the second wing on stage left. After I introduce you, the first row will come in from stage left and right, meeting in the middle. The second row, same thing. That way you'll have plenty of room, and you won't be tripping each other up. So, any questions? Your ship only came in this afternoon, so you never had a chance to rehearse with us. And one more thing: don't walk in front of the side lights. If you do, you'll cast a giant shadow on the stage, and you'll be in trouble with the lighting technicians. And don't look like you're on your way to the guillotine. There's no need to be nervous. Now line up the way I told you. And remember to look totally beatific when you sing *Ave Maria,* okay? So break a leg!"

When Lars Jensen arrived at the Sydney Opera House, the performance by Andrea Bocelli and his chorus was already in full swing. The usher asked Lars to remain in the foyer until intermission so as not to disturb any of the viewers in the audience. Although Lars understood the reason for this request, he was worried that he might miss part of the choir's performance during the intermission if the viewers leaving the Concert Hall blocked the doors and prevented him from entering. He knew nothing at all, of course, about Bocelli's decision to let the choir sing on stage *after* the intermission when the Concert Hall was full once again and the audience was attentive and silent. He paced back and forth in the foyer until one of the ushers finally suggested that he might be a bit more comfortable if he took a seat on one of the nearby benches.

When it occurred to Lars to mention to the usher in the foyer that he was the staff captain on the Cerulean Neptune, the usher apologized and led him, during the intermission, to a group of seats on the far left end of the front row of the stalls that had been reserved for people who were associated with the show. The usher gave him seat A35 next to Per Andersen, the captain of the Cerulean Neptune and a friend and compatriot of Lars Jensen's. They smiled at each other but said nothing, as the performance was about to begin.

Ted Rasmussen's singers came in from the wings and lined up on the stage in two rows, looking very choir-like in their black-and-white costumes and cerulean blue music folders. Suddenly three stage hands ran in from stage right holding a fifteen-foot, blue-and-white oil-cloth banner displaying the Neptune logo along with the words, THE SYDNEY OPERA PRESENTS THE NEPTUNE CRUISE LINE'S WORLD CHOIR.

The stage hands knelt in front of the first row of singers, holding the banner taut while the audience in the Concert Hall burst into applause. The spotlight fell on the Steinway grand piano on stage left, revealing Ted Rasmussen sitting at the piano in his tuxedo. When the applause heightened, Ted stood up and took a bow, then he sat down at the piano and waited for the applause to die down. When the audience was silent, Ted played Schubert's beautiful introduction to *Ave Maria,* then nodded at the choir for them to sing their parts.

Something came over Ted Rasmussen's choir when they began to sing. The acoustics in the Concert Hall were so stunning, so overpoweringly perfect, that the voices in the choir became muted, almost as though the members were too awestruck to sing out in the face of such perfect beauty, but when they saw Ted's encouraging expression, their voices took wing. They put all their effort, thought, and feeling into their rendition of *Ave Maria,* causing it to develop a life of its very own, a life that expressed the sudden, unexpected exaltation of all the choir members. Their voices continued to mount until, at the end of the soaring prayer, they reached a full crescendo:

Ave Maria, mater Dei
Ora pro nobis, nobis peccatoribus,
Nunc et in hora mortis nostrae.
Ave Maria.

Greetings, Mary, mother of God
Pray for us, us sinners,
Now and in the hour of our death.
Greetings, Mary.

Dominique loved those words. The name *Maria* became her real name again, for it was the name that Ted had always called her. She was no longer the fake Maria, she was Maria Trouvée, the woman who once was lost and now was found.

She looked over at Ted as she sang the final *Ave Maria,* and was happy to see that he was looking at her too. God is love, she mused, and God is eternal—therefore love is eternal too. Schubert must have had that hypothetical syllogism in mind when he composed music with such timeless beauty.

When the applause died down, Ted played the music to the first five Hallelujahs of Handel's chorus, then he signaled to the choir to come in. It was the experience of a lifetime for all the members of the choir, as they sang their various parts both separately and in harmony together.

Then the nightmare began. Just when the audience was giving the choir a standing ovation and calling for an encore, Bella suddenly fell to the floor, right behind the long oilcloth banner. Nobody in the audience noticed her go down, as she was hidden by the banner and by the Steinway piano as well. But Lars saw her fall. He jumped to his feet and bounded up the nine steps on stage right. Ted stood up just as Lars passed him, and the two men went around the piano and behind the banner to help her.

"Bella, what is it?" Lars asked her, kneeling beside her and cradling her head. "What happened?"

"I think my right leg just broke," she said, groaning with pain. "I can't move. It's that same femur, I'm afraid."

"I'll call an ambulance right away," Ted said, taking out his iPhone.

"The closest public hospital is the Sydney Opera House Hospital on Macquarie Street," Lars said, looking up at him.

"What's going on?" said the stage manager, approaching them quickly. "Did she faint?"

"No, no," Lars replied. "Her leg's broken. It's the thigh bone. Ted's calling the hospital to send for an ambulance."

"We've a fully-equipped medical office here, staffed by registered nurses," the stage manager said, flicking open his cell phone. "They'll come with a stretcher, then they'll move her to the wings and stabilize her. Ted, tell the ambulance driver to go to the main Forecourt, East Circular Quay."

"I've already told them," Ted replied. "They said that's where they're going. They'll be here in ten minutes."

"How did she break her leg?" the stage manager asked Lars quietly. "Did she trip on something?"

"No, nothing like that. She has bone cancer. The bone broke and the leg just gave way, I'm afraid."

"Good Lord. I'm so sorry, sir. I wish you both the very best. She'll be in good hands at the Sydney Opera House Hospital. The doctors will take very good care of her there."

"Good. Thank you. That's a big relief," Lars said.

Just then two nurses from the first aid room appeared on the stage platform with a stretcher, and the stage manager guided them over to where Bella was lying.

"Excuse me, Ma'am," the stage manager said, bending down so Bella could hear him. "The nurses are going to wrap you up and put you on a stretcher so you'll be ready for the ambulance when it gets here. It will arrive very soon."

"I'm sorry about all the fuss I'm causing," Bella said. "But it's all your fault, actually."

"My fault?" said the stage manager, looking worried. He was probably wondering if Bella was going to press charges against the Sydney Opera House for having been negligent in some way.

"You told us to break a leg, remember? Well, I was just trying to comply," Bella said, giving him a wink.

"You're feeling rather chipper this evening, aren't you Ma'am?" the stage manager said, smiling at her. "I hope you have a very speedy recovery."

Bella smiled and waved to him as the nurses picked her up on the stretcher and took her out through the wings.

"I have to make an announcement to the audience now," the stage manager said, turning to Ted and Lars. "Will you excuse me, please?"

"Of course. Please, go right ahead," Ted said.

The stage manager walked to the very front of the stage platform, and addressed the audience.

"I'm sorry for the delay," he began. "One of the choir members is seriously ill, and we've sent for an ambulance. Meanwhile the choir master, Ted Rasmussen, will direct the Neptune Choir in Handel's *Hallelujah Chorus*. I thank you in advance for your patience and understanding. You're a very special audience."

Ted sat at the piano and played the first five *hallelujahs* of Handel's chorus, and then he signaled to the choir to come in on the next round of *hallelujahs*.

Meanwhile, in the wings of the Concert Hall, Lars was kneeling down beside Bella and speaking quietly to her.

"Darling," he said, "I want you to have your engagement ring now, while the choir is singing *The Hallelujah Chorus*. Can you raise your left hand for me?"

Bella lifted her left hand, and Lars slipped the cerulean sapphire ring onto her fourth finger. She closed her eyes as they kissed, letting the choir's *hallelujahs* flow through her heart and body and soul.

"You've made me the happiest man in the world, Bella," Lars told her, gazing down at her tenderly.

Then suddenly an extraordinary thing happened. The Sydney Opera's choir members were scattered around in the audience that night, and they began to rise to their feet one by one, whereupon they spontaneously joined the Cerulean Neptune choir in singing the *Hallelujah Chorus*. Little by little the rest of the members of the audience arose from their seats and joined the two choirs.

It was a flash mob to beat all flash mobs, made up of a full house of some 2,679 people. The Concert Hall platform was surrounded by seats set on a steep angle, reminiscent of the arenas of ancient times. It was truly a majestic sight, with unrivaled acoustics derived from its high vaulted ceiling and white birch timber with brush box paneling.

Bella, lying on the stretcher near the wings, felt as if she were being borne away to faraway places somewhere over the rainbow of blinding lights that shone above her in the ᵉᵉᵉ

Concert Hall. For Bella it was an unforgettable moment in Sensaround Sound, close to Lars in the most awe-inspiring venue in the world, filled with the rich tones of thousands of voices singing her favorite chorus—a one-off experience that would not and could not be repeated again while she was on this Earth—a moment in eternity with Lars by her side.

*Halle-lu-**jaaaah!*** sang the flash mob, with a drawn-out final note that resonated perfectly with the triumphant piano finale by Ted Rasmussen that underscored the extraordinary moment, a moment that would remain forever in the hearts of all those who found themselves in the Concert Hall at the Sydney Opera House on that remarkable, once-in-a-lifetime occasion.

Epilogue

Bella Boorsma underwent an operation at the Sydney Opera House Hospital to clean and set her broken femur. She was released just in time for the medical staff to take her back to the Cerulean Neptune before it left the dock.

Captain Per Andersen performed a wedding ceremony for Bella Boorsma and Lars Jensen on the ship, attended by all the passengers. Captain Andersen would later say that it was the most poignant and meaningful wedding ceremony he had ever performed.

Piglet and Paloma Casablanca threw a major party for the Jensens when they eventually returned to Europe. A cornucopia of mouth-watering delicacies from the kitchen of *El Cerdito Bendito* (The Blessed Piglet) was laid out for the joyful celebrants, and Andalusia's finest wine flowed non-stop. The couple spent a week in Norway where Bella met her husband's friends and relatives, then they flew to New York where she said goodbye to her own family and loved-ones. Although the Jensens had only a very short marriage, Lars would always say they were the best days of his life.

Ted Rasmussen's career blossomed after his choir's first performance at the Concert Hall in the Sydney Opera House. He was written up in all the major newspapers, entertainment magazines and electronic media, and both the Sydney Opera and the Neptune Cruise Line enjoyed an enormous influx of customers as a direct result of his success. Ted would say that he had waited all his life for Dominique Perdue to show up, then at last he saw her one enchanted evening across a crowded Casino Lounge. Once he had found her, he never let her go—and he never stopped saying *Maria*.

Dominique Perdue sold her townhouse in Mayfair, keeping a small apartment for her own use so she could visit London whenever she wished. She spent the rest of her life touring the world on the Cerulean Neptune, never missing a chance to sing in Ted Rasmussen's choir. She learned, to her great surprise, that it was no more costly to live on a cruise ship than in an up-scale retirement home. She eventually became a best-selling author—the dream of every English professor.

Maria Morgan purchased the Mayfair townhouse from Dominique, using the funds her father left her when he died. After she got out of jail she lived a quiet life, free from her obligations in the North London mosque, and far from the consequences of the poor decisions she had made in the past. Nobody in Mayfair seemed to notice that she wasn't the real Dominique Perdue. She was never found by those carrying out the imam's fatwa.

The Ted Rasmussen Choir continued to be invited to sing at the Sydney Opera House every year. During the Cerulean Neptune's world cruises, the choir would perform all over the globe, in venues both large and small. It was by far the most popular and well-loved shore activity ever executed by the cruise industry. Although many other cruise lines tried to copy Ted's choir, their efforts failed. The proceeds from his choir went to clothing the poor and feeding the hungry.

Selim and Ahmad (alias Angel) completed their jail terms and returned to their respective home countries, where they were given heroes' welcomes.

Federico Carpaggio and **The Room Service Man** were in and out of jail for the rest of their lives. They continued to do odd jobs for shady characters in the back streets of Rome.

The Manager of *Il Fortunello* felt greatly honored when the Neptune Cruise Line recommended his bed-and-breakfast to all its passengers. His guests saw it as a safe place to stay—a place where everybody knew their names.

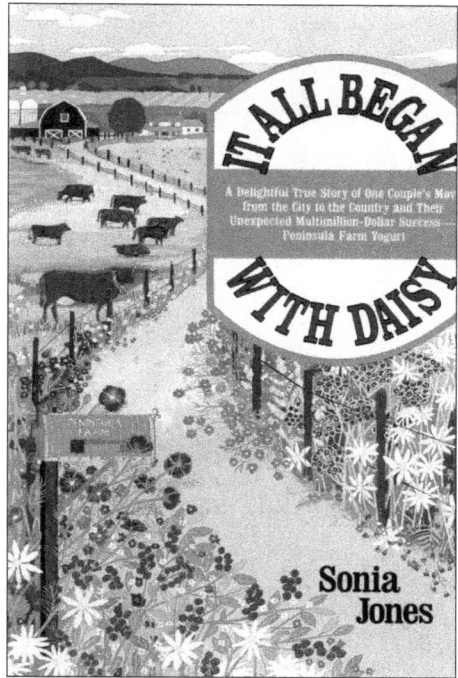

If you enjoyed reading *The Choir,* you will also like *It All Began with Daisy* (Dutton/Penguin, New York, 1987). When Sonia Jones moved with her husband to Nova Scotia to teach at Dalhousie University, they bought an oceanside farm and settled down to enjoy a life of quiet contemplation. But they bought a cow in an unguarded moment, and their tranquility evaporated overnight. Daisy quickly became the head of the household, providing them with more milk than they knew what to do with. They started making yogurt for a local health food store, eventually reaching over two million dollars in annual sales.

Featured as an alternate selection by the *Literary Guild of America,* condensed by *The Reader's Digest,* translated into 15 languages, and circulated worldwide to 28,000,000 readers.

Available on Amazon or at www.erserandpond.com

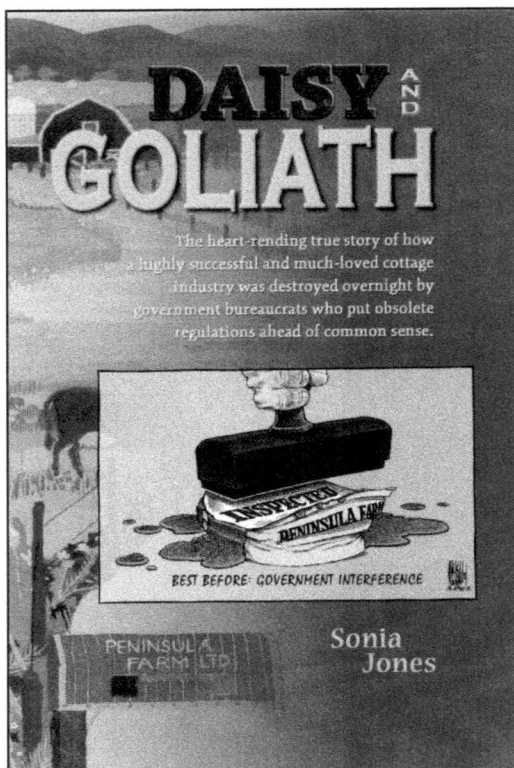

If you enjoyed reading *It All Began with Daisy,* you will also like *Daisy and Goliath* (Erser and Pond, 2007), the sequel to *It All Began with Daisy,* which describes the vandalism of Peninsula Farm by agents of the federal government. It is an informative, intelligent, and sometimes painfully humorous inside look at the struggles of one family to run a highly successful small business in spite of the current trend toward the industrialization and the corporatization of farming.

Available on Amazon or at www.erserandpond.com

The

PENINSULA FARM

YOGOURT

COOKBOOK

by Sonia Jones

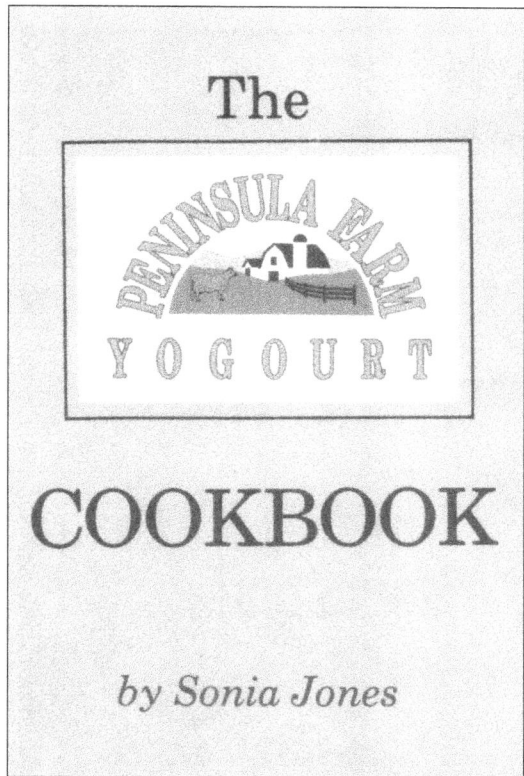

If you have ever wanted to make your own yogurt at home, this is the book for you. Sonia Jones, a highly successful yogurt-maker for twenty-five years, reveals her tried-and-true recipes along with instructions on how to make delicious yogurt (and what to do when you fail). This well-loved book is a compendium of yogurt fact, yogurt lore, yogurt recipes and all you need know to become part of the yogurt revolution.

Available on Amazon or at www.erserandpond.com

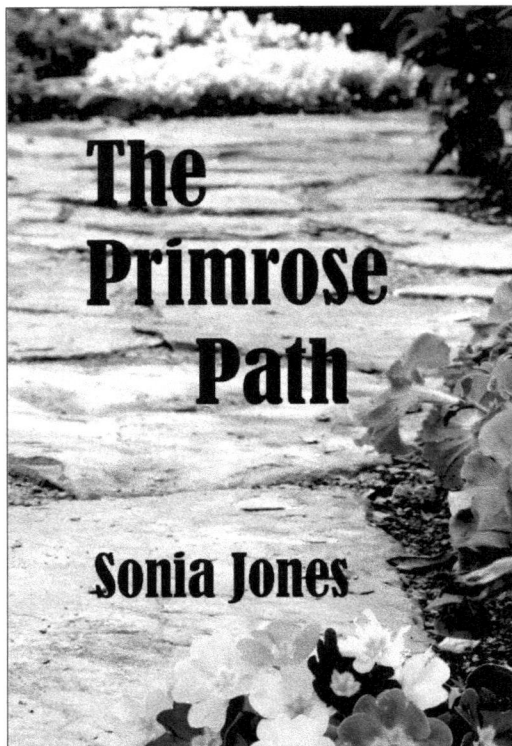

The Primrose Path (Erser and Pond, 2008) is the true story
of Percy Pond, the author's grandfather and celebrated
photographer who documented the Klondike Gold Rush, the
founding of Juneau, and the culture of the native tribes in
Alaska. It also introduces the author's father, Kay Harrison,
who was the Managing Director of Hollywood's Technicolor
Films in London, Paris, and Rome. He often went to Spain as
well, where he would confer with producers such as Sam
Bronston, who made *John Paul Jones* in Technicolor, and
Mike Todd who, before his death in 1958, was planning to
produce a spectacular Technicolor film about Don Quixote.

Available on Amazon or at www.erserandpond.com

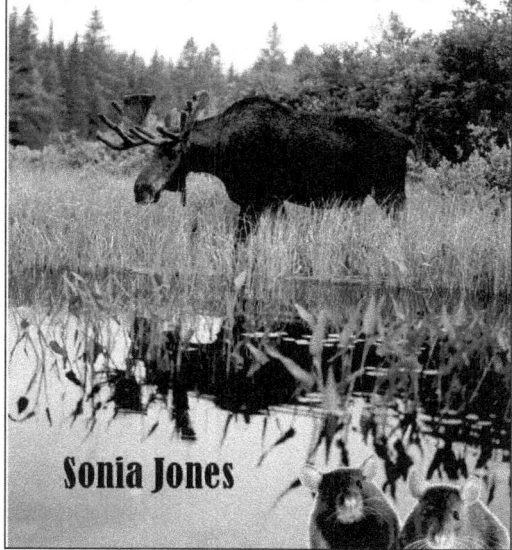

Of Mice and Moosecalls

Reflections on life ever laughing

Sonia Jones

AVAILABLE IN COLOR OR BLACK AND WHITE

If you enjoyed reading *The Primrose Path,* you will also like *Of Mice and Moose Calls* (Erser and Pond 2008), an enticing collection of the author's humor columns published in *The Banner.* The topics range from warbling church mice to operatic moose calls, and from chaos on the farm to wild roosters running amok in the Dutch countryside. Described by New York Times critic Robert Coleman as having "a born teacher's eye for the well-chosen example," Sonia Jones has written a collection of humorous and beguiling stories are sure to move you.

Available on Amazon or at www.erserandpond.com

CLONING JESUS

COLOR EDITION

Sonia Harrison Jones

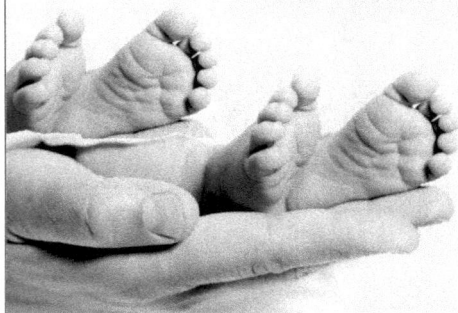

AVAILABLE IN FULL COLOR OR BLACK-AND-WHITE EDITIONS—IN ENGLISH AND IN SPANISH OR FRENCH TRANSLATIONS.

WHAT READERS ARE SAYING: I LOVED it! For me the test of a good book is that when I'm not reading it I'm thinking about it and trying to figure out when I will be able to get back to it, and that definitely happened with this book. —Julie Graveline, retired Canadian Naval officer

This is a masterpiece! It was a real gripper. My wife and I almost fought for the computer. There is much in this book about *intellect apologetics*—the tragedy of using Christianity to gain power. The last chapter highlights *living apologetics*. Great! —Rev. Clarence Vos, pastor and retired professor, Calvin College

Available on Amazon or at www.erserandpond.com

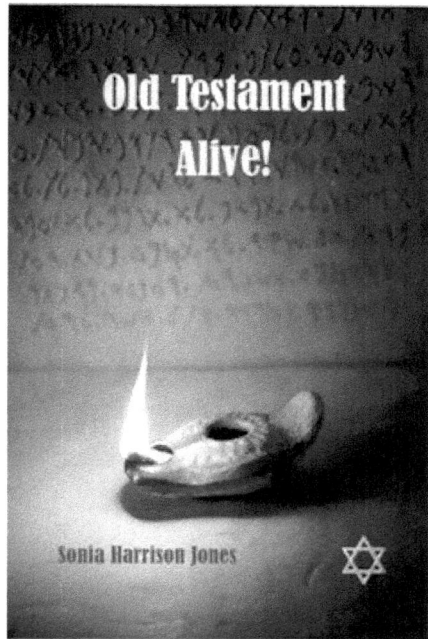

This is a poignant, respectfully humorous bird's eye view of the Old Testament, when people in the Scriptures come alive and talk directly to the reader. The prophet Hosea wonders why God wants him to marry a prostitute, and Satan boasts about winning people to his point of view. This fascinating book is illustrated with 170 beautiful color images created by professional photographers around the world. This book is available at www.amazon.com or www.erserandpond.com

What readers are saying:

As a pastor, I was delighted to discover such an interactive study. When we shared the Bible with our very bright int'l students, we used this book to inform our discoveries and launch us into discussions. —Rev Winston Clark, pastor

We found this book very informative and entertaining. It is one of the reasons why my wife and I became Christians. —Dr. Cheng Wang, pathologist

Available on Amazon or at www.erserandpond.com

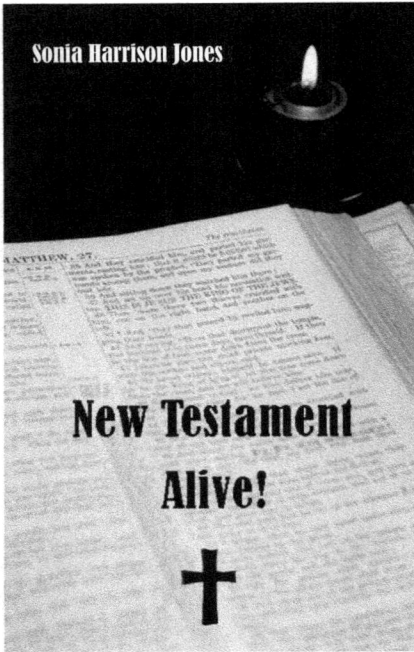

Sonia Harrison Jones

New Testament Alive!

✝

This sequel to *Old Testament Alive!* presents an overview of the main events of the New Testament, where people come alive and talk to the reader. Lucifer returns as a cool and worldly young man who presents an ironic and cynical view of the unfolding action. Judas explains his political ambitions, Peter bares his soul to you after he denies Jesus three times, and Paul plays a crucial role in introducing and explaining the Christian faith. This book is available at www.amazon.com or www.erserandpond.com

What readers are saying

When we studied with Dr. Jones, we went back 2,000 years when people in the Bible talked to us about their struggles and hopes and fears. The class reminded us that we are all one human family, no matter when and where we live. It was so joyful and fun to join this group of people to discuss the Christian faith. —Yiling Hu, MD, MSc, and Changjiang Li

Available at www.amazon. or at www.erserandpond.com

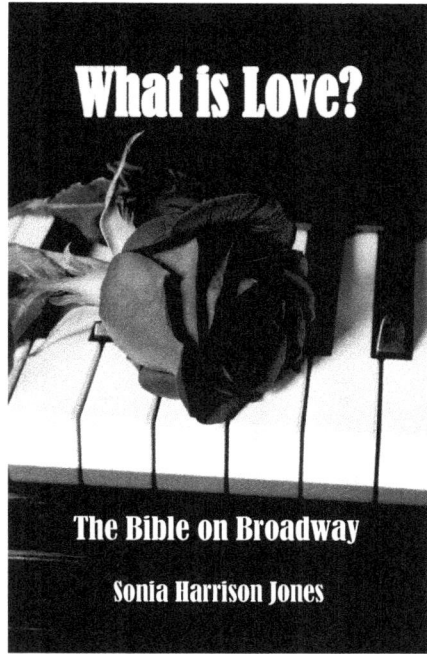

What is Love?

The Bible on Broadway

Sonia Harrison Jones

This is an examination of the many forms of love depicted in three Broadway musicals—*The Phantom of the Opera, Man of La Mancha,* and *Les Misérables.* Starting with twelfth-century troubadours and ending with comments by C.S. Lewis, this intriguing book presents the Bible in a brand-new manner, bringing an original and refreshingly new point of view to the world's most popular musicals.

The author taught this book many times in manuscript form in the Adult Sunday School program and in home Bible studies at All Nations Christian Reformed Church in Halifax, Nova Scotia. She also taught it to foreign university students under the auspices of International Varsity Christian Fellowship.

Although the songs have been summarized by the author, it is recommended that the reader purchase or rent the CDs or the DVDs of these musicals to enhance the reading experience.

Available on Amazon or at www.erserandpond.com

BOOKS BY SONIA HARRISON JONES
PUBLISHED DURING HER TENURE
AT DALHOUSIE UNIVERSITY

SPANISH ONE, VAN NOSTRAND, NEW YORK, NY, 1974; *2ND EDITION,* 1979
(adopted by over 100 universities in the US and Canada)

ALFONSINA STORNI, GK HALL, BOSTON (TWAYNE WORLD AUTHORS), 1979. Biography and literary critique of the well-known Argentine poet, playwright, and short story writer (the author won a Canada Council grant to research the project in Buenos Aires).

ABOUT THE AUTHOR

Sonia Harrison Jones was born in England, but moved to the U.S. when she was twelve. She received her B.A. from Bennington College in Vermont, and her M.A. from the University of California at Berkeley. After receiving her PhD from Harvard in Romance Languages and Literatures, she chaired the Department of Spanish at Dalhousie University in Halifax, Nova Scotia, for many years.

Now she is well into her third career, writing books a mile a minute. She has published a dozen books in various genres (see above), and is looking forward to writing many more. She has been listed in *Who's Who in the East, International Authors and Writers Who's Who, The World Who's Who of Women, and Who's Who in Canada.*